THE
OFFERING

THE
OFFERING

Tom Carhart

WILLIAM MORROW AND COMPANY, INC.
New York

Library of Congress Cataloging-in-Publication Data

Carhart, Tom.
The offering.
1. Vietnamese Conflict, 1961–1975—Personal
narratives, American. 2. Carhart, Tom. I. Title.
DS559.5.C37   1987   959.704′38   86-28520
ISBN 0-688-05753-5

Printed in the United States of America

First Edition

1   2   3   4   5   6   7   8   9   10

BOOK DESIGN BY BERNARD SCHLEIFER

When American forces went to Southeast Asia to fight in the Vietnam war, we, the individual members of those forces, offered our lives for our country. In the course of events some of those offers were accepted.

I dedicate this book to Buck Thompson and Art Parker and Johnny Hoskins and Mike Snell and Uncle Jimmy Haugh and Pappy Collins and Speedy Lopez and all the other gallant American soldiers who died violent deaths in that part of the world; your sacrifices are not forgotten.

Foreword

WHEN I RETURNED from Vietnam, there was little opportunity for me to share my wartime experiences with other Americans, so I bottled them up. But they ate at my guts, and primarily as scripto-therapy, I began to write them down in the late 1970s.

While performing our duties in Vietnam, of course, we American soldiers all retained our human fallibility. I hope a lot will be learned from the events I relate, but I have no interest in casting shadows over any of my fellow veterans. Accordingly, I have changed some names and other details to obscure identities. With that exception, here is the true story, from a rice-roots level, of my electrifying year in Vietnam.

T C.

Contents

BOOK I: WARRIOR

1. *Phan Thiet*   15
2. *Song Be*   27
3. *Ambush*   33
4. *Hospital*   41
5. *Tiger Force*   49
6. *Tiger Ridge*   59
7. *Fast Shuffle*   75
8. *Saigon*   89
9. *Jacqueline*   95
10. *Brigade Staff*   105
11. *O-Deuce*   119
12. *The Longest Day*   127
13. *Mission Impossible*   147
14. *R&R*   159

BOOK II: ADVISER

15. *Mat 85*   171
16. *The Province*   183
17. *Ruff Puffs*   189
18. *Local Color*   207

19. Dai Uy Trung   225
20. Proust   243
21. Debriefing   251
22. Phoenix   259
23. Imprudence   277
24. Refuge   295
    Glossary   303

THE OFFERING

BOOK · I

WARRIOR

*I have heard the bullets whistle, and
believe me, there is something charming
in the sound.*
                    —GEORGE WASHINGTON

*It is well that war is so terrible,
or we should grow too fond of it.*
                    —ROBERT E. LEE

*The man who cannot look upon a battlefield
dry-eyed will allow many men to be killed needlessly.*
                    —NAPOLEON BONAPARTE

Phan Thiet

I WAS AWAKENED by the pilot speaking over the public-address system: "—remain at altitude until we enter the Saigon area, at which time—" Saigon area—we must be over Vietnam! I quickly sat up, raised the shade on the window, and stared at the bright land below.

It was December 7, 1967. I had graduated from West Point in 1966, but my commission had been delayed for six months because of injuries I had suffered in a car accident. I had been impatient to catch up with my destiny and had raced through airborne school, ranger school, and the then-required troop duty with a stateside unit—in my case, the 82d Airborne Division in Fort Bragg, North Carolina. Now I was on my way to join the unit and duty in Vietnam I had chosen before graduation: 1st Brigade, 101st Airborne Division, as an infantry platoon leader.

Behind my brave face and committed manner I was frightened. I had just spent a week with my family in Tokyo, where my father, a colonel in the Air Force, was serving. All my life my father had been my hero. Unsurprisingly, I was consciously trying to model my life after his, to be better, if anything.

My father had come up through the ranks in World War II and ended up flying P–38 Lightning fighters in Italy. In the late forties the Army Air Force had sent him to the University of Alabama to complete his formal education. He thus became the first member of his family to earn a college degree. I was to become the second.

I had forever wanted to go to West Point, it seemed. I told my father of this when I was a junior in high school, and he wished me well but insisted that if I was to win an appointment to West Point, I had to do it entirely on my own. I think, in retrospect, that no child could have been better served by a parent than I was then by my father, who forced me to take responsibility for my own life.

I satisfied the eligibility requirements for West Point: high school grades, College Board scores, athletic ability, and medical requirements. That was the easy part. The actual appointments were given out by members of both houses of the U.S. Congress. But since we were constantly on the move, I found I was technically ineligible to compete for a normal appointment since I had not lived long enough in any given congressional district.

In the winter of 1961–62, my senior year in high school, I took a couple of weeks off from school and went to Capitol Hill in Washington, D.C. I knocked on the door of every senator and every member of the House of Representatives, asking their assistants bluntly if I could have his or her political appointment to West Point. Out of five hundred and something members of Congress, fourteen asked me to come back.

Eventually it narrowed down to a woman from South Carolina, whose husband had died in office, and Congressman Lucien Nedzi of Michigan, who had just been appointed to Congress to replace a man who had taken a federal judgeship. West Point appointments were political plums, and both members were besieged by other applicants.

Congressman Nedzi asked me to write a paper on my ideas about freedom and the United States government. He then sat me down for twenty minutes and grilled me hard on what I thought of the American system. I knew he held a law degree from the prestigious University of Michigan, and I was afraid I'd say the wrong thing. After I had finished, however, he smiled at me, shook my hand, and told me I had won his appointment to West Point.

Years later I stopped in Washington to see him on my way to Vietnam, and I asked him how it was that he had chosen me over all the other applicants. I knew that he had been inundated with requests, many of them through powerful political intermediaries. He told me, with a smile, that out of the dozens of applicants who had swarmed around his office seeking his appointment, I was the only one who came to him alone, without my father holding me by the hand. He told me that since I obviously had known what I wanted at age eighteen, not what my father wanted, he had thought I deserved special consideration. We both smiled: major lesson in life.

West Point had not been fun, for I was not easily disciplined. I was not a "good" cadet: I did not enjoy wearing the harness, and I spent a lot of off-duty time walking punishment tours. But I did put up with it and graduated, all for the sake of the degree and the gold bars that would make me a second lieutenant in the United States Army. Now, here I was, approaching the pinnacle of the military life I had been training and straining for. This was the whole ball of wax: life and death on the line.

My flight into Saigon out of Tokyo was by commercial airliner, and most of the other passengers were Oriental businessmen. (Can you imagine a more unusual way to go to war?) As I stared out the window, all I could see was a great green carpet below us. I started to make out black and red lines—paved and unpaved roads, I quickly realized—then clusters of buildings that must be villages and towns.

As I concentrated on the largest settlement, I suddenly saw four or five fine plumes of jet-black smoke rising from it. I had never seen smoke like that but was instantly sure I was witnessing the burning of a town during or after a battle. My heart leaped, and I spun around to see if anyone else was alarmed. But the other passengers seemed too bored even to look down with me. I considered saying something aloud but realized that I would be cynically reminded there was a war going on down there, so I said nothing. But I was stunned. Was this boredom possible while fire and death raged below?

I was quite unsettled by the time we landed at Saigon's Tan Son Nhut Airport, but as I got off at the civilian terminal, life was peaceful. There were clouds of truly beautiful Vietnamese women floating around in their lovely *ao dai* national dress—the colorful blouse and long skirt slit to the hip on each side and worn over black silk trousers.

I found the men's room inside the terminal and was stunned and repulsed by the stench, the flies, and the strange toilet basin cut into the floor of each stall. These basins were uniformly plugged and overflowing, with small porcelain squares where one presumably stood and squatted floating on the brine—a rude introduction to Third World sanitary standards. I quickly decided to wait until I reached a U.S. installation, longing for the comfort of that familiar form-fitting sit-down facility. But my biological needs reversed that decision, and I soon found myself back in one of the men's room stalls. As I squatted in that revolting situation, trying to retain shreds of dignity and not soil my pants in the sea of fecal matter that surrounded me, I realized fully that I was now in a wholly different world. It was going to be a very long year.

The bus finally arrived, and I carried my duffle bag aboard. We rode for an hour or so through hot, dusty streets jammed with trucks, motorscooters, bicycles, and the occasional horse- or ox-drawn cart. As we left Saigon, the road became a four-lane divided highway, surrounded by acre after acre of new high-rise office buildings or industrial parks. I found it hard to understand a war going on in the midst of all this apparent well-being and stability.

When we arrived at the 80th Replacement Detachment, we quickly slipped into that familiar army "hurry up and wait" mode. I relished trading in my khakis for jungle fatigues, pulling those cool green pants over my legs and rolling up the crisp sleeves until they were tight over my biceps. I had awaited this moment for some time, and every step in Anointing the Warrior for Battle thrilled me.

On the second day I was startled to see those thin black streamers of smoke rising into the sky from somewhere within the compound. I quickly learned that this was only the work of guys who literally had the "shit detail," adding diesel fuel to the daily contents of the steel drum receptacles from the latrine and burning the product. I had to laugh at myself as I watched the smoke rise which I had, from the airplane, believed to be the smoke of towns burning in the wake of battle.

A few days later I caught a plane to Phan Rang, where the 1st Brigade of the 101st Airborne Division had its rear area.

I was soon enrolled in a "preparatory" class that differed from all other army instruction in that there was no petty harassment or unreasonable pressure. This was real, and we all wanted to learn. The school motto soon became our own: "Stay Alert, Stay Alive."

The course was a combination overview of the small-unit tactics we had learned back in the World and a close-up appreciation of some of the problems we would actually face. All newly arrived officers and NCOs were required to take the course, and that included those who had been out-of-country (Vietnam) only for the thirty-day leaves they got when they extended their tours in Vietnam by six months.

The first week was all classroom. We saw the kinds of explosives we would use to clear landing zones, got tips on hurried C ration meals, were shown the kinds of snakes we might sit on, learned how to give albumin intravenously to a wounded man who had lost a lot of blood.

The second week we began to go on patrols in the surrounding hills. In five days of patrolling, we saw no enemy, but we began to pick up some feel for the kind of country we would be operating in, for the pace and scale of infantry movements, for ways to deal with the problems of survival in the jungle.

I also learned two important things in prep training that were not formally part of the course content but were central to the U.S. military presence in South Vietnam.

The first was the incredible, even by army standards, use of vulgarity. Crudity not only was used for emphasis but was also a normal, even expected part of one's regular speech. I initially decided that I would be different, that I didn't need vulgarity to prove my manhood. But that decision was short-lived, and soon enough, like everyone else, every fourth or fifth word out of my mouth was "fuck" or some variation on the theme.

The second was the strong effort made to dehumanize the enemy, which unfortunately spilled over into an unhealthy disrespect for our South Vietnamese allies and the civilian populace we were supposed to be defending.

In the early days of the Korean War, I was told by a fellow new lieutenant, the U.S. Army had run into a considerable problem: American soldiers proved hesitant to fire their weapons. For whatever reasons, our infantrymen were unwilling to take human life knowingly. The Pentagon, aided by a battery of psychologists, embarked on a major program to dehumanize the enemy. "Gook" is a Korean word which means "foreigner." This term, in accordance with orders from on high, was uniformly applied to our North Korean enemies, along with stories that pointed out the differences between Korean and American civilizations. The differences were emphasized in ways that made the Koreans appear to be vastly inferior to Americans, especially on a moral level—inferior, therefore easier to kill. The program was a success in that American soldiers began to fire their weapons.

When the conflict in South Vietnam burst in on us in the mid-sixties, the Pentagon was ready. While we were in formal classroom settings, we were never told to spit on the Vietnamese people. But that was the very real message from the sergeants, especially those just back from a tour in Vietnam: "Only good gook's a dead gook"; "never saw a gook I'd trust or I wouldn't blow away in a heartbeat."

In terms of personal survival the sergeants were smarter than the humanist school of behavioral theory: Their approach assumed an entire culture inferior to our own. Objectively, of course, this is an ugly, irrational approach to life. In context, however, I'm sure that the racist nature of the war—English-speaking round-eyes against the gooks—kept a lot of Americans alive. Hesitation or sympathy for a wounded enemy soldier was something you could do without if you valued your life.

It was difficult, of course, to distinguish between the enemy soldier and our supposed "ally" in the rear. But since the only Vietnamese seen by the infantrymen doing the fighting were enemy soldiers in the field or laundry girls/whores at their base camps, that didn't seem too important.

There were three battalions in the 1st Brigade of the 101st, one of which would be my new home: the 1st Battalion, 327th Infantry; the 2d Battalion, 327th Infantry; the 2d Battalion, 502nd Infantry. Their battalion mottoes, respectively, were "Above the Rest," "No Slack," and "Strike Force," blunt statements of unit esprit that were spoken or shouted as greetings while saluting or were hurled cynically at the nonairborne-qualified support troops in the rear we referred to condescendingly as "legs."

While there were some competitive stories about these three battalions making the rounds, there seemed little difference among them. All were filled by paratroopers who had volunteered to go to jump school and so committed themselves to serving with the most elite and most dangerous unit in the U.S. Army, and these were the men I would command in the field.

On the last day of prep training we received our assignments. I was to report to A Company, or "Abu," a nickname from World War II, 1st/327. Above the Rest! The next morning I hopped a C-130 cargo plane to Phan Thiet, where the 1st/327 was then maintaining its rear area.

When I arrived in Phan Thiet, I was taken to the rear of 1st/327, a cluster of army tents on the edge of town. I exchanged my M-16 for a CAR-15, a shorter model of the M-16 with a collapsible stock that officers were allowed to carry, packed my rucksack with Cs, and got ferried by slick—as we called the Huey helicopters—to the forward fire base. As I got out of the slick, I saw a prostrate body lying in a trench on an air mattress in front of me, naked to the waist, wearing sunglasses, and reading a comic book. It was an old high school friend and football teammate, Bob Riviello. He had gone to Notre Dame, and I hadn't seen him for about five years. He had just gotten off line and was the commander of the mortar platoon. We managed to get in some smiling backslaps before I reported to the tactical operations center (TOC). I met Lieutenant Colonel Morse, or "Ghostrider," the battalion commander; he gave me a brief pep talk.

Then I got on the slick again and was ferried forward to A Company. I met my company commander, Captain Johnson. He assigned me to a platoon, and I met my platoon sergeant, Sergeant Wilson, who was probably in his late thirties. That first day and night I did what Sergeant Wilson told me, including taking off my boots at night and sleeping on an air mattress. The next morning I was putting on my boots when Sergeant Patterson, one of my squad leaders, came over to tell me something. When he saw me lacing up my boots, he began laughing, but he quickly smothered the laughter with his hand, turning half away as he did so. I was surprised, then embarrassed.

"Hey, I'm new, Sergeant Patterson. What's the matter? Aren't we supposed to take our boots off at night?"

"Oh, that's okay, sir. You kin take 'em off if you want to. Course you may find yersef runnin' 'round barefoot on the jungle floor at night, that's all."

"You don't take 'em off, huh?"

"Sir, I don't take 'em off the whole time I'm in the field."

"Okay, I get the message."

" 'Nother thing, sir, Sergeant Wilson is gone now, so I'll tell ya: Them air mattresses is awful noisy, tells the gooks jest where we're at, 'n' you 'n' Sergeant Wilson is the only ones that use 'em."

I slashed my air mattress then and there and made Sergeant Wilson do the same when he got back. Two days later Sergeant Wilson got extracted from the field with suspected malaria, and Sergeant Patterson, twenty-two years old, took over as my platoon sergeant. I breathed a sigh of relief and began to learn in earnest how to survive in the jungle. We were making only sporadic contact with small enemy units that quickly fled; I still hadn't fired my weapon or even been fired at.

In Vietnam, an infantry battalion in the 101st Airborne Division had four line infantry companies of approximately 100 to 120 men in field strength, a long-range reconnaissance platoon of 40 to 60 volunteers, and an artillery battery of four 105 mm howitzers in direct support. But although one of our rifle companies might average more than 100 men in the field when things were going well, it might sink to a strength of 30 or 40 men when things were going badly. I commanded a platoon of about 25 men, varying from extremes of 5 to 40.

When a battalion of the 101st moved into an area of operations, the commander would normally establish a headquarters position on top of a hill. Perimeter trenches would be dug, barbed wire strung, claymore mines emplaced, and overhead-cover bunkers built. A battery of 105 mm howitzers would be dug into this new fire base. One of the four line companies would be assigned to man the defensive positions on the fire base. The other three companies and the long-range reconnaissance platoon would roam through the jungle within the eleven-kilometer—roughly seven miles—range of the direct support artillery on the fire base, usually trying to lock into combat with the enemy, whom we referred to as Charley. If we could get Charley to commit a sizable number of his troops to combat and pinpoint his location on the map, then we could destroy him. That was when we could use our massive superiority in artillery and our monopoly of air power to best advantage.

While out in the field hunting for Charley, I learned to carry and use an M-16 rifle. (I gave up on my CAR-15 for reasons that I'll explain later.) I carried two bandoliers of ten magazines each across my chest and six more magazines in pouches on my suspender harness we called "load bearing equipment" (LBE). On my right shoulder harness, I carried a compass, a yellow or purple smoke canister, and a white phosphorus hand grenade. On my left shoulder harness, I carried a bottle-in-a-can of albumen—the blood replacement—and a red smoke canister. On the web belt attached, I carried a canteen, an ammunition pouch, and an M-48 hand grenade on each side. In my right thigh pocket, I carried a plastic-covered map, and on my right hip, a sheath knife. Everyone wore a helmet and a jungle fatigue shirt, sleeves rolled up, and pants. Few people wore underwear or socks; our canvas boots dried out quickly, while socks would stay wet and uncomfortable all day long. On our backs, we carried rucksacks containing four to eight more canteens of water, ten to twenty more magazines of eighteen rounds each, a poncho and quilted poncho liner to sleep in, and C rations. We took water from jungle streams, adding Kool-Aid, if we had it, to relieve the monotony.

Each night the infantry company was usually spread into a large circle; the men dug shallow positions on the perimeter an hour or so before dark and settled in. There were three or four men at each position with ten or fifteen meters between positions. The company commander and headquarters element were in the center. The men at each position rotated three or four hour watches among themselves from full dark until just before first light. Everyone was then quickly and silently awakened.

Dawn was sudden in the jungle. At six o'clock it was still dark, but by six-fifteen full light had spread over the top of the canopy, and the sun could be felt through the thick tree branches and foliage. C rations would be gobbled, coffee drunk, cans crushed and buried. By seven o'clock the long, slow chain of men would begin to move Indian file.

The 1st Battalion, 327th Infantry, was operating out of Phan Thiet on the coast, moving toward its two sister battalions of the 1st Brigade, 101st Airborne Division around Bau Loc, farther inland. We were operating in a free-fire zone, where there was supposedly nothing but enemy. However, the gooks were running from us, not wanting to make contact. We spent whole days on trails, humping down likely valleys, but only hitting a trail watcher or small stay-behind force every few days. Charley didn't want to mess with us, and we chased him over the steepest mountains in the world—or so it seemed.

They said, and I believed, that the most dangerous time in your tour in the Nam was your first two weeks, when you didn't know anything, and your last two weeks, when you felt fat and cocky.

On my second day out we stumbled into a camp of six or eight hooches. I was the leader of the second platoon in line. There were several goats and pigs running loose through the camp, snuffling and bawling. As the first platoon got to the other side of the camp, a burst of AK-47 fire rang out fifty meters in front of us. There was no real canopy here, with the tree growth somewhat thin, but the undergrowth was chest high. The only way to see anything was to stand up. I was standing near a tree, and I assumed that to someone fifty meters away there would be little way to distinguish me from a tree trunk if I stood perfectly still. I wanted desperately to see combat.

"Get down, sir!" My legs were knocked out from under me by a hard tackle. As I was going down, a burst of AK fire hit the tree next to where my head had been. I was mad at being knocked down for about half a second—until the AK rounds hit the tree. Then I was scared speechless. Mouth agape, wide-eyed, I turned and looked at my assailant, Sergeant Patterson, who was half laughing, half mad at me. "Sir, you got to get your ass down when the gooks are shooting at ya." His smile was reassuring.

"I just wanted to see what was going on."

"Goddamn, sir, you'll see plenty! Let Scotty take care of that shit! We don't want ya gettin' killed on us first time out." A wide, life-giving, glad-you're-alive grin. I could hear Sergeant Scott yelling to his machine gunner in the first squad, returning the fire and maneuvering out to our left front.

"Thanks, Sarge."

"Don't worry about it, sir; we're all in this together. You keep me alive, and I'll keep you alive. You just gotta learn ta keep ya ass *down* when we get fired up." He grinned at me while sweat stood out on my forehead. My armpits were soaked, and I felt a tight lump in my throat. I tried to force a smile as I rolled over and cautiously raised myself on my hands and knees.

Suddenly we were under fire again from the left flank, and we scrambled behind a clump of trees. I saw muzzle flashes and movement some forty to fifty meters away and brought my CAR-15 to bear on them. But as I squeezed off the first round, the weapon jammed. I had been warned about this possibility, but I never dreamed it would happen to me the first time I fired a shot in anger. I had taped an assembled cleaning rod to the bottom of my stock for just such an emergency, and I ripped it off and rammed it down the barrel, praying nervously that I'd live. The rod finally pushed the hot, empty cartridge out of the chamber, and I struggled to get the magazine back into position and chamber another round. My fingers seemed thick and clumsy; I couldn't accomplish the simplest of tasks. Finally I got another cartridge in and opened fire. This time I got off five or six rounds before it jammed again. By now, though, the first platoon seemed to be gaining control of things, and I didn't even make the pretense of adding to the firepower. I rolled completely behind the tree and, taking my time, ran the rod back down the barrel to clear it.

"Seem to be having some problems there, sir?" I looked up at Sergeant McNeill, the company field first sergeant, crouched compactly behind a neighboring tree.

"Yeah, Top, I can't keep this goddamn weapon clear."

"I'm not surprised, sir; them things ain't worth shit. You oughta get yerself a regular M-sixteen—may keep ya alive when that little piece of shit would jam up on ya." We both tightened up behind our trees at a renewed outburst from the first platoon area. "Move yer platoon up there behind the first platoon, sir. See if they need any help."

"Okay, Top."

I reached over and took the handphone of the company net radio from my radiotelephone operator (RTO). "Buckles, this is Billy Goat; we're moving up behind you on your left." I motioned to Sergeant Patterson, who had heard me, and he dashed off to his left, yelling to the second squad as he went. The radio crackled to life.

"Goat, this is Buckles. Tell your men to watch up in the trees. We just took some fire from the left, right where you're headed."

I could see Buckles now, Lieutenant Thompson of the first platoon, crouched over some fifty meters to my right front. "Okay, Buckles, thank you much." I yelled to my men, "Watch up in the trees; first platoon just took some fire from the trees on the left!" The warning echoed down the line to the left as we began to waver forward. The adrenaline was flowing now. I began to feel that I was part of the war.

I began to swagger in my mind as I squeezed off the first few rounds. Within seconds, thirty men were firing on the tree line. Suddenly there were two bursts of AK fire from a tree in front of us, and the wrath of the platoon turned on it. I saw the muted explosions of two M-79 grenade launcher rounds in the tree branches and then saw a flash of green and black as something fell. When we got there, two of my men reached under the tree and dragged the body out in front of me. It was a small, young-looking man with greasy black hair. Half his forehead had been blown away, and his brains were spilling out over the side of his head. He was wearing a filthy olive drab uniform, boots, canteen, knife, AK ammunition pouch; he was clearly a North Vietnamese Army (NVA) regular.

A mass of guts began to slop out from beneath his shirt and onto the ground at my feet. I felt nothing. Appreciation of the Vietcong (VC) or NVA as human beings was only an academic exercise to me; here, on the ground, they were a dangerous strain that must be destroyed.

The few gooks who had fired us up as we came through the camp drifted quickly into the jungle, and we set up a hasty perimeter. Captain Johnson, the company commander, called a meeting of the platoon leaders (myself, Lieutenant Thompson, Lieutenant Baker, and Sergeant Queen) in front of the hooches. I was the last to arrive, and everyone gave me a wide grin as I approached. "You get shot at there, Tom?"

"Shit, yes, he got shot at—almost got blowed away."

"Well, now you know what it's like."

"You'll get used to it, don't worry."

"Welcome to the club!" I was somewhat flushed after this, my first brush with life-and-death combat but tried to act unaffected and professional. But they all knew and smiled sympathetically. I couldn't keep from breaking into a wide, self-conscious grin.

I heard Captain Johnson through a fog: "Well, we'll put you in for the Combat Infantryman's Badge now, you can relax. Didn't take ya long. I can remember eight long, scared-shitless days before I got shot at." I laughed nervously with the others, who were much more relaxed.

When the wounded were extracted after that firefight, I kept the M-16 that belonged to one of them and gave him my CAR-15 to take to the rear. I wasn't going to take any more chances with a flashy-looking weapon that might not work when I needed it most.

Song Be

AROUND JANUARY 10, 1968, after chasing Charley around the jungle fruitlessly for several more weeks, we were extracted. I had seen two wild elephants, but we hadn't been able to run Charley down in his own backyard. Now the 1st Brigade of the 101st was to be sent to the Song Be Valley on the Cambodian border some 300 kilometers north of Saigon. We spent a few days relaxing in our encampment at Phan Thiet. Frank Cosentino, one of my roommates from West Point, was there, his signal unit supporting our battalion. We drank some beer together, then recorded a cassette for his wife, Marlene, whom he had dated since high school and who had become my close friend as well. It seemed kind of silly as we laughed into the microphone in the little hut made of wooden ammunition boxes where he slept. Not so long ago we had been young princes in gray, and now we were dirty, unkempt, sleeping on the ground like animals, and grateful for the illusory protection offered by a quarter-inch-thick pine box.

The next morning there was a memorial service for the fifty or so men of the battalion who had been killed during the last operation, which had lasted some five weeks. That night there was a formal officers' drunk in one of the tents. We toasted General William Westmoreland, our senior commander and our hero, an old paratrooper himself whom we'd have followed into hell. Then we toasted Colonel Rip Collins, the Iron Duke, our brigade commander. He responded with a toast to Joe Tentpeg, "the lowest enlisted man who is fighting the war without recognition." Another toast was proposed to "Ho Chi Minh Sucks," and then all the new lieutenants had to drink glasses of straight hard liquor mixed with hot sauce and vinegar and everything vile that could be found.

The next morning I had an eighty-pound head. We packed our gear and were trucked over to the airstrip. We climbed into the cleared cargo space of a number of giant C-130 aircraft with all our combat gear and rode like baggage for two or three hours.

The landing was rough, and the airplane strained with reversed prop pitch to stop on a short runway. When the cargo doors opened, we found ourselves in a heavily jungled valley. The next day my platoon took over a defensive position in the trenches at one end of the airfield.

I had talked to a number of officers and sergeants in the brigade, and it was the accepted opinion that we would be able to stay in this area for years and be busy fighting every day. We were in the middle of a major North Vietnamese Army staging area and also one of the primary resupply points where the Ho Chi Minh Trail crossed into South Vietnam. I was assured that I would not find Charley running from us here; he would close with us without any hesitation. He had excellent artillery support, and two North Vietnamese helicopters had been sighted the day we arrived. The other two battalions in the brigade, the 2d/327 and the 2d/502, were out in the woods and had been getting chewed up. Now we, the 1st/327, were going out to help them.

I went over the plan with Captain Johnson and the other platoon leaders the night before our combat assault (CA), a helicopter-borne insertion of troops into a contested area. We were going to be inserted into a cleared area of land just outside a large Montagnard village. The Montagnards, a nomadic tribe of native mountain people who hated and were hated by the lowland Vietnamese, had abandoned their camp; our intelligence said that a North Vietnamese regiment was using it as one of its base camps. We were going to land there with another company from our battalion and try to force the NVA to commit themselves to a fight. Our leaders were confident that with the use of our tactical air support and artillery, we would be able to crush them.

We were ready to move at dawn the next day. We filed quickly out onto the airfield and lined up in our prearranged helicopter loads of six men each. As I stood talking to Sergeant Patterson about the distribution of our machine guns, First Sergeant Dayoc, a grizzled veteran, came strolling over. "Morning, sir. How ya feelin'?" Already I was feeling competent in the field, and I told him I felt good. "Okay," said First Sergeant Dayoc, "but I just wanna make sure you know what's goin' on and get the word out to your men.

You've got quite a few cherries goin' out with ya this time." He looked at me for a moment. "You're gonna be all right, sir. You were in the shit in Phan Thiet. But this time Charley ain't gonna run."

The slicks were dropping out of the clouds in formation a few hundred meters away. "If ya get on the trails, make sure your shit is straight, sir." The slicks were beginning to settle onto the ground, and my men were boarding. "Good luck, sir, and keep your ass down!" I smiled and waved to Top as I ran under the blades of my slick, bent over, holding my helmet on with my left hand, my new M-16 in my right, my rucksack on my back, and the rest of my combat equipment strapped to my webbing or to my body.

We rode for no more than ten minutes, just above treetop level over thick jungle vegetation. Suddenly we veered sharply through a narrow pass and sailed down the throat of a steep-sided canyon. After about two or three thousand meters the canyon widened into a flat-bottomed valley. One of the pilots turned and gave me the high sign that indicated we were near our landing zone (LZ). I slapped a few men, and the word was quickly passed. As the slick slowed down some fifty meters off the deck, I eased my legs out the open side and braced myself. My RTO was on my right; one of my machine gunners, on my left. As soon as we hit the clearing, we were to move some twenty or thirty meters forward and set up on its edge. Out of the corner of my right eye I caught sight of purple smoke a few hundred meters to our front marking our LZ. I heard machine-gun fire on the ground. The door gunners opened up, and we dropped to a few feet above the prop wash-blown thick grass. The pilot honked the slick back, and suddenly we were moving at what felt like only a 5 to 10 mph clip. Time to get out.

I turned to check with the pilot, but as I did, the Plexiglas canopy was shattered over him on the left side, and the slick shuddered like some great beast. I looked back at my men, but they were already out the door. I thrust my body forward out that door without even thinking about it.

I had thought that this grass was only a foot or two deep; but it was elephant grass more than six feet high, and it swallowed me up. I fell hard on my back, slamming the breath out of me. I was startled for a moment, hearing only the slick beating its way down the valley, clawing for life-preserving altitude. Then that slick was lost in the noise of the fifteen or twenty others that were bringing the rest of the company in.

The grass was too deep for me to see anything but the other slicks. The noise of an intense firefight raged all around me. Where was my radiotelephone operator? "Gramelspacher!" No answer. "Sergeant Patterson!" No answer. I crawled some twenty meters until I got to a sort of dike, where the elephant grass ended. I saw three figures in olive drab fatigues scrambling off to the right as I came out of the grass and figured they were men from my company. I had started to turn and yell to them when I realized they weren't Americans. One of them raised his weapon to his shoulder and turned toward me. I threw myself off the dike and back into the grass even as I realized who those men were. The burst of AK fire sailed harmlessly over my head as I scrambled.

Out of nowhere Sergeant Patterson came crashing through the weeds and fell over me. "Sir! You all right?"

"Yeah. Where is everybody?"

"Shit, sir, everybody's on the side of the ridge, like we planned. Jesus, we thought you were hit!"

We plunged into the deep grass and up a steep grade. After about fifty meters we came out of the high grass on the edge of a clearing. My men were set up facing off to my left; I had completely lost my bearings during my fall from the slick.

Gramelspacher came running over with my radio. My platoon was not drawing fire, but we had no contact on our left with the third platoon. Combat is the mother of confusion. The first platoon on our right had no other contact, and nobody knew where Captain Johnson ("Warhawk") was.

"Warhawk, Warhawk, this is Billy Goat, over."

"Billy Goat, this is Warhawk. Where the fuck are you? Over."

"This is Billy Goat. We are in a cleared field about two hundred meters due south of the purple smoke markers. Where are you? Over."

"This is Warhawk. I got out in some deep grass on a hillside in what looks like the same spot you're in, maybe closer to the smoke. Who ya got with ya? Over."

"This is Goat. Buckles and his unit are here with me and mine. Do you want us to pop smoke? Over."

"No, hold on that. I just got word that we have your unit in sight. We're coming up the hill to you out of the weeds to your south. Don't fire us up. Out."

Abu was soon massed around the small clearing, and we moved into the edge of the jungle in the agreed direction with C Company.

Then we had a platoon leaders' meeting for both companies together. Captain Johnson took charge. C Company's commanding officer (CO), Captain Butler, had broken his ankle on the CA and was to be evacuated on the medical evacuation, slicks we called "dustoff" that were coming for our three dead and eight wounded. His face was etched with pain, and he could do nothing but grunt. Warhawk got right to business. "Lieutenant Traspen, you're the ranking platoon leader, so you'll take over command of C Company for now. Our standing orders are to move on an azimuth of one hundred and thirty-five degrees until we get up on a ridge, if we don't find any gooks in the village. Well . . . did you guys see a village anywhere?" Cynical laughter met this. C Company had been hardest hit: Two of the Dogwood eights (wounded), and all three of the Dogwood sixes (dead) had come from one platoon. Abu had suffered only two Dogwood eights, both men from the weapons platoon, hit before they ever got out of the slick. "Okay, they seem to have broken contact and drifted away. We didn't think they'd do that, but now we gotta run 'em down. Abu will lead out after the dustoff comes in and pulls our wounded out; C Company will follow. Traspen, get all your shit together. How much time we got?"

"First dustoff just called in, said he's about zero-five out."

"Okay, let's get ready."

In about an hour we reached the trail atop the big ridge shown on the map.

The battalion commander moved us about eight kilometers down it, and then we set up on the ridge crest for the night.

The next morning we were moving at first light. C Company stayed on top of the ridge line, and Abu went three or four hundred meters down the steep western slope into the bottom of a small valley. The gooks often put their larger camps on streambeds in the bottom of valleys, and the intelligence we had said there would be plenty of activity.

But as usual, Charley fooled us. We ran those valleys for almost two weeks without making serious contact. We walked through major camp areas, sometimes with zigzag trench lines running for hundreds of meters in all directions, but all deserted. The only gunfire was from sporadic snipers, although we could almost feel Charley's presence in the air.

Then, on January 24, we walked into a buzz saw.

Ambush

IT WAS AROUND ten o'clock in the morning. We were moving down a major trail that ran along a stream through a thickly jungled valley. Our pace was very slow and cautious. Even so, we walked right into a major ambush.

My platoon was second in line on the trail behind that of Lieutenant Baker, or Tin Drum. We had stopped at a point in the trail where the front man in my platoon was atop a small rise in the jungle floor. Tin Drum was beyond that rise and out of sight. Suddenly it sounded as if someone had turned on five or six enormous machines in front of us; there was a staggering roar from beyond the rise, where Tin Drum was. Everyone was instantly flat on the jungle floor. "RPD fire!" The North Vietnamese used the RPD machine gun, which was the same basic action as the AK-47 with a longer barrel and a bipod mounting. I had been told that it was the fastest-firing individual weapon in the world. I believed it. The roar we heard from the other side of the rise was immense, thunderous, paralyzing.

I didn't know what to do. I grabbed my radio handset from Gramelspacher and pressed the key. Nothing. My radio was dead. I couldn't understand it. Gramelspacher played with it for a minute and was dumbfounded. "I don't know what it is, sir. Something is jamming us. We can't use the radio."

I still didn't know what had happened to Tin Drum. I crawled up near the hillock over my men. Two men from Tin Drum's platoon had gotten over to our side of the small hill. "What happened?"

"Big ambush, sir. They've got bunkers on the hill across the stream on our left, and we were drawing fire from somewhere on the right, too."

I turned toward Tin Drum and yelled to him, "Tin Drum!" No answer. The RPD roar went on undiminished, and there were precious few M-16 rounds being fired in response.

I quickly stood up and immediately came down, trying to see something beyond the hillock in the ambush area. I caught an eyeful of eight or ten American soldiers lying inertly on the ground and intense small-arms fire coming from the left front. I was so scared I could barely talk, but I yelled to my platoon, "Second platoon, listen up. Our radio is out; the fourth platoon hit an ambush. On the left is a small stream. Everybody break brush and get down to the edge."

Out of the confusion that seemed to be controlling events, I remembered a trick I had learned in ranger school. It had not been part of the formal instruction but rather was something that had been volunteered by one of the students. He was in the British Army and had gone to the Royal Army survival and tracking school in Malaysia some years before. We were learning how to cross a contested roadway with a large force, and the U.S. way was to use brute force to barge across in a square formation. Our British friend volunteered a way to cross more safely if the crossing was expected by the enemy; the force simply lined up on the side of the roadway and, on a given signal, crossed as one man.

I expected that the open streambed would be covered by automatic weapons fire, and the gooks expected us to try to cross it in order to relieve the ambush pressure. "All right, Sergeant Patterson, is everyone down to the edge?"

Sergeant Patterson was at the back of the platoon and was the farthest away from me. "Yes, sir, we're all set."

"All right, second platoon, I'm going to start to count; when I hit six, everybody jump in and get your asses across. I'm counting now: one, two, three, four, five, six, seven . . ." My voice was drowned out by the roar of two RPDs that covered the streambed. I stopped breathing, stopped feeling, stopped caring. All I wanted to do was somehow pull my leaden legs through the syrupy water and get to the other side alive.

I made it unscathed and threw myself into the bushes, then turned and saw we hadn't left anyone in the water. "All right, second platoon, anybody hit?"

Sergeant Patterson answered immediately: "We got two hit down here, sir, Dogwood eights."

Sergeant Scott chimed in: "We got one more here, sir, Dogwood six."

I grimaced. That meant I had twenty-five men able to fight on this side of the stream. "Roger that. I will stay where I am at the edge of the stream. I want the rest of you to swing around on me so we're facing uphill."

From where I lay, I could look back across the stream and up beyond the hillock at Tin Drum's position. There was a small open area of thirty to forty meters in breadth where the path crossed the stream. It was in that clearing that Tin Drum had been hit. I could see ten or twelve bodies lying in the open, and Charley was riddling them with RPD fire. I could not see anyone firing back, and I didn't even know if anyone in the fourth platoon was left alive.

Suddenly there was an explosion in the canopy over our heads. I winced. We had a sixty-millimeter mortar, which we couldn't fire because of the trees and canopy overhead. But Charley had a mortar set up in a clearing somewhere and was getting lethal airburst with every round as the shells were detonated by the canopy. Sergeant Patterson and the ten or twelve men at his end of the platoon were getting chewed up. We had to get up and close with the enemy.

I yelled to my men, "Everybody up! On line! Let's take that hill!" As I said that, I stood up and roared as loud as I could, dumping a magazine on full automatic into the woods in front of me. The twenty-five men in my platoon followed suit, and we poured fire into the jungle. We couldn't see more than about ten or fifteen meters into the trees, but we knew the gook ambush positions were somewhere to our front.

I was wound tight as I continued to walk forward. I could hear the RPD fire off to the left some fifty meters or so, where the other end of my platoon was. I had no radio, so I had to rely on yells for communication. "Sergeant Patterson, you okay?"

"Sergeant Patterson is Dogwood six, sir," said a voice on my left. "There's a bunch of gooks over here trying to go around us."

Patterson dead! Oh, my God! What next? "All right, set up one machine gun there, five men, hold that corner, don't let them get around you. The rest of you stay on line with me, and let's take that hill!" Another RPD opened up somewhere on the left front. "If you can't hold, back up the way you came, but don't go across the stream!" I turned back uphill and dumped another magazine into the trees.

After we had moved together for ten or fifteen meters, we suddenly came to an open, apparently defoliated strip of jungle some twenty meters wide. I stopped for a minute but could see nothing beyond it. I hesitated, but I had to stay up with the men moving forward on my left. Gramelspacher and I moved into the clearing, and a burst of AK fire came out of the trees on the other side. Life itself suddenly slipped into a sort of superslow motion. I could see five green bees coming at me, but they slipped by on either side, all save the fifth one. That one hit my right leg and knocked both legs out from under me.

A combination of things happened. First of all, I was hit with a jolt of pain that radiated up my leg like juice out of a car battery. It was the sort of initial shock of pain that paralyzes, but you know it will immediately pass because it is too intense to last. But the pain didn't go away. It hurt like nothing I had ever known before in my life, and it didn't lessen; it seemed to get worse. I couldn't yell. I couldn't scream. I couldn't cry. I couldn't even breathe. Simultaneously time disappeared. As my legs were knocked out from under me, I instantly believed that somehow, in the middle of the jungle, we had stumbled into a group of baseball players. One of them had hit a hard line drive, and it had hit me squarely on my right thighbone, the only similar pain I could relate this to from my past.

As my body was hurtling through the air, I more rationally rejected that thought because a baseball didn't hurt that much. Now I decided that someone had shot me with an M-79 grenade launcher. The M-79 fires a large projectile, twenty millimeters in diameter, that explodes, like a small hand grenade, when it hits something. I was revolving slowly in the air now and caught half glimpses of the ground, the jungle, and then the sky. On my back now, I reached both hands down and grabbed my leg. It had not been blown off, so the M-79 round must have failed to explode. The pain was all that mattered, and it wouldn't go away. Dear God, what's happening? Then I realized that my hands were wet and warm. I must be bleeding!

I looked down at my red hands and red leg. I looked up at Gramelspacher, who was pumping rounds into the jungle. We were both in the cleared strip, and there was no place to hide. Then AK fire poured out of the trees—green and white and red tracers.

I was going to die; I knew it. I heard someone yell, "Billy Goat's hit!"

Then Sergeant Scott shouted, "Come on, second platoon, let's take that hill!" I turned over and picked up my weapon and emptied the magazine up the hill.

Gramelspacher was lying beside me, firing. He looked at me. "You all right, sir?"

"Yeah, I got hit in the leg. How 'bout you?"

"I'm okay, sir." The RPD fire in the ambush area had stopped, but it had gotten much more intense over on my left, where the rest of my platoon was moving. No radio.

"Sergeant Scott," I screamed, "where's that machine gun I told to hold the corner?"

"They couldn't hold where they was, sir, so they swung back. You okay?"

"Yeah, I'm hit in the leg. How are you?"

"We got tore up bad, sir. We can't hold out here. We got to drop back by the creek. That okay?"

"Yes, Sergeant Scott. Stay together and pull back."

Everywhere confusion. The men of the fourth platoon who had tripped the ambush were no longer drawing fire, but most of them were probably dead anyway. The left flank of my platoon was drawing intense fire, and somewhere off in our left rear was more gunfire, lots of it. Was that Buckles's first platoon, which had been bringing up the rear, or was it Warhawk and the command unit in front of them? Where was Bulldog, Sergeant Queen? He had been right behind me. The roar of gunfire on my left grew in a crescendo. Gramelspacher was tying a bandage around my leg, hands shaking.

"Sergeant Scott, what's happening?"

"Bulldog coming up on our left, sir. We're gonna slip back down to the creek."

"Okay, stay together. Where are our medics?"

"Both of 'em in our platoon got hit, but there's a couple more over here from Bulldog. You okay, sir?"

As he spoke, a medic crawled out of the woods. "Where you hit, sir?"

"In the leg. I'll be all right, but I'm bleeding a lot." Blood ran down my lower leg like wine. The medic tore my pants open, checked my wound, then resecured the bandage.

Warhawk was now crossing the area where Tin Drum had been

ambushed and crossed the stream. There was little firing there now, but it sounded as if all hell had broken loose over in Bulldog's area on my left. The medic slipped back off in that direction, crawling through the weeds on his belly. Gramelspacher grabbed me. "Sir, we got radio contact again." Warhawk was talking to Bulldog, who was now in the shit.

Sergeant Pearson, the head medic in the company, appeared from across the stream. "Sir, we got radio contact again, and Warhawk is bringing in tac air. He wants you and all your wounded to come over to Tin Drum's position." I leaned on Gramelspacher through the bushes, and we stumbled into the stream. I didn't dare look up but held my breath, waiting for the RPD fire. Nothing happened, and we made it through the water and up the far bank. Behind me I could hear the comforting whump! of tactical air delivering its ordnance. The RPD fire slackened, and I hoped Charley was breaking contact.

I was directed to the side of the clearing, where I joined about twenty other wounded men. Ten meters away they were slowly lining up the dead and covering them with ponchos. I counted sixteen. Poor bastards! Another twenty wounded were being brought over from Bulldog's platoon. Jesus, Warhawk would be lucky to have sixty men left on the ground. Buckles was the only one of his officers who hadn't been killed or wounded.

Things were getting tight, but I was strangely elated. Surrounded by the dead and dying, I felt good because I had somehow managed to stay alive. Four or five men were chopping down a bamboo grove nearby for an LZ, and the RPD fire on the left had ended. So had the artillery, but there were a lot of fighter planes dropping their loads in the contact area. I felt good, still alive, but I also felt helpless. I thought the gooks would never let the dustoff slicks come in to pick us up. I was not going to get out of this alive. We all were going to die together. I wanted to laugh and cry.

Someone handed me a cigar. The pain in my leg had turned to a dull throbbing when the medics came by, changed the bandage, and several times sent sharp stabs of pain through me as they did something to my wound.

Sergeant Scott was squeezing my hand. "You're gonna be all right, sir. I came over to tell you that Sergeant Patterson is gonna make it. He took a couple of RPD rounds in the gut; but the medics gave him two bottles of albumin, and I heard him talk a minute ago. Not making much sense right now, but if we can get him on a dustoff soon, the medics said he'll probably make it." Patterson was gonna make it! Although only twenty-three years old, he had been over here for two years and was very war-wise. But he was going home now. Thank God!

Warhawk came over to me with First Sergeant McNeil. "How ya doin', Goat?"

"Fine, sir, I'll be all right."

"Well, if your leg is really fucked up, you'll go back to the World. Otherwise, you'll spend a coupla months in the hospital, and then you'll probably be back on line with the 101st, so take it easy while you got the chance."

Overhead we heard the first dustoff approaching. "I'll be back, sir!" As the slick settled through the trees, two AKs opened up from the trees on the other side of the LZ. Warhawk disappeared; the air was filled with gunfire and obscenities, and the dustoff never faltered as it smoothly slid into our postage-stamp LZ. Oh, God! They're gonna shoot that dustoff down, they won't be able to get any more in, and we'll all die! I gripped my M-16 tightly, palms sweaty. The slick touched down, and our medics instantly loaded four stretchers and jumped back out. The slick had never really stopped moving and quickly clawed its way back up through the tiny hole in the canopy. I breathed a great sigh of relief. Maybe I would get out. The AK fire was still crackling in the woods as the next slick came in, but this time we had somebody over there shooting back.

When my turn finally came, Scotty helped me across the LZ. I crawled onto a litter inside the slick and was strapped down.

Then the slick began to rise, and my heart rose with it. I looked down at the receding images of Warhawk and his men. I was struck by the messy future they seemed to have in front of them, but I didn't care. My face had burst into an uncontrollable, all-consuming grin. I was alive! I thought I had received a classic "flesh wound" that hurt and would log me some safe time in the hospital. But I wasn't dying. I wasn't blind. I had both arms, both legs, my genitals, and I probably would have nothing to remind me of this wound but a scar—and a Purple Heart. Wow! I had bled for my country; but the wound was sort of numb now, and I was very proud.

We were high over the jungle and the five o'clock sun was low in the sky to our right, bathing the lush green carpet with a fire-orange glow. The cloudless sky before us was flushed the same color. My heart was bursting in my chest, and I wanted to laugh and cry and sing and shout; but the guy below me had taken a bad gut shot, and the guy below him had lost a hand. I turned my body as much as I could to look over the pilots' shoulders at the rest of the world. I curled up, content and smug inside myself.

Hospital

AFTER ABOUT A ten-minute ride we arrived at the battalion fire base and were off-loaded at the aid station. I was carried on my stretcher into a bunker, where a medic changed my bandage, tied a summary card to my shirt, and gave me some shots. Then I was back on a helicopter again, headed for Tay Ninh.

After we arrived, my wound was cleaned and debrided by army doctors in a large tent. I hadn't been able to feel my leg since I'd gotten those shots at the 101st aid station, but I was still nervous about what was going on, especially since the doctors wouldn't let me watch. I spent that night traveling, heavily drugged. When I awoke in the morning, I found myself in a brightly sunlit ward of the 94th Evacuation Hospital at Long Binh, outside Saigon, near the 80th repo depot where I had initially arrived in country. I ate every scrap of the hot bacon and eggs served to me in bed, then asked for and received seconds on everything. Soon three doctors came to my bed and examined my wound.

I had briefly seen the wound while it was being treated in the field. I had been hit on the right front of my thigh, about two inches above the knee. The bullet had made a nasty red entry hole, but it had tumbled as it went through my leg (as our bullets did) and made an exit hole in back I could have stuffed with a tomato. At Tay Ninh the doctors had told me they were cutting away all the "dead" flesh to clean my wound and I wouldn't be sewn up for several more days. Now, as the doctors unwrapped my wound, I was stunned to see how much flesh had been cut away. The small entry hole was replaced by a trough cut around the side of my leg, removing all the flesh from the side of my leg between the holes and about a one-inch margin on both sides for good measure. The side of my leg resembled a cold, gristly pork chop. I expressed some concern, and the doctors smiled. "Actually you're pretty lucky," one of them confided to me. "We'll sew you up tomorrow, and you'll be back on your feet a few days later. Within a couple of months all you'll have left will be the scar." I grinned widely. I had suspected as much, but it was nice to hear a doctor say the words.

I was still pretty heavily drugged and slept most of the day. The next morning I was taken to surgery. I remember the shot, the cold of the operating room, then black.

When I awoke, it was close to suppertime. I had been on the table for two and a half hours, I was told, but was doing fine. I dozed off, but someone made me wake up and drink a bowl of something. It was vile. I was awakened later by the surgeons who had done the work. When they unwrapped my wound, they all mmmed and ahhhed in self-satisfaction.

It wasn't pretty to look at, but the trough was gone. My whole lower thigh and the knee area were bloated death-white with a touch of purple bruise here and there. There was an angry red line running from just above my knee around the side of my leg and out of sight on the back of the leg. The slit was held together with two kinds of stitches. The first kind was clear filament. The second was a series of ten heavy-gauge metal wires that bridged the slit and disappeared at right angles into my leg about an inch on either side of the wound. I was told that the gut stitches would be taken out in four or five days but that the wires would stay in for three weeks. I could expect to stay in the hospital for another two months or so, recovering full use of my leg.

I slept most of that day, but I got out of bed the next afternoon and walked to the john on crutches. I couldn't feel my right leg and swung it along like some heavy, insensate appendage. It felt as if I had lost my leg at the groin and someone had tied a sack of grain to that hip, allowing it to swing in balance against my remaining leg. I vividly recalled the gouge in my leg I had seen after I arrived at the 94th, and it wasn't the sort of thing that looked to me as if it would *ever* heal! What did they mean, "full use in a couple of months"? Christ, I'd be lucky if I ever walked again! I couldn't even feel my leg as I walked down the ward, even when I banged it on the nurse's pill cart. Then I tried to get my leg back up into the bed and under the sheet before I started to cry. I didn't quite make it, but no one said anything.

The next day was better. A medic wheeled me over to the MARS (military affiliated radio system) station, and I got to talk to my parents at Yokota Air Force Base in Tokyo. My youngest sister and brother were also there with them, so I talked to my family for ten or fifteen minutes. My father asked if there was any chance that I might get sent to Camp Drake or Camp Zama, army hospitals in Tokyo where wounded from Vietnam were often sent. I said I didn't know but would find out. That night I told my doctor about my situation, and he said he'd see what he could do for me.

I was transferred on January 30 to an air force staging unit hospital at Bien Hoa airfield, only a few miles away, from which I would be loaded on a medevac flight and soar off to Tokyo and my eagerly waiting family. I was carried into a ward and placed on a bed, but my high spirits were quickly suppressed; the other patients here were seriously wounded, and there was more than enough moaning to drown out any wish to laugh at my outrageous good fortune. These were patients who would be leaving the country, many for the States and unending years of pain; I was embarrassed by the full recovery I knew lay before me.

There were wounds of all descriptions here in the staging unit: head wounds; sucking chest wounds; multiple fractures in traction; burns; traumatic amputations—you name it. Men were hooked by tubes to bottles of fluid that dripped precisely into their dying bodies, keeping them just this side of Jordan. Most slept or simply had never regained consciousness. It was brutal; it was real, and we were alive. That was the main mission of the staging unit, of course, to keep these men alive until they were flown out of country. Still, the predicament of some was bleak, and the sight of blunt white stumps with blood oozing through the bandages was painful.

That day passed slowly. But it was impossible to kill the bright anticipation of seeing my parents in Tokyo. It was the thirtieth of January. Tomorrow, I thought as I slipped under with the sun, tomorrow . . .

I was awakened by hushed shouting. Then three dark figures ran by the foot of my bed. Flashlights briefly shone, then were gone. I was confused and disoriented. What's going on? Where am I? Then reality flooded back: the hospital. But what was going on? I called to the next figure that ran by, "Hey, what's going on?"

"The airfield is getting attacked."

I was dumbfounded—airfield getting attacked? But we were in the middle of the big annual Tet holiday cease-fire that had started a few days after I got hit; nobody was really going to start fighting. I lay still and tried to listen. Sure enough, after a few seconds I could hear explosions in the distance, and the ground shook slightly. Must be mortar rounds or maybe rockets. Great. I had heard that the North Vietnamese had cheated on cease-fires before. They'd probably sent a squad inside the perimeter with a mortar and a few rounds, trying to hit an ammo dump or a group of planes while nobody was on guard, then scoot before they got caught. But that's the problem of the airport security troops, I thought; why are we getting worked up? We're in a hospital; they're not going to hit us. I looked at my watch: ten after three. That's a hell of a way to spoil a man's sleep, I thought, then slipped back under.

I awoke again suddenly when the main overhead lights in the ward came on, and I lifted my head, bleary-eyed. Someone roared: *"Turn off those lights!"*

The lights were soon off. Then came loud stage whispers and more figures running by the foot of my bed. Outside, there were more explosions, but these seemed much closer now. Then I heard AK-47 fire in the distance, lots of it. The guy in the bed next to me had lost his left leg up to mid-thigh, and his angry question was loud: "Hey, what the fuck is goin' on?"

A medic hurried over to his bedside, and his stage whisper filled the air. "Some of the other wards have taken mortar fire, sir, and we gotta get—"

Then a booming voice from the end of the ward took over: *"Everybody listen up. Some of the other wards have taken mortar fire and small-arms fire. Everybody that can manage it get under your bed and lay down on the floor. Leave the mattress on the springs, and get under it. The medics will be coming around to help those that need it."*

Sleep and drugs blurred my eyes and my mind as I fought to wake from the worst dream ever. What's going on? Are they really attacking us in a hospital? There was a stillness outside. Then two explosions ripped the air, and for the first time their light flashed grotesquely through the ward. This is for real, I thought, suddenly cold and scared. The cement floor was icy as it lurched up to meet me, graceless as my good-leg-bad-leg tandem clattered crablike under the bed. The whole ward seemed alive as men scrambled around, and my mind was flashing hopelessly through desperate survival questions: Where's my weapon? Where can I get cover and a weapon? But there was no answer, and we all were helplessly dependent on support from unknown U.S. troops who, we hoped desperately, were out there somewhere to protect us.

The same loud voice came from the end of the ward: *"Those of you who are in traction, don't try to get out of bed. Stay where you are. We'll be coming around to—"*

His calm, loud rhythm was interrupted by the voice of a wildman screaming from one of the other wards that seemed connected to us beyond my view: *"That ain't no fuckin' mortar fire. That's hand grenades or satchel charges. They're in here with us, get some men outside with weapons 'fore they get to us!"*

Some battle-savvy sergeant, and he was right. There was no earthshaking impact as rounds hit the ground, just the high, flat roar of hurled explosives. All drugs and weariness had been swept away by the tide of cold fear. A guy across the aisle roared from his bed: *"I'm Major Wallace. Don't send anybody outside. Get those doors bolted and windows secured, and get under your beds like he said to do. Now move!"*

Muffled pandemonium set in as people scuttled around the ward, helping each other out of bed and closing the shutters over the windows. Medics were running back and forth down the aisle. Then one of them was struggling into a flak jacket as he went by, a heavy M-14 in his hand. He stopped and leaned his rifle against my bed as he wrestled with the flak jacket in the dark. Major Wallace was half curled under his bed across the aisle as he barked at him: "What're you doin', soldier?"

The medic's voice trembled as he answered: "Sir, I'm supposed to secure the door at this end of the ward, then guard it."

"Well, leave your weapon there. Then get down to the door and lock it up tight—you got any chain?"

"No, sir."

"Okay, well, secure it as best you can, then get back to helping the men in traction under their beds. We must have somebody here can handle that weapon better'n you can, don't we?"

I rolled over to the base of my bed and reached up to the medic. "I'm Lieutenant Carhart, medic, gimme that weapon."

He handed it to me, and I whirled it around in my arms and drew back the bolt. There was no magazine in it, and the chamber was empty. I looked up at him in the dark.

"You got any ammunition?"

"Yes, sir, here."

He dropped four full magazines on my good leg, and they crashed on the cement floor. I groped for them as I sent him away. "Okay, go secure that door."

He hurried away as I seated a magazine, chambered a round, flipped the safety switch on, and clutched the three other magazines in my left hand. A tedious, breathless crawl after him ensued, fear clawing at my throat with each move. I couldn't feel my injured leg, and in the heavy metal frame it dragged like a wet sandbag. I reached the third bed from the door, then swung my legs around in front of me, raised my left knee, and leaned back against the base of the bed. I pointed the weapon at the door some fifteen feet away, cradling it across my waist, my hands loosely grasping the small of the stock and the upper hand grip, ready to quickly lift it to my shoulder and fire. It was much heavier than an M-16, and the magazine held only eight rounds, rather than the eighteen or nineteen we could use in an M-16 magazine. The bullets were bigger and heavier and hit harder; but it was only semiautomatic, and an M-16 that could dump six or eight rounds through that door in one burst would have been preferable. But never mind that, you play with what you get, and this would work just fine.

The medic seemed to be tying a rope to the doorknob, then turned and started back down the aisle.

Then he was gone, and I flipped the safety switch off. There was still a lot of muffled noise coming from the other wards, but our ward had gotten quite still. Somebody was softly sobbing, and the low rhythm of several men reciting the Lord's Prayer together reverberated under the beds. There was an explosion, very near, with a flash of light that lit up the frightened faces on the floor, then two more, very close together. Jesus, I thought, we're really helpless. Where the hell are the security troops? There must be units assigned to the hospital just for the purpose of defending against ground attacks—hell, that's what the MPs are supposed to do, isn't it? The rails of the bed were biting into my back now, and a throbbing ache ran over my hips. My back was killing me as I turned to the guy under the bed behind me.

"Hey, can you reach a pillow for me?"

He turned his head and looked at me, but in the dark I could see only that he had a tube coming out of his nose, and his head was quivering. Jesus, I thought, there's one man in a world of trouble. A whisper from across the aisle told me a pillow was on the way, and I stuffed it behind the small of my back. Only small cries and whispers broke the silence as we all prayed to be safe and back in bed.

There were two or three more loud, flashing explosions and several bursts of AK-47 fire. A few minutes of silence followed as we wondered aloud where the security troops were. Then an enormous flash lit the ward like daylight, and the explosion rocked the beds. Smoke and dust filled the air as eight or ten M-14 rounds rang out from the end of one of the wards connected to ours. Shouts told us that a satchel charge had blown their door off, and they needed more medics to take care of the freshly wounded. There was quite an uproar now. Then another patient with an M-14 crawled toward me from the hallway connecting us to other wards. I reached out and grabbed him. "Watch my leg! Watch my leg! What happened?"

"Satchel charge blew the door out, fucked up a couple of patients. They say they got the sapper who threw it, but I dunno. Can you cover the windows?"

"I can cover the ones on the other side, but I can't turn around so good."

"Okay, I'll cover the ones behind you, but we both cover the door, right?"

He slid himself to the other side of the aisle, then turned facing me and leaned against the base of a bed, his rifle pointed at the door to his right, his left hand on the small of the stock, his right arm a bandaged stump at mid-forearm.

"I hope you're a natural lefty."

"Well, I am now, and I guarantee you I can dump some lead through that door if they hit it."

We smiled wanly at each other, then fell silent, listening for sappers outside. The ward that had taken the satchel charge was still loud with shouts and groans, but silence reigned where we lay.

We sat frozen like that for some time. There were more explosions outside, but none so close that they flashed light through our ward. The AK-47 fire was gone.

Around five in the morning, a medic replaced me and I dragged myself back to my bunk. The explosions had ended, and patients were allowed back in their beds. I eagerly fell into mine and right to sleep.

I slept for only a few hours, then awoke unrested and edgy. The news of the Tet offensive was just reaching us. We knew about the attack on the embassy in Saigon from the radio; but that was still going on, and we didn't really know how things would turn out. We heard garbled reports about attacks taking place all over the country, about a major battle raging through part of Saigon, and no one really knew what was going on.

The next morning the gut stitches were taken out, and that afternoon I was flown to the 5th Convalescent Center in Cam Ranh Bay. Because of the wave of casualties from the Tet offensive, I wouldn't be going to Japan, but would stay in-country. I felt bad, but at least I was still alive.

I was assigned to a ward, then taken to the physical therapy room and set up a schedule to exercise my leg for an hour each morning and each afternoon. I was depressed that I couldn't even move my leg, but the physical therapist assured me that within a month or six weeks I would be as good as new.

Time dragged on. We learned that the Tet offensive had been quickly blunted, but life in the hospital was tedious. After a few weeks the doctor took my metal stitches out, but physical therapy seemed slow. By the end of February, however, I could walk without a limp, run, and almost do a full knee bend. We heard that the 101st was getting hit hard up in I Corps, and I was eager to get back.

Tiger Force

WHEN I REPORTED back in to my battalion, I learned that Lieutenant Colonel Morse, Ghostrider, had been wounded, and the new battalion commander was Lieutenant Colonel Block, or Red Grizzly. I was assigned to duty in the tactical operations center as an assistant operations officer, meaning I pulled radio watch from midnight until eight in the morning. After three or four days of this I was getting edgy. After a week I was ready to puke. I hated leading my life inside a bunker like some goddamn little mole. This was almost as bad as the hospital! I wanted to go back to the field. But unfortunately a new batch of lieutenants had come in, and Warhawk had four, all he could use, out in the field with him now. Then, one day about two weeks after I had come back, Lieutenant Blank was medevacked out with suspected malaria. Blank was the guy who had taken over the long-range reconnaissance platoon known as the Tiger Force when his predecessor, Captain McGaha, had been killed a month or so earlier. The Tigers were then pulling guard duty in the battalion fire base defensive positions. I immediately asked Red Grizzly if I could be the new commander of the Tiger Force. The next morning, as I was finishing my radio watch tour, Red Grizzly came and told me I was now the new Tiger six, or commanding officer of the Tiger Force. He told me to go down to meet my men and to be ready to go to the field within a few days. I got a set of the camouflaged fatigues worn by the Tigers from the supply sergeant and slipped them on, as well as a floppy-brimmed jungle hat they wore instead of helmets. I was fiercely proud when I went down to the bunker where the Tiger platoon sergeant was and introduced myself around. I was now the commander of our battalion's elite long-range reconnaissance platoon.

Like all LRRP's, the Tigers were a different breed of cat. They numbered sixty-eight at that time, but there were only two officers, as in all such units—myself and a lieutenant in the artillery who acted as a forward observer. The rest of the men were all volunteers who had served at least one year on line. The Tigers were further subdivided into four "patrols" of fifteen men each, which roughly reflected the platoons in a normal company, only without any lieutenants. We were somewhat smaller than a line company but operated freely like one.

And the Tigers had a reputation for ferocity and accomplishing the impossible that made them powerful beyond their numbers. Over the next few days I wandered through the bunkers, meeting the men and trying to get comfortable with them.

A few days later Red Grizzly went to join his wife for a week in Hawaii on rest and recreation (R&R) leave. The day he left, the battalion executive officer, Major Green, became the acting commander. He and Major Tan, the battalion operations officer, were new, and they had decided they would take this opportunity to show their skill as combat leaders. Most of the experienced people in the battalion took deep breaths when these two took over. Red Grizzly, like most battalion commanders, was just the right age to have seen combat as an infantry lieutenant in Korea. Green and Tan, however, had never heard a shot fired in anger until they had just recently arrived as majors. Commanders with personal combat experience as young officers in the field were always more realistic and demanded only reasonable things from their men. But young majors who didn't know what it was like on line tended to be the fire-eaters who, without a moment's hesitation, would throw their men into impossible situations and expect things to work out just as they plotted them on their maps in the TOC with a grease pencil. If they moved a small, square infantry company marker from one ridge to another on the map, they expected it to be done automatically on the ground. They had never humped a rucksack up and down hills in a combat zone, so it was perhaps a bit much to expect them to understand. We didn't know if this was how Green and Tan would turn out, and we hoped for the best. But when I was called to the TOC with Sergeant Haugh, the Tiger platoon sergeant, we weren't sure what to expect.

Our fire base was then located on the site of an old French fort, about ten kilometers inland from Highway 1 just north of the Hai Van Pass through which ran the Da Nang–Hue highway. We were situated at the mouth of a large valley that opened before us to our south. From the air the valley looked somewhat like a giant Playboy Bunny head, with our fire base on its neck, at the northern end, and the bunny's head valley dividing into two long ear-like valleys some ten clicks (kilometers) south of us. The western valley extended in the north-south direction for about eight to ten clicks and was about two to five clicks wide, with steep sides rising to peaks of perhaps several thousand meters. On the valley floor we were nearly at sea level. The eastern valley curved somewhat and ran off in an east-southeast direction for about six clicks and was nearly that wide at points. The actual position of the bow tie on a Playboy Bunny head was taken by the sharply rising precipice which blocked much of the main valley from view when on the fire base. Some of this main valley was rice paddies, but the rest of it was farmland that had been abandoned years earlier and was now partly grown over by the voracious jungle.

At the TOC Green and Tan told us they'd take us up in a slick in a few hours to look at the valley floor and plan our movements. That night we were to slip out of the perimeter after dark and move down the valley floor some five or six clicks. Then we would set up an ambush for the rest of the night and would send scouting parties up the sides of the ridges during the day. Thereafter we would continue to move down the valley or detour up the ridges depending on what our scouts uncovered.

As we moved out the front entrance to the TOC bunker, we saw an explosion on top of one of the perimeter bunkers a hundred meters below us and in front of us. The yell "Incoming!" was being echoed as I quickly looked up and saw the clear mortar muzzle flashes against the steep side of the hill a thousand meters across the mouth of the valley. We dived back into the TOC as our mortars limbered up and answered. But everyone knew that Charley would dump five or six rounds into our camp, pick up his mortar tube, and run. Within a few minutes the all-clear signal had been passed, and we went back outside and down to our perimeter positions. We had taken five rounds, and they all seemed to have hit harmlessly. But the first round had hit a bunker right at the seam of a layer of sandbags and burst through, killing a marine truck driver who had been inside.

Our mortars were now raging over the side of that hill, but we all knew that the probability of catching Charley was limited.

At around three-thirty the slick arrived, and I went on an aerial reconnaissance ride with Major Green (Cottonmouth), Major Tan (Sidewinder), and Sergeant Haugh (Tiger Five). Once we were over the main valley, we could see a main east-west trail, three or four meters wide, its dark, pounded mud giving evidence of heavy travel. "That, Tiger, is the main Hue to Da Nang highway for Charley. He hasn't used it much over the last few weeks, and we want to find his alternate routes. Now A Company is about eight or ten clicks back to the west, there, just north of that big rocky knob over there on the left, see it?" Cottonmouth said, pointing his arm out the open door.

"Yes, sir, I see—they're just over that ridge, right?"

"Right. Now C Company is right in front of us here, high up on the side of that big ridge there. Neither one of them has found anything much, so C Company is going to move west across the highlands, and A Company is going to move up into the farmland on the north, up there by Highway One. I think D Company may be swinging over near you on the west, but we won't send them into the valley unless you run into a hornets' nest or something."

We all smiled as the slick swung in a large arc. We sailed down both canyons, but the ground was so densely overgrown that we couldn't see much. We flew back into the main valley and found the large trail and several others crisscrossing on the valley floor. Tiger Five and I agreed on one intersection as a destination for the first night's movement, about six clicks south of the fire base in the main valley.

As we slid back into the fire base, the sun burst from behind a cloud for a few startling moments. It had rained twice that day, and the full rainy season would arrive soon. I wouldn't say that we enjoyed the dry season because we liked the weather, but I would say that we enjoyed it because it was not the rainy season. The rainy season meant heavy rain several times each day and night, overcast and usually drizzling the rest of the time. The rainy season cranked your emotions down a few notches: You could be only *sort of* happy if something good happened to you, like you were going back to the World or getting off line. But if something unpleasant happened to you, say, you lost your C ration cans of "GI cheesecake"—one of peaches and one of pound cake, which, when mixed, could produce tears of joy from the saltiest of line doggies—then you might start to consider suicide. "Dear John" letters during rainy season probably reduced the recipient's chances of survival by a factor of ten. Or a hundred.

The sun was welcome on my face when I got out of the slick, but it was gone again within ten or fifteen minutes. It was fully dark by six and Sidewinder called me on the radio at six-thirty and told me to move out. We slipped silently, stealthily, through the main gate, our faces and hands smeared with green-and-black camouflage stick. Flowing smoothly around the fire base, the Tiger Force crept into the valley.

The point man was the front man in the Indian-file formation we most commonly used. He was the main man, and he moved slowly and attentively and kept his weapon safety switch on full automatic. The slack man carried his weapon on semiautomatic to be able to support the point man quickly, and everyone else in the field carried his weapon with the safety switch turned to "safe" while moving.

The point and slack positions were much sought after in the 101st; that was where the action was. Back in Abu there were sets of people who walked point and slack together as teams for several hours at a time. The Tigers also had fiercely proud point and slack teams. There were four full-blooded American Indians in the Tiger Force: Specialist 4th Class Sohappy, from a Washington State fishing tribe; Private Jacaraw, an Apache from Flagstaff, Arizona; Specialist 4th Class Horsehead, a Sioux, from Minnesota; and Private Warder, a Cherokee from Oklahoma. Then there were two Cajuns, Perreau and LeBlanc, high school buddies who had grown up in the swamps around Lafayette, Louisiana, and now hunted the jungles together; four blacks from Los Angeles, New York City, and Chicago; Jackson, Farmer, Bad Ass Brown, and Razor Williams, the street-wise big-city dudes who had quickly picked up the new rules and became ruthless killers in the jungle; the Chicanos, Rivera from El Paso and Pico from Denver, who communed in Spanish; the "Texas Rangers," Baker from Dallas and Hall from Waco; and the "redneck" team, Jones from Little Rock and Crawford from Montgomery, who walked point and slack simply because they loved to kill.

The ethnic and cultural identity of these teams had been long encouraged, and I wasn't about to fool around with whatever sort of social leavening these teams provided for the unit. And a good point-slack team was hard to beat. "Pappy" Collins, the sergeant who commanded the first patrol, loved to walk point himself when things were tight. He was twenty-nine years old, the oldest man in the Tiger by five years (I was just twenty-four myself), and I heard he had been with the Tigers for close to three years, since the 101st had first come to the Nam in the summer of '65. After his first year he had been given thirty days' leave back in the World because he had extended, and another thirty days every six months after that.

Horsehead and Warder took the point that first night out. There was no moon visible through the clouds, and vision was restricted to one or two meters. The point was being directed by Sergeant Swenson, the second patrol leader who was walking right behind Warder, the slack man. Swenson, a young Viking from the Minneapolis suburbs, had a compass and was following the azimuth we had shot that afternoon to the position we wanted to reach on the first night.

We reached the trail intersection by around three, and huddled in an L-shaped ambush until dawn. Nothing walked up on us, and that morning I began sending ten- and fifteen-man patrols into other parts of the big valley, scouring out the smaller valleys by night as well as by day.

On the second night one Tiger patrol nailed three men in black pajamas who were really no more than boys, capturing the canvas bags they carried that were filled with some forty American claymore mines. They carried no personal weapons, and I openly mourned the apparently innocent deaths of these young human packhorses to Sergeant Haugh. He gave a cynical laugh, then shared the wisdom he had acquired long ago: "There ain't but one rule over here, sir: You kill the gooks, or they're gonna kill you, and that's the way it is."

There was a lot of enemy movement through the valley, which made it ideal for ambushes. We had good hunting for close to a week, scoring a body count of nine, capturing quite a bit of hardware, and suffering only two Dogwood eights, lightly wounded men who were evacuated.

Then, one day, the roof fell in on one of the line companies. At around four o'clock C Company walked into an ambush. They were badly mauled and in danger of being overrun, some twelve kilometers away from us over rough ground. Abu and the Tiger Force were called on to rescue them.

We got across the main valley and started up the ridge before nightfall. There was no trail, and we were fighting our way through thick jungle, trying to move too quickly in the pitch-dark. The temperature dropped into the fifties, and it started to rain hard. Every man was soaked to the skin, and the sodden rucksacks on our backs took on the weight of the world, carving trenches in our shoulders as rainwater streamed off bearded faces.

We clawed our way up that agony slope for endless hours, quickly bone tired and then completely exhausted.

Still the rain fell. The only noise was that of the point man's machete, interspersed with the occasional grunt and smothered obscenity as someone slipped. Suddenly there were two bursts of AK fire, green tracers, from a point that must have been a hundred meters in front of me. Everyone was down instantly. I tried to get the point team on the company's net when Haugh was beside me. "Who's on point, sir?" Two more bursts of AK fire, green tracers streaming off to our left.

"I think the Cajuns. Pappy's up there, can't be that far ahead."

Parker, my RTO, shoved the handset to me, and a low, hushed voice spoke over the radio. "Tiger, this is Pappy. Those bursts were at least fifty meters in front of us. I don't think they were shootin' at us, either, 'cause we could see the muzzle flashes from the side. Over."

I looked at Haugh quizzically. "Pappy, this is Tiger, roger that, wait, out." I then got on my battalion radio to call the TOC in the same hushed voice. "Bandbox, this is Tiger, over." The green fluorescence of my watch told me it was five after three. "This is Bandbox, go." The radio was being handled by some faceless infantry captain who was pulling radio duty in the TOC. "This is Tiger. Is Cottonmouth or Sidewinder there? Over."

"This is Bandbox. They're in the sack. Do you have a contact? Over." "This is Tiger. We just got fired up by one man. Over." "This is Bandbox, roger that, wait."

Sergeant Haugh's voice broke my stumbling reverie: "Shit, sir, I don't think that gook was shootin' at us either. First thing he woulda done is lob a coupla grenades. No reason for him to mark his position like that at night."

I saw immediately that was true . . . maybe. "Yeah, but we can't afford to fuck with him tonight. I'm gonna propose to Cottonmouth that we just lay up here till dawn; we've only got about three hours, and from what we been hearin' on the battalion net, C Company has been out of the shit for a couple hours now."

The radio crackled to life. "Tiger, this is Cottonmouth. Over."

"Cottonmouth, this is Tiger, we took two bursts of AK fire about zero-five ago, no Dogwoods, but we're still waiting in place to see what it is. Over."

"This is Cottonmouth, how far away was the source of fire? Over."

"This is Tiger, it's hard to say, maybe fifty meters in front of our point element. Over."

"This is Cottonmouth, roger that. We can't afford to get you hung up on that ridge; Charley Company needs you. I'll leave the decision up to you, but I want you to figure out some way to go around that contact. Maybe you ought to go back down the ridge a couple hundred meters, then go off to one side or the other for a couple hundred meters and come up the ridge a different way, see what I mean? Over."

My heart fell through my stomach. Go back *down* a couple hundred meters? What the fuck is wrong with that jerk? Doesn't he realize what our pace is out here?

"This is Tiger, roger that. Maybe you don't realize what our position is out here. We are in the complete dark, with heavy rain; the only way we can keep contact in our column is to hold on to the guy in front of you. The hill is very steep. We are moving maybe a couple hundred meters an hour. If we do what you say, it will be dawn before we get started up the hill again. Over."

"This is Cottonmouth, roger that. What do you propose? Over."

"This is Tiger. I propose that we stay where we are until dawn. I'll set up a hasty perimeter, but my men are exhausted, and if we keep this up, they'll be worthless when and if we get to Charley Company. I would remind you that you can run a racehorse to death. Over."

"This is Cottonmouth, wait, over."

Sergeant Haugh was perched over me attentively. "Is he talkin' to Sidewinder?"

"I don't know, I suppose so. Asshole is probably wearin' pajamas." The radio was dead for more than five minutes.

"Tiger, this is Cottonmouth, over."

"Tiger, go."

"Cottonmouth. I have discussed your situation with Sidewinder. I realize the extremity of your situation, but you are on a rescue mission. It is imperative that you get to Charley Company as soon as possible. Abu got tangled up at a stream crossing, so we're expecting you to get there first. Do you roger? Over."

"This is Tiger, I roger that. Is Charley Company still in contact? That isn't what I've been hearing over the battalion net. Over."

"This is Cottonmouth, that's affirmative. They're still taking incoming fire. Spooky has cleared up a lot of it, but they're still in need of all the help they can get. You will let us make the decisions, all you do is obey your orders, do you roger that? Over."

"This is Tiger, I roger that, over." Fuck! That fat bastard!

"This is Cottonmouth. Your orders remain to proceed to the rescue of Charley Company. I'll leave it to you how to get around that contact position. We don't really know how much farther you've got to go to the top of that ridge, but you've got almost three hours of darkness left. That should be long enough for you to get to the crest of the ridge. Now drive on, over."

I began to slip out of control. "This is Tiger. I don't think you know what you're saying. My men are collapsing all over each other. We're huddled together like a pack of wet rats. If we run into an ambush now, we'll all be killed! Every one of us! Over."

"This is Cottonmouth. Now *calm down*! You're not going to run into an ambush because they're not sitting up waiting for you to come up that steep ridge. Now you take charge, Tiger. I want you on top of that ridge by dawn. Do you roger? Over."

"This is Tiger, roger."

I was disgusted, but I was so bone weary that it just didn't seem to matter anymore. I turned and picked up the company net radio handset. "Pappy, this is Tiger, over."

"Pappy, go."

"Pappy, we've been told to press on and make it to the top of the ridge by dawn. I want you to head off to the left for fifty meters or so, then start back up the ridge. We've got to get around whoever fired those AK bursts without gettin' hung up. Do you roger? Over."

"This is Pappy, roger. I think we can slip by okay, 'less they got a whole shit pot of gooks on line up there waitin' for us. I'm going to move two machine guns up with my point element. Stay tight. Out."

I turned and began to lurch up that eternal hill, all sensory input coming from my blindly stumbling feet, my hand on the rucksack in front of me, the rain drumming rhythmically on the brim of my jungle hat. I retreated once again into myself, trying to wall off the pain in my legs and shoulders, to ignore the agony that washed through my body with every step as I grabbed at vines and branches with my free hand, tried to dig my toes into some sort of foothold in the mud and stone and trampled bushes. It was torture. And the rain came down.

Tiger Ridge

DAWN WAS GRAY rain around six, but we didn't reach the crest of the ridge until after seven. Then we headed down the game trail we found there toward C Company, now only five or six clicks away. After almost a thousand meters everyone froze on a signal from the point element. I met Haugh coming back to me as I crawled forward.

"What's up?"

"Found some sort of gook camp up ahead on a saddle of the ridge. If we get some men off on the left side here, we can get right up on 'em before they see us."

"Okay, do it."

Sergeant Haugh was quickly past me, and I crawled forward another thirty meters with my two RTOs, slipping up beside a prostrate Sergeant Collins.

"What's happenin', Pappy?"

"Right down there, sir, in that little depression in the ridge, see that pointed—wait, there—see 'em?"

A Vietnamese man in an olive drab uniform had just walked around a tree and was talking to two others who were squatting next to what appeared to be a campfire. I turned my head and saw Sergeant Haugh some thirty meters back waving his arm. Six or eight Tigers were loping down the side of the ridge, heading off to the left and toward the far side of the gook position. Soon there would be Tigers on two sides of the little campsite in an L formation.

I looked back at the gooks. All three of them were standing now. Two of them were holding rice bowls and looking off in the direction of the Tigers who were moving up into an enfilading position; the other was looking to my right. As I watched, all three

59

picked up AKs, and two of them headed for the moving Tigers, still on the other side of a small rise from them. The other gook kept his eyes riveted to my right.

Then suddenly he lifted his AK, but Pappy unleashed a burst of red tracers from his M-16. They were instantaneously soaked up by the shirt of the falling gook.

Then, in a flash, the Tigers came to life. The four or five other men in the point element were on their feet, firing and roaring as we swooped down the slope. The enfilading force rushed over the small rise on the left side of the camp and got to the fire as we did. There were only a few bursts of AK fire coming back now, from down the steep far side of the heavily overgrown ridge. There was one body next to the fire, another at the base of a large tree.

Parker, my battalion net RTO, grabbed my arm. "Sir, Sergeant Collins wants you."

I turned and saw Pappy, thirty meters away, beckoning me. I left Sergeant Haugh and walked back to Pappy, standing near the fire by an open bunker ringed with sandbags.

"Look at this shit, sir." Sergeant Collins was pointing into the sandbag-ringed open bunker, and as I walked up to him, I saw that the bunker held a wicked-looking well-oiled heavy mortar, mounted on its base plate with full sight attached, pointing menacingly down the ridge toward where Charley Company must be. Holy shit! An 82 mm mortar, intact! Wonder how many of these have been captured in the whole goddamn *war*! What a prize! I looked back at Sergeant Collins, and we both were stunned, laughing openmouthed. Wow! Well, maybe that night of misery on the ridge had been worth something. The gooks had obviously been caught with their pants down. They think they can keep tabs on us, but this night movement is something new on them. I called Parker over and got on the horn to Bandbox.

"Bandbox, this is Tiger. We have just surprised the Hanoi coastal artillery over breakfast. We have no Dogwoods, body count of two, two weapons, both AK-forty-sevens, and an eighty-two millimeter mortar, complete with baseplate, sight, about forty rounds of ammunition, and staring right down Charley Company's throat. Over."

"This is Sidewinder. Well done, Tiger, wait, out."

Now the adrenaline was pumping, and I laughed out loud, joined by all the Tigers around me. Then Sergeant Haugh was beside me, grinning hard. "Shit, sir, looks pretty good."

"Yeah, I just called the news in to Sidewinder. Wonder if we'll get to take it back with us."

As we talked, a tall Vietnamese soldier suddenly strode into view from behind a bush forty meters away, walking down the middle of the ridge trail as bold as brass, his AK slung over his shoulder. There was an instant of hesitation as he and we realized at the same instant what we were looking at. Then he dived into the downhill bushes, clutching for his AK as a fury of M-16 bullets followed him. There were Tigers no more than twenty meters from where he had appeared, and as they quickly recovered from their shock, they unleashed waves of M-16 fire into the vegetation. Several bursts of red tracers came out of the bushes, but they sailed harmlessly into the trees. Everyone knew that he was going to die, and the bloodlust was quickly boiling. Sergeant Collins was firing semiautomatic, squeezing off single rounds into the bushes, screaming to his men, "Kill him! Kill him!," the veins on his red throat standing out like knotted cords. Then he scrambled into the bushes with three other Tigers to finish him off. There was a brief flurry of violence; then they were dragging his blood-soaked carcass out of the bushes. Two of them dragged it by the feet down the small rise and into the camp clearing.

As Sergeant Collins passed me, I looked up at one of the Tigers, who had followed the body out of the bushes and stopped twenty meters away from and slightly above me. He carried his M-16 in his left hand and a gore-dripping knife in his right. He slowly raised this red appendage in front of his face, eyes closed to slits, head and hand trembling ever so slightly. Even with my eyes locked on him, I sensed a hush falling over the other Tigers, as if we were in the presence of and about to witness something mystical. I half expected him to make the sign of the cross with the hand that had just slashed life out of a chest. Instead, he slowly extended his tongue from his mouth and, with a long, soft stroke, licked the blood from his steel blade. Fierce, growling roars of approval sprang from the Tigers all around me. Frost descended on my heart, immobilizing it. I flashed back to my religious childhood: "Take and drink of this, for this is my blood. . . ." I turned my head away, stunned, shaken, soulshivered.

"Sergeant Haugh, get a patrol down that trail, see if he had any friends!" Sergeant Collins was already moving past the contact point, the members of his patrol ranging out loosely on either side of him. Everyone else was down now, still and waiting.

Then the radio crackled to life. "Tiger, this is Sidewinder, over."

"This is Tiger, we got a contact, I'll call you back, out." Let him cool his heels, I thought.

Within a few minutes Sergeant Collins came up on the company net. "Tiger, Pappy, over."

"Tiger, go."

"This is Pappy, nothin' up here now. No way we can tell if he had any friends with him, but if he did, we ain't gonna see 'em today. Over."

Sergeant Haugh was crouched next to me. "Sergeant Haugh, whaddya make of that?"

"Shit, sir, I don't know, but he lost his stripes real fast for stupidity." We both laughed quietly, somewhat relaxed now, letting the tension dissipate. "Probably just strolling back down the trail whistlin' 'Dixie,' comin' back to the safe rear area to get him some chow. D'ja see the look on his face when he come around that bush and seen the Tigers standin' on his breakfast?"

I grinned as I took the radio handset from Parker. "Sidewinder, this is Tiger, over."

"Tiger, this is Sidewinder. What's happening? Over."

"This is Tiger. We just had some NVA sergeant come strolling around the bend into camp for breakfast, so we greased him. Add one more body to our tally, one more AK, no Dogwoods, over."

"This is Sidewinder, roger that, well done. As for that mortar, we don't want you slowed down, so blow it in place. Then hook up with Charley Company, out."

We blew the mortar tube in place, then moved down the ridge. The linkup with Charley Company was effected without further problems at eleven-fifteen. We walked through the ambush area and then up onto the hill Charley Company had pulled back to. Abu had hooked up at about ten-thirty, and I met Warhawk—Captain Johnson—on the crest of the hill. We shook hands warmly, and I felt some of the tension flow out of me as I relaxed.

Within an hour Cottonmouth and Sidewinder had arrived in the Command & Control slick. They huddled on top of the hill with the captains, lieutenants, and some sergeants from Abu, Charley Company, and the Tiger Force, asking questions about the previous night, contacts each unit had had, and the mortar that the Tigers had captured and blown.

Then they began to talk about tactics. The 1st Battalion, 327th

Infantry had orders to evacuate its position and move by truck convoy to Camp Eagle, the division base west of Hue some fifty miles to the north. The Marine Corps would be sending trucks to transport us the next day, so all units were to return to the fire base that day. Charley Company was to return with Abu, moving up the ridgeline to the north and then sweeping west across the small plain that separated the fire base from the ridgelines. We in Tiger Force would move down the same ridgeline to the south, retracing our steps and checking on the mortar position we had been through that morning, then swinging down into the main valley and sweeping back north to the fire base.

I was uneasy about this. "Sir, I don't like the sound of that. Everything I've ever heard says you don't go back the way you came in this country."

Sergeant Haugh was even more outspoken. "That's right, sir, we move back down that ridge, and we'll be ambushed just bigger'n shit!"

Sidewinder spoke with authority. "Relax, Tiger, and you, too, Tiger Five. We're moving only a couple of clicks down the ridge in broad daylight. We just want to check on enemy activity, see if he's been back to that mortar position. We don't want him operating too freely. If you expect an ambush, then you know what to do. It's going to be your responsibility to keep him off guard here. We're leaving, but we want him to think we're still around. Now, we haven't been getting much body count out of the Tiger Force lately. Let's see what you're made of. Get things going!"

I bit back my anger. You dumb shit, I thought, if you expect to get ambushed on a ridge trail, you don't go down that trail!

The C&C slick soon clattered away, leaving us in jungle's silence. I talked to Warhawk, who agreed to stay in place for a few hours, just in case we walked into an ambush. Charley probably had trail watchers keeping an eye on us, and if we went back that way, it spelled trouble. My sergeants were edgy, too, but we had our orders.

The rain began to come down in earnest as we moved out. I was so tired I could barely keep my mind focused on even the genuine life-threatening dangers before us. I moved blindly for more than an hour, my body screaming for rest. I knew we all were out on our feet.

Then a bloodcurdling yell from the front startled me wide-awake:

"Claymore! Claymore!"

Pappy's shrill scream had barely registered in my mind when I was nearly blown down by an enormous explosion from the front. A blast of hot air rushed by my face as I was throwing myself down thoughtlessly. The impact of what was happening had not yet fully registered. My God, what? There was the roar of RPD fire from the front, another explosion, and another, then more RPD fire in a relentless blur of deafening noise. I was stunned, my exhausted body not realizing what was happening. I groped at MacGregor who was extending the handset to me. The roar of noise from the front told me we had walked into the dreaded ambush. Goddamn Sidewinder, that sorry motherfucker!

"Pappy, this is Tiger, over." No answer. I turned to my left rear as Sergeant Jackson frantically crawled past me with four men. Only Pappy's patrol was in front of him, maybe twelve men, spread out at five- to ten-meter intervals, just to avoid an ambush. I yelled at Sergeant Jackson, now five meters in front of me. *"Starbuck! Starbuck!* Come up on Pappy's left! Get your patrol over on the left!"

Sergeant Jackson instantly scuttled off to his left with his men, over the edge of a steep slope that leveled out some ten meters below us.

I turned onto my back and began to wave my arms frantically as Jackson's men came crawling up madly behind me. "Over there! Over that drop-off! Starbuck is over there. Get over to him!" Eight or ten men disappeared over the edge as Sergeant Swenson came crawling up behind them. "Viking, I got no radio contact with Pappy. See if you can get up there and find out what's going on!"

"Roger, sir. How many witch doctors up there?"

"Just one with Pappy, and I think one went by with Starbuck. I sent him over the edge on the left there."

Sergeant Quartz, the head medic in the Tigers, was suddenly on my left. "I'm goin' up with Viking, sir."

"Okay, then leave his medic here. Gimme a shout if you need him."

Up front we could hear one of our M-60 machine guns open up, from Starbuck's unit off to the left, then another, their deep roar balancing the much faster, sharper RPD and AK fire from the enemy.

"Where's the FO?"

"Right here!" He came plunging up behind Viking, green but eager, followed by his calmer experienced NCO. "You've got a prearranged target down this ridge. Put a marking round in down there, and then walk it down the ridge. And walk it slow!"

"Roger!" Then the artillery forward observer lieutenant got on his radio to the battery at the fire base.

The fire from Starbuck's area intensified, and the company radio crackled to life. "Tiger, Starbuck over."

"Tiger, go."

"Starbuck. We got a bag of shit over here. I can see where Pappy's unit is pinned down, but I can't get to him yet. I need more men to hold my left. Over."

"This is Tiger, roger that. I'm sending Viking up the trail to Pappy. I'll have him send some men over to link up with you, out. Break. Viking, this is Roger, did you monitor my call to Starbuck? Over."

"This is Viking, roger that. Starbuck is off to my left, I'll send some men to him. Pappy is Dogwood six. Maybe seven or eight other Dogwoods. We've got to get—"

The radio went dead. "Viking, Tiger, over."

"This is Viking's Oscar. Viking is a Dogwood. We need more witch doctors up here, beaucoup Dogwoods, over." Fuck I thought. Pappy Collins dead! That bastard Sidewinder and his goddamn Napoleon games!

"Viking Oscar, this is Tiger, roger that. We're gonna walk some Red Leg down the ridge to help out. Hold tight. Break. Polar Bear, Tiger, over."

"Tiger, this is Polar Bear. I'm forty meters behind you, over."

"This is Tiger, get about ten men over the edge of the ridge on the left and up to Starbuck's position; send the rest up here to me. Over."

"This is Polar Bear, roger, wilco, out." Jesus, I thought, now where's Sergeant Haugh? "Break. Uncle Jimmy, this is Tiger, over."

I looked back to my rear and saw Sergeant Parsons (Polar Bear) lunge over the side of the ridge with a group of his men in pursuit. Good to have a kamikaze once in a while when you need one. The rest of Polar Bear's men were flooding up the trail toward me. Behind them, some fifty meters away, I saw Uncle Jimmy loping up the trail in a deep crouch, a group of men strung out behind him. Thank God! The RPD and AK fire had shifted somewhat, most of it now coming from off to the left. Jesus! Pappy dead, Viking hit, at least a half dozen other men hit. What a fuck! We've got to get out of this shit!

I grabbed the battalion net radio, that was tuned to another agreed frequency so I could talk to Warhawk, from Parker, who had been keeping Warhawk advised.

"Warhawk, Tiger, over."

"Warhawk, go."

"This is Tiger, we're in some shit. 'Preciate it if you could help out. We're about fifteen, eighteen hundred meters down the ridge from you. Over."

"Tiger, Warhawk, roger that, we're on our way—" The world stopped as I was lifted off the ground by an explosion that came from behind me. Three simultaneous explosions hit between me and Starbuck. I was stunned, unable to think. What the fuck was that? Could only be artillery. Jesus, they had big guns somewhere! Who got hit? God Almighty, where is our own artillery? I depressed the key on the handset. "Warhawk, this is Tiger, we just took artillery fire, direct hit. We're in real trouble. I'm going back to the battalion net, out." My hands were shaking as I twisted the dials, bracing myself against the expected next barrage.

"Bandbox, Bandbox, this is Tiger, we're in deep shit. Over."

"Tiger, this is Cottonmouth, whaddya got? Over." As I listened to Cottonmouth, I heard my own FO sobbing twenty feet away as the artillery NCO talked to the artillery battery: "I say again, do *not* repeat that target, you got a direct hit on friendly forces, over."

That was our own artillery! My rage was cooled only by concern for my men. "Cottonmouth, we walked into the expected ambush; we just took four rounds of direct-hit artillery fire, suspect that it was friendly. If not, they've got our range perfectly with hostile artillery. Over."

"This is Cottonmouth, wait, out."

I turned around. Uncle Jimmy was crawling toward me some thirty meters away, his face white as a sheet. Behind him were five or six men; over on my right were another ten or twelve from Polar Bear's patrol. "Sir, we got to pull Pappy back, we're takin' Red Leg fire!"

"I know, get up here, we're going to assault on the right." I was so scared I had trouble breathing. But there was no time to worry about that. "All right, Tigers, everybody crawl up here. When I give the word, everybody up on line."

I was breathing fast and shallow now, feeling my thighs tremble like leaves in the wind. The Tigers quickly threw themselves across the narrow ridge. "All right, don't shoot until you can see that you're shooting at gooks. Pappy and Viking are in front of us, Starbuck and Polar Bear off to the left. We're gonna move through them. Wait a minute!"

I lurched over to the artillery NCO and took the handset from him and depressed the key. "Red Leg, this is Tiger, do not fire anymore in support of us until I tell you to. Do not take any fire direction orders from our Foxtrot Oscar, do you roger? Over."

"Tiger, this is Red Leg, I would remind you that you are using the Red Leg net without authorization. If you want to talk to me, have your Foxtrot Oscar call me or ask to talk to me over the bandbox net, over."

I was incredulous. I keyed the mike. "Listen, you motherfucker, this is life and death. Do not, I say again, do *not* shoot until I tell you to, out."

I threw the mike down in disgust. "All right, everybody up on line." I stood up shakily. "Let's go. And roar like Tigers!" And I roared as I hadn't done since high school football. The line wavered forward, bellowing. Within thirty meters we came to Pappy's pinned-down patrol. Viking had moved most of his men off to the right to get flanking fire. His men stood up as we reached them and joined us, roaring and spitting fire from their weapons. Starbuck was off to the left, slightly below and in front of us. The bulk of the hostile fire was coming from down the ridge and the jungle-covered high ground that could be seen off to our left, some thirty or forty meters beyond Starbuck. I poured lead at muzzle flashes, fury and terror coursing through my head. As the rage of our assault washed over Pappy's position, the RPD fire abated, and the enemy fire was soon only scattered AK bursts.

Some twenty meters beyond the front of Pappy's position, we stopped and got down. I yelled to my sergeants aloud, asking for a situation report. Then I left the assaulting force in position and scurried back with my RTOs to just behind Pappy's patrol but still in sight of Starbuck and Viking's units. I called Red Leg and told him to take fire orders from our artillery reconnaissance sergeant. Then I began to assess our losses, talking to Pappy's Oscar and the other patrol leaders.

Pappy was dead. As they were moving down the trail, he had had his favorite point team, Horsehead and Jacaraw, the Indians, up front. He was walking in the number five position. They had entered the killing zone of the ambush when Pappy saw a Chinese claymore mine tied to the trunk of a tree behind a screen of cut branches. It was circular, two feet across and six inches deep, looking like nothing so much as maybe a small archery target. It was supposedly lethal at two hundred meters, and when Pappy saw it, his entire patrol was within the killing zone. He had screamed a warning and rushed over to pull it off the tree. But just as he reached it, it had been detonated, and then the unsuspected others followed in quick succession. The first had disintegrated Pappy's head, left arm, and left shoulder. Because of his warning, everyone was flat on the ground when they went off—everyone but him.

The gooks had been waiting as supporting forces moved up on the left and they walked into a hornets' nest. Over the next hour or so, complete with a friendly artillery barrage right on top of us, a lot of Tigers had gone down. Three more had been killed; eight or nine, seriously wounded. Our artillery recon sergeant was able to call in effective supporting fire, and the enemy drifted away. A platoon from Abu had been sent flying down the ridge and arrived just as hostile contact was dissolving.

Starbuck came back up the ridge with his men. Four dead! Fuck! I got on the horn to Cottonmouth and told him the bad news. Ten meters away Jacaraw and Starbuck were carrying a poncho containing a body, blood running freely out the tail end. Tears were running down both men's faces unashamedly. Uncle Jimmy was rooting around in the bushes another twenty meters down the trail. Then he followed them, opened the poncho, gently placed a piece of a hand and a piece of hair-covered scalp inside, and just as gently pulled the poncho closed. He stood up, snuffled, wiped his now-bloody arm across his tear-filled eyes, and absentmindedly wiped the blood from his hands on the seat of his pants. Then he turned away as tears began to fill his eyes again, hawked deep, and spit into the bushes.

I took the handset from Parker and talked to Sidewinder. "I think we're gonna have to take our Dogwoods back to the Lima Zulu we used this morning, over."

"This is Sidewinder, roger that. Warhawk should be at your location soon. I think you should let him take all of your Dogwoods back to that Lima Zulu, and then you finish your sweep. It's hard to take all those Dogwoods, I realize, but you've got to remember your mission. I know the men are probably feeling tired now, but this is where real leadership comes out. Let's see what you've got, over."

I was dumbfounded. Did that dumb shit really mean what he was saying? I turned on my other side, saw Warhawk coming up the trail to me some thirty meters away. I couldn't believe what I had just heard. "Tiger, this is Sidewinder, do you roger my last transmission? Over." Warhawk was holding his hand up in the air and yelled, "I heard that, just give him a 'Roger, out.' I'll talk to him later. Now let's get your Dogwoods ready, and we'll get them back to that LZ. Then we'll all get back to the fire base."

I grunted. "Yeah, okay," then picked up the handset again. "Sidewinder, this is Tiger. Roger, out."

I gave the handset back to Parker, then stumbled wearily to my feet. "Shit. Well, let's get outa here. Sergeant Haugh, Dogwoods ready to go?"

Sergeant Haugh was still standing next to Pappy's shrouded body. "Roger that, sir. We could use some help from A or C Company carryin' 'em, though."

Warhawk waved his arm. "That's no problem." He half turned and shouted over his shoulder. "Lieutenant Shields!" A man raised his head thirty meters down the trail. "Get your platoon down here. Tigers need some help carryin' their Dogwoods." He turned back to me, his eyes ranging across the canopy overhead. "Doesn't look like we'll be able to chop an LZ anywhere up here. Guess we'll have to take 'em back to that hill we were on this morning. Got any critically wounded?"

I turned and looked down the trail. The Dogwood sixes were neatly wrapped in ponchos and stacked along one side of the trail. The Dogwood eights were on the other side of the trail, being treated, now, by the Tiger medics as well as several from A and C companies. I couldn't see Sergeant Quartz anywhere. "Sergeant Quartz!"

The nearest tiger-suited medic with his back to me turned and looked at me, still holding something in his hands over the wounded Tiger he was treating. "Sir?" I walked down to him.

"We got any Dogwood eights we've got to extract here? We're gonna try to get back to the Lima Zulu we used this morning for dustoffs. Anybody can't make it?"

"Yes, sir, we got two, maybe three are bad. Robbins is unconscious, pretty nasty head wound. Johnson's got a bad gut wound, internal bleeding, and we really ought to get Sergeant Parsons out, lost a lot of blood and he's in shock."

Warhawk had brought air support with him, and now the F-4s were droning overhead, roaring in on a line parallel to the ridge, plastering the plateau a hundred meters away. We had taken this for granted, crouching and tensing for the explosion on each pass without even thinking about it. Sergeant Haugh moved up beside me. "Sir, about that air support—we got no contact left now. Whyncha move it down the ridge a couple hundred meters?"

I felt numb. I looked at Sergeant Haugh blankly. "Here," I said, handing him the handset, "you do it. I wanta see if I can talk to Polar Bear."

Sergeant Haugh got on the line to the forward air controller (FAC), circling overhead in his little Piper Cub-like 0-1 and controlling the flight of F-4s.

The air strikes soon moved down the ridge as I got to Sergeant Parsons's litter. Two medics were working on him. One of them was holding a bottle of albumin in the air, the tube out the bottom extending down to his arm, a big needle inserted into the inside of his forearm. Parsons's eyes were closed. His legs were swathed in bandages, the stumps grotesquely chopped short just above his knee. "Is he okay?"

"No, sir, he's not too good. Doesn't know what happened to him yet."

Polar Bear's eyes opened, and he started to jabber. "Never get me down in that mine again, no, sir. Cedric 'n' Rachel was here, said they was comin' back on Sunday. . . ."

I looked at one of the medics. "Still in shock, sir."

"God, I'm cold, sir. I'm dreadful cold. Cedric oughta be here soon, don't know what we're gonna do. . . ."

I felt helpless. The rain started to come down in earnest now. I pulled the edge of the poncho one medic was holding over Parsons's face up a little farther, knowing there was nothing I could do. The medic with the albumin bottle reassured me. "He's gonna be all right, sir."

"Yeah, he'll be all right." I got up and started to move back to Warhawk.

Polar Bear was yelling after me. "Don't let Mama come in here, sir."

I yelled to Warhawk, "We need an extraction here 'fore we move, three men, maybe more, I dunno."

Warhawk waved his hand. "No sweat, Tiger, we got a dustoff with a basket that's about zero-five out." I turned and went back down the trail.

Robbins was lying unconscious, Sergeant Quartz squatting next to him. "How is he?"

"Dunno, sir, he's gotta get out first. Are we gonna get an extractor?"

"Yeah, we got a dustoff with a basket about zero-five out."

"Good."

I went to the next man, Johnson, fresh-faced teenager, his gut ripped open by two or three RPD rounds, now swathed in blood-soaked bandages. He had been given albumin and was able to talk somewhat, but was flat on his back. I knelt next to him and bent over close to his death-white face. "How are ya, Johnson?"

Johnson's face was wet with tears, snot, and blood. Raindrops splashed lightly, unnoticed. He looked desperately at me. "I don't wanna die, sir."

"You're not gonna die, Johnson, you're gonna be okay."

I was distracted by the roar of the dustoff, now dropping to tree-top level thirty or forty meters up, the blast from the rotors blowing crap around in the rain. I squinted and looked up, seeing the stretcher basket being dropped down on a cable. A couple of medics grabbed it as it got down to them and swung it over to Robbins. He was quickly loaded and strapped in, then was being winched up through the trees. Johnson's voice caught my attention again. "Don't let me die, please, sir, please."

I turned and looked down at Johnson. "You're gonna be all right, don't worry."

I looked at the bulging white bandages stretched over his guts, the red stain spreading through the bandages faster than the medics could put them on. I stood up uneasily and went to the next man: Sergeant Swenson, a sucking chest wound. He was flat on his back, an albumin bottle almost empty, still draining into his arm as the medic held it aloft. "How are you, Viking?"

Viking's face was blanched now, but he was in control. "I'll be all right, sir. We got hit pretty hard, huh?"

"Yeah, I guess we did. But don't you worry about that. You just take care of gettin' yourself all fixed up."

Viking grunted and looked up.

I turned and watched as they strapped Johnson into the basket. I felt uneasy about this kind of extraction. But they hadn't drawn any fire as yet, and the F-4s were back hammering the ridge to the south and the plateau a few hundred meters to the west.

After Viking and Polar Bear were evacuated, we moved back down the ridge to that morning's LZ. The rest of the Dogwood eights were evacuated from there, along with the bodies of the Dogwood sixes. Then we all began to move back to the fire base. The Tiger force quickly fell into line behind A Company on the trail. I moved like a zombie, one foot behind the other, not knowing what was happening, not even caring. It seemed like an eternity down that ridgeline, across the lowlands, then up the road, and suddenly we were through the concertina wire that surrounded the fire base.

I was still somewhat dazed when Captain Kobiyashi, the headquarters company commander, grabbed my arm. "Tiger, we want you to put your men in one of those big storehouse bunkers over by the TOC. They've been emptied for the move, so you should be able to get everybody inside one of them. Then Cottonmouth wants to see you in the TOC."

I nodded silently, then turned to the line of Tigers that was beginning to form into a knot behind me. I mustered all the strength I could but still felt half dead. "All right, Tigers, we're gettin' one of the warehouse bunkers. Everybody inside; then you can sleep or cook Cs or whatever you want." I turned a quizzical eye to Kobiyashi, who nodded in affirmation, and continued. "Any of you Tigers haven't got enough Cs, let me know, or Sergeant Miller here. We're gonna be moving by truck tomorrow, so get all the rest you can now. We expect you to be bright-eyed and bushy-tailed in the morning."

A chorus of mumbled groans came from the Tigers as they moved fifty meters to the bunker and disappeared inside. I dropped my rucksack and my load-bearing equipment web belts at the door, then turned with just my weapon and trudged over to the TOC. Fuck, I thought, here we go. Well, I don't give a shit; they can say anything they want to me. I stumbled on the sandbag threshold as I stepped into the familiar coolness of the big bunker. Cottonmouth and Sidewinder were sitting in a corner on camp chairs, talking to Warhawk. Cottonmouth looked up as I stumbled over to them. "Tiger! You look exhausted. We'll let you go get some sleep in just a minute. We just wanted to tell you 'well done' before you turn in. You had a tough job out there, and you handled it well. We're proud of you."

What? What kind of shit is this? You're supposed to chew me out! Sidewinder turned in his chair. "Good job, Tiger. Now before you turn in, we just want to make sure you understand we'll be leaving in the morning, so make sure your men get plenty of rest. They deserve it!"

I was totally disarmed by this surprising approach. My mind

fumbled for a response. "Yes, sir, thank you. I'm sorry about all that shit up by—"

Cottonmouth broke in. "Relax, Tiger, you're exhausted, but we think you did a good job. Now go get some sleep." They both were smiling. I didn't know what to make of it.

"Yes, sir," I mumbled, then wearily stumbled out the door and over to the warehouse bunker. It was raining hard again now, but I barely even noticed it. Fuck, I mumbled under my breath. A few Tigers were heating Cs as I dragged my rucksack into the bunker, but I didn't even know what food was; all I wanted was some sleep. I threw my ruck against one wall at the first open space I came to, wrapped myself in my poncho liner, and fell into a deep sleep.

Fast Shuffle

I AWOKE THE NEXT MORNING just before noon, when a convoy of marine trucks came rolling through the wire. Then Captain Kobiyashi appeared. "Tiger, this convoy is gonna be leavin' in about three-zero for Camp Eagle. The Tiger Force will be on the last three trucks; just have 'em throw all their shit on the trucks. It should be about a two-hour drive. Any questions?"

"Hnn. No, no problem." I stood up and stretched, still exhausted, and walked outside. "Sergeant Haugh! Our trucks are here. We're on the last three trucks; we're leavin' in about three-zero minutes. Make sure everybody gets all their shit up on those trucks."

Sergeant Haugh came over to me, looking nasty in his Tiger suit with about three weeks' growth of beard. "Okay, sir."

I found the next-to-last truck and wrenched my way up into the cab. There was no glass in the back window, and Parker and Mac-Gregor were seated in the front of the truck bed, just outside the open window, where they could quickly pass their radio handsets to me. There was a delay of another ten or fifteen minutes after all the Tigers had been loaded, and then a quick commo check with the convoy commander, Lieutenant Wayman, the marine rear-echelon motherfucker (REMF) in command of the convoy. Soon we were headed out through the wire. I felt like hell and laid my head back against the worn canvas seatback, hoping I'd be able to get some sleep.

It was early in April 1968. We would come to Highway 1 within a few clicks, follow that north for fifty miles or so to Hue, then travel the well-used road out to Camp Eagle. Convoys used these roads every day of the week, the road was lined with U.S. installations, and there hadn't been an ambush on this road in months, since the big Tet offensive on the last day of January. I was drained and dozed off quickly. But within a few minutes I was startled awake by gunfire from the truck behind ours. There was one truck of Tigers in front of mine, and one behind it, and short bursts were being fired off to the right from the latter. I quickly sat up, turned, and looked out the back window.

Now my own truck and the one in front had also opened up, and the .50 caliber machine gun, manned by a marine in a cupola on the roof above me had opened up as well. Then I saw tracers going out to the right side of the road. I looked out the door window. In the distance a click or so was the ocean. Three or four hundred meters away, however, a railroad trestle, built by the French but no longer in use, rose a few meters above the rice paddies that covered the area between it and the roadway. In this enclosed area there was a herd of fifty or so big black water buffalo. The Tigers were shooting at them, and they had begun to charge around wildly, many of them going down in the waist-deep paddy water now churned to a bloody froth. I hesitated, but then I was horrified and threw my torso out the back window and into the truck bed, screaming, "Cease fire! Cease fire!"

My truck quickly stopped firing, but the truck behind me was still pouring death into the paddy when I grabbed the driver and told him to stop. As the trucks screeched to a halt, I got out and stumbled back to the truck behind us, my head pounding like a trip-hammer, feeling sick and pissed-off. The firing had stopped as the trucks stopped, and as I came alongside, I yelled into the truck bed, "Goddammit, I said to cease fire!"

Sergeant Haugh was sitting on the side of the truck bed, nonchalantly clearing his weapon and seating a fresh magazine. "Shit, sir, we got fired up."

"Anybody hit?"

"No, sir, but we better move on. This is a bad spot for us to be sittin'."

Lieutenant Wayman had turned his jeep around and pulled up next to me in the road. He was mad as hell. He yelled directly up into the truck, "What the hell was all that firing about?"

That pissed me off, so I turned to him. "Just a minute, Lieutenant. I'm in command of these men. You want to talk to them, you talk to me! They were fired up, so they returned the fire."

Now the only noise was from the other side of the truck, where we could hear the wounded water buffaloes' death agonies. I stared at Wayman for a few seconds; then the marine had his driver turn around. He stopped by my truck on his way back to the head of the column and yelled at the marine machine gunner on top of the cab, "What the hell were you firing at?"

"We got fired up, sir. I just fired back."

"Did those water buffalo shoot at you?"

"Yes, sir, I mean, there was somebody shootin' at us from over there." Fat chance, I thought.

"C'mon, Wayman, let's get outa here, we're sittin' ducks." We exchanged scowls; then his jeep pulled away toward the front of the column. I didn't really know what to do as I swung back up into the cab of my truck. I looked over to the right at the herd of water buffalo milling around. I could see five or six down in the water, others struggling and thrashing around, the water churned white and red, not a gook to be seen. I had to take care of my men, but Jesus what a ruthless bunch. They were very good at their job, which was killing the enemy, but God Almighty, this was just random violence.

When we arrived at Camp Eagle, I found that it was little more than a huge, sprawling encampment of long army tents pitched along the sides of a dirt road. I never really learned what the north-south dimensions of the camp were, but the tents ran seemingly for miles along one road. As one approached from Hue to the east, first there were several kilometers of open grasslands. There was a major Special Forces camp on a small hill off to the north of the road, and then the clay road ran over a small rise and through a barbed-wire perimeter, on the far side of which some giant plowman seemed to have ripped the red earth open and left it to bake in the sun, pock-marked by the canvas measles of countless identical rectangular army tents.

Once into this morass of olive drab, one quickly forgot about direction, save that the U.S. presence seemed stretched along the ground like some giant dry slug. Beyond our own unit's 1st Brigade area, was the 2nd Brigade of the 82d Airborne Division encampment, with all its associated administrative service areas. Beyond that was the main 101st Airborne Division forward base area. First were the helicopter service areas, then the motor pools, and finally the division administrative area. Beyond that were the headquarters areas for the other two brigades in the division. In short, it was a very large U.S. military installation, with certainly many thousand support troops stationed there in support of the troops in the field.

As the marine convoy carrying the Tiger Force pulled into

Camp Eagle, I got my first glimpse of it, but I was no sooner aware of its immensity than we had arrived at the base camp for the 1st Battalion, 327th Infantry, two rows of eight or ten large tents. It took us less than ten minutes to clear everything from the trucks, and then they were gone. A couple of sergeants directed us into two big tents, where we laid our gear on the ground, and the Tigers were soon put to work, cleaning their weapons and other gear and preparing to return to the field.

I went back to the administrative tent where the Tigers were staying and got an update on the wounded who had been evacuated. I had just heard that Polar Bear died in Da Nang the night before when a sergeant came in the tent looking for me: Cottonmouth wanted to see me. It was five minutes before four o'clock. I stood up, stretched, and followed the sergeant back outside the tent into the pale light and soft mist.

I walked inside the dark tent and reported. "Sir, Lieutenant Carhart reports to the battalion executive officer as ordered."

My salute was quickly returned by a half-smiling Cottonmouth. "C'mon in, Lieutenant Carhart, sit down." Here we go, I thought, as I gently perched on the edge of a folding metal chair. "You had a tough time, Tiger, and as we told you the other day, we think you did all you could. Still," he continued, looking blindly up at the top of the tent, folding his hands behind his head, "you got into a real mess there—and that wasn't your fault. Don't get me wrong; there wasn't anything anyone could have done."

Like hell, I thought. Sidewinder ordered us to walk into that ambush, and you probably concurred, you bastard! "No, sir."

"Anyway, we've decided you need a rest. A man can't take too much of that, and you sure got more'n your share of death the other day." He was smiling again, throwing me off guard. I smiled with him, thinking, What the hell are we laughing about? Those men are dead!

"Lieutenant Blank got back from the hospital yesterday, and as you may recall, we gave you the Tigers only until he was ready to go again. He's still the number one Tiger, and he's gonna take 'em back to the field in a few days. We didn't forget you, though, and we got you a job in the personnel shop at Brigade. I think you might be pleased to know that your old friend Major Wallace is the brigade S-one. He'll be your boss."

Major Wallace! Snake Eater, the old battalion S-3! He had been wounded soon after I had, and had spent several weeks in the Cam

Ranh Bay hospital with me. An unexpected stroke of luck, but I still didn't like what was happening. "Where's the battalion commander, sir?"

"He got back from R and R a few days ago, but he's still down in Bien Hoa taking care of personal matters. You can talk to him when he gets back, of course, but I think he'll back me up on this. Want me to see if I can get you an appointment to see him when he gets back?"

I was in a box, and I knew it. "No, sir."

"All right, then you just go back to headquarters company. The first sergeant will send you up to the brigade area in a jeep. It's only a few hundred meters down the road. You've been through a pretty rough experience. I think you'll find that the pressures here aren't nearly what they were on line, and maybe you'll be able to relax." He was speaking in a quiet voice, his tone almost soothing.

I was furious, and my clenched teeth and hot eyes spoke my bitterness. You goddamned mealymouthed REMF! "What about my men, sir?"

"What men are you speaking of?"

"The men who got killed when we walked into that ambush, sir!" I felt a strand of cold snot on my cheek that I had snorted out in fury as I spoke.

"Carhart, you've got to settle down!" Cottonmouth half snarled. Then, in a softer more conciliatory tone: "I already told you, there was nothing anyone could have done about that. That's war, and as Sherman said, war is hell! You, of all people, ought to know that. Now I know you're a little bit overwrought, and maybe you've got some reason for that in your own mind. But a leader can't think like that. You can't pay any attention to the men you lose because if you start worrying about every man that dies, then you'll be consumed! The only thing a leader can pay any attention to, especially an infantry leader on the ground here in Vietnam, is the mission! What's your mission? That's all you can do. Do you think Napoleon would ever have gotten to where he did if he'd worried about casualties?"

I was stunned. "How can you say that, sir? How can you say their deaths don't count?"

"I didn't say that, Lieutenant. I said you can't let those deaths affect you. Of course, those deaths bother me. Do you really think that didn't bother us? We were bleeding with you in the TOC. I'll bet we were hurt as bad as you by what happened out there." LIAR! my mind screamed. LIAR! LIAR! LIAR! "Of course, that hurt us; it hurt every man in the battalion. But we could stand back and see more of the big picture. *We* knew what was important for us, not just for the Tiger Force or a company or even for the whole battalion, but we could see a little piece of what the American presence here is all about. And *that's* the only important thing—not what happens to you or me, or *any* individual soldier, even General Westmoreland, but what happens in the war! And the only way we can have even the slightest effect on anything is to perform our mission without starting to feel sorry for ourselves."

I felt stymied. You know everything, you bastard, I thought. I didn't know if what I was hearing was right or not. It sounded crazy. Maybe the generals did have to think like that, but anyone who could coldly ignore the men whose lives were snatched away from them out in the jungle wasn't worth talking to. And I was sure that most of these bastards in the rear didn't even know what was going on out there.

"But, sir, what about those men who died? They were good, brave men—boys, some of 'em—and they gave their lives!"

"I know they did. They gave their lives, and that's the greatest bravery you can ever ask of a man. But then you've got to ask yourself what you're doing here. You know the opposition to the war is starting to heat up back in the World, but that doesn't matter. Warfare is as old as mankind, and it'll probably still be part of life as long as anyone is left around on this planet. And in this case our leaders decided the United States had vital interests at stake in this little, shit-eaten country, and they sent their young men here to fight for those interests. I don't know whether they're right or wrong, and neither does anyone else. But the question comes down to whether or not you trust your leaders. I agree with you, the deaths of your men are tragic if you think about them. They didn't want to die; nobody does! But if you're a leader, you accept the deaths of all your men before you get here, and then everyone who survives is a bonus! It doesn't matter if they die in an ambush, like your men did, or the airplane bringin' 'em over from San Francisco crashes in the middle of the Pacific. They're just as dead. But you can't allow yourself to get caught up in deaths of your men if you're a leader. Do you begin to see that?"

I was stunned and confused. He was probably right, at least in part. But what about those guys Sidewinder sent to their deaths by ordering us to go back down that ridge? They might have lived through the war and gone home to their families if it hadn't been for that! "I don't know, sir. Maybe part of what you say is right. But what about the poor bastard who gets greased because his commander fucks up? What happens when somebody makes a mistake and gets people killed?"

"I already told you, you offer your life the minute you put on a uniform and get on the airplane that brings you over here. The offer of your life for your country has been accepted, that's all. Nobody likes to see their soldiers killed, and nobody knowingly sends soldiers to their death ordinarily. But sometimes they even do that, and there can be justifiable reasons for doing that, too. It all depends on the situation and your mission. I know you and some of the other men on line get a little bit upset with us and the other guys who are pretty safe inside the TOC while they're getting shot at. But that's all chance, the luck of the draw. I'll tell you something, I'd give anything to be in your boots, a young infantry lieutenant who actually gets the chance to fight and kill and risk his life for his country. That's a real honor and a privilege! And you're especially lucky; you were wounded once, but it wasn't too bad, and you came back to fight again. Now you have that red badge of courage, and nobody can ever take that away from you or what that says about your patriotism. But I didn't get that chance, so I'll never know if I'm that brave. I'm a major, not a lieutenant, so I have to sit in the rear and sweat things out for you guys. And you may not believe this, but that's not easy. Now take back the life you offered and be grateful. You may live through this year, and if you do, you will have lived through a noble and honorable experience."

I was unsure of what to say or do. "I don't want to leave the line, sir. I want to stay in the field until my year is up."

"Well, that's another thing about this war and the way of the world, Carhart. We're not handing out choices. Now when you get told to do something by your commander, you don't question it, you *do* it! Y'understand that?" Cottonmouth had suddenly changed from patient, fatherly counselor to hardass, and I was just as suddenly back in my underling role.

"Yes, sir!"

"All right, now as I told you, you did a good job while you were here, and you'll get a plaque and a certificate through channels. Just try to calm down a little bit and get some of the violence you've been living out of your system. There'll be plenty for you to do as S-one without having to worry quite so much about survival on a daily basis. Now you'd better get your gear moved up to Brigade. Got any more questions?"

"No, sir."

"Okay, that's all I have. First sergeant'll have a jeep waiting for you."

I stood up stiffly and saluted. "Above the Rest, sir."

"Above the Rest."

I turned and strode back out the doorway of the tent, ducking to miss the canvas folds that blocked my way. I smoldered as I walked back to the headquarters company area, but I didn't know what I could or should say or do. I decided I'd just better follow orders. There was a jeep parked in front of the main orderly room tent, and as I walked up to it, the first sergeant came walking out. "Lieutenant Carhart. We got word to have a jeep here to take you up to the brigade area. You leavin' us, sir?"

"Yeah, Top, looks that way."

"Well, I'll sure be sorry to see you go, sir. Any of the Tigers know about this yet?"

"No, I just found out about it myself."

"Well, most of 'em are layin' around in those two big tents on the end. I think they'd like to hear about it from you."

"Yeah, I guess you're right."

I turned and walked over to the rear tent. I had to pick up my gear anyway. Shit, I thought as I walked, I don't even know all of 'em yet. I was the Tiger commander for one lousy operation, and now I've got to leave. It took me a few seconds to get used to the darkness as I walked into the tent filled with Tigers milling around. "Sergeant Haugh around?"

"Right here, sir." He came walking over with Starbuck.

"I'm gonna be leavin' the Tigers, goin' to Brigade. Lieutenant Blank is out of the hospital; he'll be the Tiger six again."

"Yeah, we heard, sir. Blank's already been here, chewing ass on Mickey Mouse garrison soldier shit. They say we're goin' back to the field tomorrow, and we'll miss you."

Starbuck pushed his hat to the back of his head. "Yeah, that's right sir. We're gonna miss you when we're in the shit."

I was slightly taken aback by their candor. "Well, thanks. You'll be all right. Blank's not so bad; he just wants to make sure his unit is under control, that's all."

"Yeah, I'm sure we'll find out where he is pretty quick. We're having a command meeting of all the patrol leaders after supper."

Sergeant Haugh folded his arms and kicked at something. "Next time we come in, whyncha see if you can come down 'n' get drunk with us, sir? I know the men'd like that."

"I'd like that, too, Sergeant Haugh. I'll try to keep track of where you are, see if I can arrange that." I waved my arm as I turned to walk out the front of the tent.

"Good luck to you, sir."

"Above the Rest, sir. And keep your ass down."

Then I was out in the strained sunlight, hoisting my rucksack and load-bearing equipment up on one shoulder, carrying my weapon loosely in my free left hand. I caught the jeep up to the brigade area and walked into the S-1 tent. It was lit on the inside by a string of bare bulbs that ran down the middle of the top of the tent. A tall, middle-aged black sergeant wearing glasses came over to me. "Can I help you, sir?"

"I hope so, Sergeant. My name is Lieutenant Carhart. I just got assigned to you from the First Three-two-seven."

"Oh, yes, sir, we knew you were coming. Major Wallace knew you down there when he was the S-three, ain't that right?" I grinned. "He sure did. Is he around?"

"Oh, yes, sir, he's in the squad tent down at the end of our tent. Whyncha report in to him first? Then we can take care of all the rest of your stuff. My name is Sergeant Connors, sir."

I turned, and we shook hands, then continued down the middle of the tent. At the end he pushed the tent flap out of the way as we walked into a smaller tent. "Major Wallace, sir, Lieutenant Carhart is here from the First Three-two-seven." I came through the door and saw Major Wallace sitting behind a desk. A captain was sitting next to him behind another desk.

I stood at attention and saluted. "Sir, Lieutenant Carhart reports to Major Wallace as ordered."

"Above the Rest, Carhart, come on in. Welcome aboard."

"Thank you, sir. Glad to be here."

"This is Captain Smith, the assistant S-one. So how are you? Last time I saw you, we were both in the hospital, isn't that right?"

"Yes, sir, I'm all better now. How 'bout you?"

"Oh, I'm all recovered now, just counting my days. I'll send you up to your billets with one of our clerks. Then we'll see if we can put you to work."

Major Wallace had stood up and come around his desk, and he and I shook hands warmly. "You look a little worse for wear, how ya been?"

"Well, shit, sir, not so bad. We had a pretty messy couple of days within the last week or so. I was the commander of the Tiger Force, and we got chewed up pretty bad. I don't have too many good things to say about the man who took your place when you got medevaced."

"Yeah, I heard from Major Green that you got kinda beat up. But it's no sense blaming it on anybody; those things just happen."

"That's right, sir. I don't mean to blame it on anybody; but someday I'll tell you the whole story, and maybe it'll make a little more sense to you."

"Yeah, okay, maybe some other time. But right now you look whipped. Wanna take a shower or anything?"

"Shit, sir, I'd love to take a shower!"

"Well, the shower is right near the billet tent. We'll be eating supper in about an hour, so you just take your time, soap your butt down, get something to eat, and I'll see you back here about seven o'clock. Okay?"

"Yes, sir."

I turned and walked out, following Sergeant Connors. "Your desk is right here, sir." He indicated a small folding desk just inside the main tent. "You'll meet everyone after supper. For now, let's just try to get you settled. Rodrigues!"

A small dark soldier searching in an open field file cabinet at the far end of the tent turned around. "Yes, Sergeant?"

"Rodrigues, this here is Lieutenant Carhart, the new assistant S-one. I want you to show him where the company-grade billet tent is." He turned and looked at me. "You got your gear with you, sir?"

"Yeah, it's in a jeep out behind the tent."

"Okay, Rodrigues'll show you where to put it."

We went outside and hopped into a jeep, which drove maybe fifty meters to another row of tents, just over the rise. I carried my crap into the designated tent, helped by Rodrigues, and threw it on the first empty bunk I came to. Then Rodrigues took me down to the brigade supply tent, where I acquired mosquito netting and an air mattress to lay on top of the stretched canvas cot on which I would sleep. No sense in failing to take advantage of whatever creature comfort was available.

I then went and picked up the canvas bucket from the water

trailer next to the shower point, filled it with cold water, and hung it from a peg on the tent pole that had been set up behind two stretched-out tarps. Privacy was kind of ridiculous at this point; but the wind had picked up a little, and the sun was now hidden behind the omnipresent clouds. It hadn't started to rain yet, but rain was in the air, so I hurried.

The water was icy, but the soap I scrubbed into my skin was wonderful. When my whole body was lathered up, I turned the valve on the shower head at the bottom of the shower bucket and stepped into the fine spray. God, it was cold, but it felt so good, the grime crusts unpeeling and sliding to the ground, that I stood there for several minutes, exulting in the cathartic feeling. Finally, I began to feel the chill enter my bones, and I stepped from under the spray, only then realizing that the rain had started. I grabbed my towel and scurried over to the tent. I busied myself with searching through my duffel bag, finally coming up with a pair of dry cushion socks. I left the sleeves on my fatigue jacket rolled down as I pulled it on, then pulled on the clean pants and laced my boots up tight over my warm feet. I flexed my toes, rolling them around in soft-sock joy. First time I had worn socks in years, it seemed, and they felt great. Finally I stood up and pulled my baseball cap on. It wasn't raining too badly yet; I could probably make it to the mess tent without getting very wet. I took a deep breath, lowered my head against the offending raindrops, and jogged out the door and down the slight incline.

The mess hall tent was no more than a hundred meters away, and when I got there, I was able to get inside the tent to stand in line without getting wet. I picked up a tray and followed the line to where the servers were dipping food out of big vats.

At Brigade things weren't too bad. Everyone was eating B rations, rather than the Cs we had to eat in the field. B rations were simply dehydrated food that was reconstituted in large vats, heated, and served. Mystery meat, with gravy, sliced potatoes, peas, canned fruit, reconstituted milk. Not bad—pretty goddamn good actually. Hell of a lot better'n Cs, and you could eat as much as you wanted. Man could get fat fast if he didn't watch himself.

The rain had disappeared as I ate, and after I was through, I took my tray and silverware over to the cleanup area, dumped them in the appropriate barrels of boiling water, and walked back up the slight rise toward the brigade area.

When I got to the S-1 tent, it was six forty-five, and had been fully dark for some time. The S-1 office was the personnel office. I knew it handled replacements, reassignments, decorations, and other miscellaneous stuff, and I wondered what my own job would be. I wandered into the tent, and the only man there was Sergeant Connors. He turned, recognized me, and smiled broadly. "Good evening, sir, d'ja enjoy your supper?"

"Yeah, it was okay. Beats the shit out of Cs."

"That's for sure, sir."

"Major Wallace back yet?"

"No, sir, he's not. I understand the field-grade mess is having lobster tonight, so I wouldn't expect him to be back real soon."

"Lobster?"

"Oh, yes, sir. General Matheson had got some kinda 'in' with the Navy, and they send the food up here for the brigade commander and his staff, which means all the field grades on the brigade staff. There ain't but about ten or twelve of 'em, and they eat pretty good!"

I sat down at my own desk, laughing and small-talking with Sergeant Connors. Soon enough the other clerks began to drift in, and then Major Wallace was there, smoking a cigar and waving me into his private tent behind him as he walked by, smiling. We were alone, and I spilled the whole story out. Major Wallace was understanding but didn't think I had much chance of going back to the battalion and getting Red Grizzly to believe my side of the story in preference to what his two majors told him. Thinking that Red Grizzly would differ in outlook really was a little silly. He had had the battalion for most of a month, working with these two guys, laying his heavy leadership line on them before he went on R&R. "And you don't think they didn't act just the way Red Grizzly did just so they'd get patted on the head when he gets back, do ya?" Wallace was trying to laugh me out of my depression. "No, you got your time on line, even got a Purple Heart. You're better off in the rear, now. You'll be surprised how fast time will go by.

"For now, I want you to meet Lieutenant Clark, the brigade publications officer. He handles all our relations with the press. He's got to make a run to Saigon here pretty soon, and there's some stuff I want picked up in Bien Hoa. It'll take forever to get here unless I send somebody down there to get it for me, so I thought I might send you. Give you three or four days in Saigon, depending on how fast you can hustle yourself a ride."

"Shit, sir, thanks!"

"No problem. I think the standard time frame now waiting for a ride in the regular air terminal is something like two or three days. Clark knows some of the guys in the scheduling office, though, and gets rides on generals' planes, so he ought to be able to get you down there quick, give you some slack time in Saigon."

"Shit, sir, when do we go?"

"I don't know. You'll have to check with him. Why don't you go over to the PIO tent and meet him? After you're through setting things up with him, c'mon back, and I'll tell you about what you have to pick up for us."

"Okay, sir."

I walked uncertainly out of the well-lit tent into the night, stumbling toward the long tent Sergeant Connors had pointed out. When I walked into the public information officer's tent, a baby-faced sergeant nearly ran into me, then stood aside. "Good evening, sir."

"Good evening. Is there a Lieutenant Clark over here?"

A surprised-looking face appeared around the partition midway down the tent. "That's me; what can I do for you?"

"My name's Tom Carhart; just came to the S-one office from the First Three-two-seven. Major Wallace told me I'm going to Saigon with you."

Clark was up on his feet and walking toward the front of the tent, smiling broadly. "Yeah, shit, my name's Dick Clark, Tom, glad to have you at the brigade." Clark grabbed my hand and shook it, squeezing hard.

We hit it off well, and within a few minutes we had agreed to have a beer together while we discussed the upcoming trip to the Paris of the Orient. It had stopped raining now, and Clark led the way through several rows of office tents, all of which seemed to be operating on a less-than-full-blower level. We soon arrived at a small hexagonal tent on the side of an uncluttered hill. Inside, a floor, several tables, and a bar had been hewn out of rough pine. This was the brigade officers' club, and there were ten or twelve other officers inside drinking when we arrived. We ordered two beers and, to determine who would pay, were quickly caught up in a game of liar's dice, a game that seemed to honor duplicity and deceitfulness; the most convincing liar could theoretically drink all night for free. This bothered no one, however, and we lost count after about four beers.

Drinking was heavy in the Nam, so long as you were in what you considered a safe area, where there was a significantly smaller probability that your life depended on your reflexes. Camp Eagle was a major installation, and there was no records of the gooks' having attacked an American base this size, so we all felt pretty safe in getting drunk.

Saigon

As THE SUN was breaking free of the jungle-covered hills the next morning, I joined Clark and sat down with my breakfast tray of chipped beef on toast or SOS (shit on a shingle). Didn't taste all that bad, and it was hot. And there was all the coffee and reconstituted milk you could drink. Clark had one of his clerks drive us over the nearby Phu Bai airstrip, some twenty kilometers away. The sun was disappearing behind light haze that wouldn't thicken into rain for several more hours, but we hoped to be in the air and far away by that time. We both were wearing our standard uniform of jungle fatigues and the rear-area baseball hats rather than helmets. The only baggage we each carried was an M-16 with one magazine holding eighteen rounds and a toothbrush in a shirt pocket. It was the norm for troops in the Nam to carry their weapons with them wherever they went. It was one thing to get drunk in a "safe" U.S. base area, but something else to travel in-country without your weapon. After all, there was a war going on, and Tet was still very bright in everyone's mind.

When we got to the airstrip, we walked into the huge, warehouselike passenger terminal. Several hundred troops were sprawled on the few benches and the floor, playing cards, reading, sleeping, waiting the short eternity to get on a passenger manifest, board an airplane, and leave. I let Clark handle things, and he strode over to the main counter, where he talked to one of the few sergeants standing behind it. I couldn't hear them, and I gazed around the cavernous building at all the bored men. Jesus, I thought, I hope we don't have to go through this! Then Clark was moving past me, and I turned and walked with him. "What's the scoop?"

"Ah, that sergeant said we'd have to wait twenty-four to thirty-six hours to get on a flight to Saigon. I signed us both up, which you've gotta do anyway to be legal about leaving. But now let's see if we can find our own ride."

We walked out a back door of the terminal, through a gate in the fence that led to the flight line, and down a row of aluminum hangars to a small white trailer. Clark smiled to me as he opened the door and climbed the few steps into the cramped trailer. "Warrant Officer Kelley around?" Within a few minutes Clark had talked us into a ride on a general's plane that was heading for Saigon in twenty minutes.

We both stepped back outside the trailer, then walked two hundred meters to where a brown and white twin-engine lightplane was parked. The pilot and copilot were sitting in their seats, headsets on, talking into the microphones that were attached to their earphones. They waved us aboard. There were eight passenger seats, all empty, and we flopped into the two right behind the pilot. A soldier carried a box of forms on board and plopped them into one of the empty seats, then climbed out and slammed the door. I felt a knot of tension in my stomach as excitement started to mount. The right propeller started to turn, then the left. Clark nudged me with his elbow. "Better put your seat belt on."

"Seat belt—oh, yeah, seat belt." I fumbled foolishly with the hardware, thinking how silly it was, remembering the rides I had taken jammed into helicopters with other troops, not only without seat belts but without seats or doors, everyone scrambling intensely and grabbing whatever he could. That was like a forgotten world now as I finally got the silly thing hooked. Goin' to Saigon! Hot damn!

The small plane taxied out onto the runway, turned, and took off, giving us an impressive view of the old imperial city of Hue from the air. We finally leveled off far above the thin, intermittent cloud cover and began to talk about the specifics we would go through in Saigon. Clark, because of his job as public information officer for the brigade, had met many of the TV network correspondents who were assigned to Saigon. The people from ABC had leased a floor in the Caravelle Hotel in Saigon, and since they were often out traveling, there were usually extra rooms left empty each night. They had invited Clark to use them if he was ever in Saigon, and now he and I were going to take them up on their offer.

The Caravelle was one of the only two hotels in town that had not grown neon bars on the top floors that doubled as whore outlets, the other being the Continental Palace across the street. Both were expensive but provided a seemingly safe Western island in the eye of the storm. The other hotels in town had realistically perceived their task as that of separating a lonely GI Joe from his money. There were six or eight modern high-rise hotels of ten or fifteen floors, each with a fantastic bar and restaurant on the top floor, a veranda from which you could look over the French-built city of Saigon and all its bright new American appendages, such as the new and impressive U.S. Embassy. My tongue was hanging out as I listened to Clark talk, and I made him swear that we'd head for one of the pleasure pits as soon as we got to Saigon.

We both were laughing about the good times we were going to have when the pilot turned around and got our attention. "There's an air strike going on over here on the right if you want to see something to remember from this ride."

Far below, the clouds were only thin white streamers. We saw nothing at first. Suddenly a giant black-tinged orange slug appeared and swelled across the crest of a thickly wooded ridge. Then the crack and thunder roll of the explosion hit our ears, and I quietly shuddered. It seemed to me that we were watching a war on television now, somehow insulated from the brutal life-and-death struggle that must be going on down there under the canopy. Poor bastards, I thought almost wistfully. Poor bastards!

"That, gentlemen, is napalm from above." The pilot had taken his headset off and was talking to us as I turned away from the window.

"Yeah, shit, I've seen it from the ground, but this is the first time—" Another crack-roar told of another strike, and I whipped my head around to watch another slug grow and swell, then seemingly evaporate and settle into a nasty, dark-burning, slick scar. I saw a wicked-looking green-and-brown-winged dagger darting above the trees on the same ridge. F-4 Phantom, I thought. That's what my father flies. That's what was supporting us on the ridge that day! Then the green mosquito laid its poison egg, and it blossomed in a stream of fire as it touched the treetops.

Suddenly, for the first time, I realized how the pilots here felt about the infantry. From up here it looked as if all hell were breaking loose down there. But you couldn't really tell. They had put in six napalm strikes and I knew there must really be a world of shit going on down there. I shuddered, my eyes riveted to the exploding hilltop. Poor bastards, I thought, not even knowing what was going on down there or who was killing whom. Poor bastards. Within a few minutes we had flown by, and the snarling hornets branding the earth were gone from sight, the explosions muffled and then finally smothered by the thickening clouds. I smiled and laughed, releasing my emotional confusion, unsure of what to make of this brief view of the war from God's chair. But after a few awkward laughs the pilot turned back to his instruments, and we all fell silent.

As we approached Saigon, we began to drop softly but steadily downward. Ahead the high-rise hotels and office buildings of downtown Saigon glinted in the midday sun. The morning rain had been light, and Saigon was just drying off. Dick and I got off at the small army hangar where the plane parked, then caught a ride from the first passing truck to the main gate. Once there, we walked out the gate, across some busy streets, and then Dick was talking to a little gook driving a motorcycle-powered three-wheeled ricksha. Dick turned and waved to me to join him as he climbed in. I had the distinct impression that I was stepping into a coffin as I put my feet into the passenger compartment. Dick and I were sitting side by side facing forward between the two front wheels, which were in place of the front wheel on a motorcycle. The driver sat behind us, his handlebars attached to our two-wheel coffin. There were no seat belts, and the beat-up tin trough Dick and I had our feet in was the front bumper. Dick turned and nodded at him. "Hotel Caravelle."

As Dick turned and settled into his seat, the driver shot forward, made a steep turn, and we were suddenly moving in the middle of the stream of traffic. Alarm leaped in my heart as I turned wide-eyed to Dick.

"Shit, this is crazier'n hell. If he hits anything, he hits 'em with *us*! We're the fucking front bumper!"

"Ah, relax. We got a star driver here. He's gonna take care of us, ain't that right, Nguyen? Numbah wan taxi, ya?"

The driver was grinning and waving his index finger. "Numbah wan, numbah wan!"

"Bet he's on our side, too," Dick confided, then turned and shouted back, "Hey, VC numbah ten, VC no good, huh?"

The driver outperformed Dick, grimacing and shaking his fist in a thumbs-down sign. "Oh, Trung Uy, VC numbah ten, numbah ten, VC no good. Numbah *ten*!"

Dick turned back, still smiling. "Son of a bitch is probably a major in the NVA."

"And he probably speaks English better'n either one of us, too."

We had suddenly cleared the dusty stretches of low gray and yellow buildings that lined the road, and now we were racing through the cool shade of enormous hardwood trees—planted by the French a hundred years ago—as the street widened into a boulevard and the main downtown area erupted out of the European forest. As we sailed past a large park, Dick told me it belonged to the Cercle Sportif, an exclusive private club built long ago by the French, where the idle wealthy lolled around the pool, played tennis, rode horses in this, their own guarded private park in the middle of downtown Saigon. I could see only a corner on one side of a building as we passed a side entrance, but I saw guards walking around outside the barbed-wire- and broken-glass-topped high brick wall that surrounded a small forest. I realized that some power was talking here. Then we had glided through an area of large private houses on large lots, all enclosed behind high stone walls. Except for the barbed wire and the armed guards, we might have been in a wealthy section of Paris. We soared down another wide, tree-lined avenue, veered around an enormous cathedral, and my heart was beating like a hammer, my breathing light and high in my chest, my smile hurting my cheeks. I laughed for no particular reason, and Dick laughed with me. The world was good; Saigon was the promised land.

We pulled up in front of the Caravelle, and Dick gave the driver a hundred piasters, roughly one U.S. dollar. The National Assembly Building was down the street to the right, the Saigon River down the street to the left. Huge French-built stone buildings lined an elegant boulevard; tall trees and lush flowers were everywhere. I had to laugh at myself as I remembered how I felt as we left Tan Son Nhut: a little uneasy, gripping my weapon tensely, feeling sweat on my fingers, half waiting for the expected ambush. But during the ride I had loosened up considerably, and now I was ready to taste Saigon. We went inside, and Dick called one of his friends from ABC, who came down and met us in the lobby. We were shown to a room that had somebody else's books on shelves and clothes in dressers, but clean sheets on the beds. That was all that mattered.

By eleven-thirty in the morning we were back rumbling through the streets in a tiny Renault taxi, heading for the Hotel California, one of the more renowned pleasure domes in the city. It was a new high-rise building, but it looked somehow unfinished. Raw mortar that had been trimmed off when the building had been built years earlier lay about the building in hardened, immovable slag heaps amid the weeds and gleaned-over refuse. Dogs and children scrambled over a jeep carcass on one side of the building. There was a military police station outside the front door, and we had to check our weapons: If you had worn your guns to town, you had to leave them outside the saloon with the sheriff before you indulged yourself. We rode up to the penthouse restaurant on a somewhat tacky elevator, but I had gotten used to imperfections by our standards and felt elated. Once upstairs, we sat on the veranda and had a drink, following which we had an exquisite shrimp and lobster casserole with a fine bottle of blanc de blancs.

Saigon was stretched below us, its lush green branches fluttering delicately in the sly breeze, spires and high-rise granite and red tile roofs basking and glistening in the warm sunlight. We drank heavily that afternoon and evening, but an unexpected handicap sent us reeling back out on the street before we were ready to leave. Since the Tet uprising there was a curfew at nine o'clock. Everyone had to be off the streets by then, and since we weren't staying there, we had to get back to the hotel by nine. That meant we had to leave by eight-thirty to make sure we caught a cab. We went outside, very drunk, and got our weapons back from the military police. We didn't need to use them to get a cab, but we kept a barrel pointed out each side of the cab as we sped through the streets. We may have been drunk, but we weren't gonna get ambushed, no sir.

Jacqueline

THE NEXT DAY Dick borrowed a jeep from ABC and we drove up to Bien Hoa, where the 101st Division base camp had been established. There wasn't much to it, lots of tents and trailers, nowhere near the comforts of Phan Rang. When we finally located the right personnel office, we learned that the material Major Wallace wanted had been sent by courier a few hours earlier. But the major had left a message for Lieutenant Carhart: Be back by the twenty-first. That day was the eighteenth. Dick and I grinned at each other as we eased our borrowed jeep back down the road toward Saigon. That afternoon Dick had some errands to run that didn't particularly interest me, so I elected to walk around town, agreeing to meet him at five o'clock in the sidewalk café outside the Continental Palace Hotel.

There were many tall stone buildings in the city, obviously built by the French and later by the Americans. The city itself had really been built by the colonial French, back when they could afford to be lavish, both in public buildings and in the many palatial houses that one could see only at considerable range through the guarded gateways that opened on public streets. There were a lot of guns being waved around, some by obvious show troops with starched uniforms, spit-shined boots, M-16s, and sunglasses. There were knots of three and four troops stationed at every other street corner, and jeep loads of them cruised through town with sirens on like eager hounds searching for a fresh scent in their own backyards. Barbed wire was strung everywhere. It was piled at every street corner, and at curfew the street guards would pull it across the street, then guard it (sleep next to it) until the curfew was ended at 7:00 A.M. But those wire webs pulled grotesquely across Saigon's delicate features could scarcely hide her beauty. She was an exquisite, mysterious lady, and I drank her in in great gulps.

In the business district the sidewalks were lined by black-market stalls, either a single woman selling cigarettes on a small mat or rows of waist-high stands filled with black-market merchandise, most of it allegedly stolen from the American PX and other supply systems. You could find there almost anything you wanted, from cameras to air conditioners to weapons to clothes to special-order anythings made anywhere in the world—or so promised the five or six hustling kids who flocked up every block. No, I don't want any marijuana, any whiskey, or their virgin sisters/mothers. At three-thirty I was taking a cab back to the Caravelle.

When I got there, I just walked across the street and sat down at a table on the sidewalk outside the Continental Palace Hotel. I was having my first beer when a group of five middle-aged white women came out of the hotel and sat at a table next to mine. I thought nothing more of them until I overheard them speaking to each other in French. As a child I had spent three years in French schools when my father had been assigned to Fontainebleau, France. My French was quite good, and after another beer I decided, what the hell, so I turned and asked one of them something trivial in my most Parisian accent. The ladies had already had some wine elsewhere, and I was quickly swept up by them, soon moving to their table. It was a splendid game, speaking French to Frenchwomen at a sidewalk café on a bustling Saigon plaza splashed with warm afternoon sunlight.

When Dick showed up, I was too engrossed by them to pay him much attention. He didn't speak French, so was sort of left out of things. It was understood among all doggies in the Nam that under the canopy everyone relied on everyone else, but once you got to the rear, everyone retained the right to splinter off from any group and do his own thing. Dick pulled me over to one side of the table. "Hey, listen, man, I don't speak French. I can see that you're really gettin' off on this, but I'm gonna go over to one of the other hotels and see what's going on. You wanna come?"

"Well, lemme see. . . . Nah, I don't think so. I'd rather stay here and talk to these old French broads."

"Well, shit, you might screw one of 'em. They say that older woman stuff is supposed to be nice."

We both were laughing conspiratorially as we huddled together, but the five women were drinking and chattering brightly as we talked and didn't seem to notice as I looked around at them. They were nice enough looking, but all were in their forties or fifties. One of them looked particularly lovely. She had delicate features and a clear, easy flashing laugh. Only thick glasses seemed to mar an otherwise angelic face. I was staring at her when she turned and looked at me directly in the eye. I turned away and started blushing as she laughed. I looked back at Dick. "I don't know ... I don't think it'll happen, but I wouldn't mind slippin' it to the one with the glasses. Christ, look at her tits!"

"Shit, Carhart, she's gorgeous. You're lucky I don't speak French! I'm probably gonna stay out at another hotel tonight. If you want the room, just get the key at the desk. I'll be back at the Caravelle tomorrow night for supper. No, better still, I'll meetcha right here, at this table, tomorrow at five o'clock, just like today, okay?"

"Okay, Dick, keep your ass down."

Dick stood up.

"Bonsoir, madame!" He bowed deeply to the table and was gone.

But even as he was leaving, two of the women were getting up to leave, and I was soon left alone for another beer before supper with Glasses and two other women. I was enjoying myself immensely, and in time we walked a few blocks to a Spanish restaurant they frequented, which was both splendid and expensive. It turned out that one of my companions was Camille Lebrun, the wife of the senior man in the Michelin Rubber Company in the Republic of Vietnam; she had borne him two daughters and was now trying to get them through junior high. Glasses was Jacqueline Desmarais, and her friend was Françoise Thierry. They and the two women who had left our company at the hotel were teachers at the local French lycée that served the Saigon French community of five thousand.

For supper, we had crabmeat in a thick, creamy sauce. The four of us quickly polished off a couple of bottles of cold white wine; but then it was getting close to eight o'clock, and Jacqueline and Camille had to hurry to run errands before curfew set in. Before she left, Camille invited me to a party the following evening at her home. Then she had the maître d' charge the meal to her husband and sailed out the door on a gust of thank-yous and farewells. Jacqueline flashed a brief wide smile at me; but then she and Françoise left, and I strolled back to the Caravelle.

The next morning I slept late, then killed most of the day walking around the streets of Saigon, another tourist in fatigues. I bought a map and tourist booklet at a newsstand, although I really didn't believe there was much in the way of a tourist trade. There weren't many Americans on the street at all, although there were plenty of Vietnamese walking around with loaded weapons slung over their shoulders. At five o'clock I was working on my second Carlsberg at the Continental Palace when Dick walked up. He decided he wouldn't get off at a party where everyone was speaking French and opted for another night at the Hotel California. We laughed and scratched for the better part of an hour. Then I hopped into a cab and soon arrived at the party. Monsieur Lebrun was back in Paris, so Camille was in charge. The occasion was the thirteenth birthday of the son of some eminent Frenchman in Saigon. The Lebrun house itself was a large, graceful white building inside a high-walled compound. I had worn my fatigues since I had no other clothes, and I was the only American there among perhaps twenty French adults and another twenty or so children. I met Camille and Jacqueline again, and as I relaxed, I was able to mix with the other guests. Unfortunately the party had been going on for most of the afternoon, and people were beginning to leave in anticipation of the impending nine o'clock curfew. However, the wine flowed freely, and around eight-thirty Camille invited Françoise, Jacqueline, Jacqueline's five-year-old grandson Jean-Michel (whose nickname was Kinou) and me to spend the night, so that we might stay and socialize after the nine o'clock curfew. We all quickly agreed, and suddenly everyone else had left, and we were alone on the wide veranda above the manicured gardens. As we laughed and chattered, the head of the private Michelin security force came over to Camille's side and respectfully but firmly asked that we all move inside. As we did, I watched other servants, who attached heavy metal shutters across all the doors and windows on the house, making it look like a fortress rather than a mansion.

Jean-Michel was an angelic little boy with full golden ringlets, bright blue eyes, and cherry lips, but after a full day of play he was exhausted. One of the housemaids whisked him off to a bedroom, and the four of us retired to the drawing room, where we sat in Louis XIV chairs while Camille rang for champagne. We slowly sipped Dom Pérignon as we discussed anything and everything I could think about that was French. I was delighted and entranced. And of course, they played with my mind, that of a callow youth of twenty-four. During the evening I learned that Françoise was forty-eight and had never been married; Camille was forty-six and had been married for twenty-two years; Jacqueline was forty-seven and had been married and divorced from a French diplomat.

While we opened our fourth bottle late in the evening, Camille excused herself to check on the rooms. She dismissed the house servants who were still about, then disappeared upstairs. I was feeling no pain, and neither was Jacqueline nor Françoise, who had drunk just as much as I had. I still didn't know if I was going to get laid or not, but I really was getting the hots for Jacqueline. She was clearly smarter than either of the other two, and her face was really rather exquisite behind those thick glasses. She had that rare kind of skin that almost seems to glow with the texture of fine soap. I felt myself being entangled in her web when Camille returned and told us our bedrooms were ready.

The laughter rang out freely as we navigated those wide stairs. Somehow, leaning on each other, slopping champagne over everyone and everything, we made it. Camille led the way down a high-ceilinged hallway. Then, suddenly, we were inside a large bedroom without windows that was, Camille told us, the safest room in the house in case of a mortar attack; if one should erupt, that's where everyone would gather. In the meantime, Françoise and Jacqueline were to share the large postered bed that occupied the middle of the room. As for me, unfortunately, there was only one room without windows in the whole house, but a doorway led to a small antechamber where a single bed had been prepared.

I was beginning to feel kind of silly now as I closed the door to the other bedroom, slipped off my clothes, and crawled between the cool sheets. With the lights off, my small room was bathed in moonlight, and I was smiling to myself and just drifting off when a tiny rap at my door brought me back. It was Françoise, and she told me, in a half-frightened voice, that there was a cat in their room, and she and Jacqueline wanted me to chase it out. All right, I thought, fuck it. I was naked but never even hesitated as I slipped out of bed and opened the door. The large bedroom was pitch-black, but I followed half-laughing Françoise into the room, then reached under the bed, where I discovered a very fat, very long-haired drowsy cat. I picked it up with one hand, opened the main door into the darkened corridor, and threw it out. Françoise was back in bed, and she and Jacqueline were whispering and laughing to each other as they lay stretched out on the vaguely white sheets in the dark room, the only light coming from my open doorway.

I was feeling pretty loose and felt that the cat rescue had been a contrivance to get me into their bedroom. I walked over to their bed, reached over Françoise, and vaulted over her body into the middle of the bed. We all were high, and they both laughed as I rolled onto my back. I turned my head to Jacqueline, finding her ear with my lips. *"Tu viens dans ma chambre?"*

"Oui, je viens, dans dix minutes."

I turned back to Françoise and kissed her cheek. *"Bonsoir, chéri."* I turned and rolled over Jacqueline, brushing my lips over her ear. *"Dix minutes."*

She squeezed my hand as I stood up, then drunkenly stumbled to my room. As I fell into my bed, I really didn't know whether Jacqueline would follow me. But soon the door opened silently, and she slipped into my bed.

Until that moment in life I had been a naïve young man of twenty-four with only a handful of sexual experiences behind me, all with equally naïve young American girls or with uncaring whores just hustling another trick. But this, this was a woman, and the splendors of life that night in her arms were beyond my wildest dreams. We truly visited paradise together.

As dawn began to filter through the window above my bed, she slipped away and I fell into a deep sleep. Around ten-thirty I awoke, dressed, and crept downstairs. In the dining room I blushed when I was met by hoots of laughter and welcome from the three women as well as Camille's two teenage daughters and Jacqueline's grandson, Jean-Michel. But Jacqueline's wide, sweet smile was warm and reassuring. God, what a woman!

I had coffee and croissants with them, then was back out on the street with Jacqueline and Jean-Michel. I was king as I lit a cigar and we strolled down the wide, treelined boulevards. The sun filtered through the fluttering leaves above and dappled our faces and the whole world around us like a Renoir painting brought to life. I took Jacqueline's hand, and all was right with the world. Life was good.

Jacqueline showed me her Saigon that day, and it was a delight. We had a delicious lunch in a small French restaurant in her neighborhood. As we ate and then strolled the boulevards of the city, I learned quite a bit about her. She had been married for fifteen years. She had had a son and a daughter, but the son had died of a fever at the age of eight in Tahiti. Her daugher was now twenty-five and had two sons. She showed me a picture of her daughter, a younger, more gorgeous version of Jacqueline whose elder son was Jean-Michel, who had just reached the French school age of five. Unfortunately Jean-Michel's daddy was a French businessman in the Ivory Coast. The schools in Saigon were thought to be far superior to those in the Ivory Coast, so Jean-Michel lived with Grandma during the school year, attending the school where she taught. Jacqueline also had a young Vietnamese maid who lived in her apartment and slept on a mat in the kitchen.

Jean-Michel and I had quickly hit it off. As we strolled down the avenues and stopped at shops to examine goods, the shopkeepers were quickly attracted to him and were soon squatting next to him, trying to speak to him in French or Vietnamese.

By four-thirty, as we strolled over to the Continental, where I was to meet Dick, I felt like God, and I didn't want to go back to the war. We were due back the next day, which happened to be a Monday. That didn't matter to us, but Jacqueline had to teach. It didn't seem that there would be much else to do anyway, so what the hell. I was brooding over my second beer and laughing at Kinou's antics when Dick was suddenly there at our table. He sat down and had a drink with us, and I reintroduced him to Jacqueline and Kinou. I was amazed to find out that Jacqueline spoke very good English, but quickly decided I didn't like that very much at all. Our intimacy and, yes, our love were French and French-speaking, and I was much more secure staying on known ground with her.

After Dick and I had agreed to meet at the Caravelle at nine in the morning, I danced off to a night in Paris, inside Jacqueline's air-conditioned apartment with Charles Aznavour, Jacques Brel, and Edith Piaf crooning to us, served at table by Thi Teu, the French-speaking and French-keeping-her-place housemaid who crept around almost without a sound, then slipped off to her mat in a corner of the kitchen at night like some great Siamese cat. Jacqueline's apartment was on the fourth floor, and behind the building outside her living room window was the Majestic Hotel, a Vietnamese hotel that had been leased to the U.S. Army to house American officers who worked in Saigon. There were three or four of these hotels in town, and I knew exactly how things were organized over there. I realized that if I ever got a jeep in Saigon, I could drive it to Jacqueline's apartment because I could leave it in the guarded motor pool at the Majestic overnight, and that might prove to be convenient. But the most exciting thing became apparent about eight o'clock, when we heard loud music coming from the window. Four floors down and forty meters away was an open courtyard behind the Majestic, with the bright colors of Hollywood flashing across a movie screen facing us, the sound track loud enough for the whole block to hear.

Tonight's flick was *The Green Berets,* starring John Wayne. I was really excited as I sat in a large, comfortable chair I had pulled up close to the window. But after about half an hour the movie had become sickeningly unrealistic. It had been filmed in the scrub pine and red clay of Georgia, entirely dissimilar to the terrain in Vietnam, with clusters of eight and ten actors walking around together in some seemingly suicidal stand-ups and sit-downs. I was amazed that Hollywood seemed to know so little about the war. It was depressing to think that back in the World, people were going to the movies and seeing this crap and thinking that they were seeing the war in Vietnam. The war was nothing like what John Wayne made it look like. Nobody made valiant, hard decisions that led to triumph and glory. No, we just did what was required to stay alive and do our jobs, trying to hang on, to make it through 365 days. American soldiers in the Nam weren't sitting around in their free time talking about upholding liberty and defending democracy. We talked about home and when we were going back and what we were going to do when we got there, with maybe an occasional stray comment about the fleshpots of Bangkok or Sydney or Hong Kong.

By eight-thirty Ol' John the War God had made the last daring dash into the Valley of Death that I could endure.

Jacqueline put on a dream-inducing Mireille Mathieu record. Kinou and I played on the floor like bear cubs, and he listened wide-eyed while I told him about paratroopers who jump out of airplanes and ride down under parachutes like snowflakes. He was such a radiant sun-child, bright pink skin and golden halo, with laughter spilling out like a stream of gaily colored soap bubbles. My emotional snake half uncoiled and stretched in in the psychic sunlight. I didn't know what lay in front of me, but this night, this place, I lived fully.

Thi Teu put Kinou to bed at nine and then slipped silently off to her lair. I took my olive drab suit of armor off at the door of the bedchamber, feeling it graceless and out of place in this pleasant setting, but Jacqueline brushed my fears and confusion away with her soft lips, then led me out across the sea to nirvana, softly, patiently, lovingly.

The next morning I walked over to the Caravelle in the bright morning sun. Dick and I took a cab to Tan Son Nhut. We bypassed the passenger terminal, where we were supposed to wait, and headed straight for the flight line, where we lucked into a C-130 that was running supplies up to Phu Bai. Soon we were once again climbing into the fluffy-white-cloud-strewn sky. We laughed in delight at our memories, never willing to consider the fact that we were going back to a war that might kill us.

Brigade Staff

AT 1530 HOURS, 21 April 1968, I reported back in to Major Wallace. It didn't take me long to settle into an underworked rut of three or four hours of paper shuffling each day, filling the rest of the day and evening with paperbacks and letters. On the second night back I was visited by an old friend and classmate, T. K. Kinane, who had been in the 1st/327 six months ago and was now running the brigade long-range reconnaissance platoon, a group of some fifty men similar to the Tiger Force but run from the brigade level. T.K. was a great bear of a man, an Irish Catholic rogue rugby player from Brooklyn who could drink all comers under the table or would "die" trying. We had shared an Irish Catholic heritage and a fondness for hell-raising at West Point. T.K. had just come out of the field with the LRRP and would be staying in the brigade area until he and his unit were called back out; that could be any time.

T.K. knew all the officers on the brigade staff, and he suggested that we retire to the chaplain's tent after supper. Actually there were three chaplains, each of whom had his own small tent pitched in a loose cluster down the hill and across the road from the S-1 office tent. There were two Protestant chaplains and one Catholic priest, but one of the Protestants, Captain Grit, was gone on R&R. The rest of us gathered in Father Torer's tent with a bottle of Canadian whiskey and two cases of beer to discuss life, the war, and the NFL.

Chaplains were in the business of making people relax, so the evening turned into a genuine gala affair, reliving the last football season in all its color and glory. By midnight we were dancing across the Sydney Harbor in a hydroplane ferry as T.K. sang the song of his R&R in Australia, with round-eyed women, a few months before. By two o'clock we had decided that California was about to break loose from North America and the rest of the continent would sink into the ocean. By four o'clock T.K. and I had decided to run away and join the French Foreign Legion in Africa but figured we had better stop by the tent and get our weapons. We started to low-crawl on our bellies the two hundred meters back to the billet tent. We changed our minds en route, climbed onto our respective cots, and fell asleep.

I quickly slipped into the staff officer role, taking long lunch breaks, riding around with no particular direction in mind, and reading everything I could get my hands on, from *Playboy* to Plato, from *Sports Illustrated* to Spillane, from *Motor Trend* to Machiavelli. During the morning I spent about two hours signing orders that would allow soldiers to fly anywhere in-country and perhaps one or two more hours handling administrative matters that came up involving personnel and assignments. Sergeant Connors was true to his word, and he took care of most of the administration. Every few days Major Wallace would ask for lists or rosters of some sort, which made me scurry around to the battalion rear areas some three or four hundred meters away. It was generally a low-key life. Meanwhile, the war was being fought a few kilometers away.

The first break in routine came when Red Grizzly finally returned from R&R and rejoined his battalion, which had now moved to Fire Base Birmingham down the road leading to the A Shau Valley. As soon as I heard about it, I went to see Major Wallace, who counseled caution. "But if you want to go back to the battalion, the commander has got to clear it. You really want to go back, don't you?"

We both knew how important an experience it would be to command a line company if I stayed in the service. If I lived. But the gambit was taken as if it had to be.

"Shit, sir, I gotta get back to the battalion so I can get in line for a company."

"Hunh. Well, there's a convoy goin' out there from Camp Eagle tomorrow morning. I'll put you down as the officer in charge if you want, but first call the battalion and see if Red Grizzly will talk to you tomorrow before lunch. You bring the convoy back in the afternoon; then we'll see where we go from there."

I was suddenly enthusiastic, and after I had talked to a sergeant in the rear requesting an audience with Red Grizzly, I began to convince myself that I would be accepted back into the battalion with open arms. I got a call back from the battalion rear an hour later confirming my appointment, and my heart soared.

The next morning at 0-nine-thirty hours the convoy of five-ton dump trucks pulled out of Camp Eagle, their beds bristling with three or four riflemen each, several of them mounting .50 caliber machine-gun turrets above the driver. I rode in the cab of the third truck, uncomfortably bound up in the first flak jacket I had ever worn but grateful for it and my helmet in case we drew hostile fire from the jungle that bordered the forty kilometers of road. The fears came to nothing, and at ten thirty-five hours the lead jeep entered the perimeter of Fire Base Birmingham. The grade required the use of four-wheel drive, but soon I found myself walking up to the TOC, a sweat just beginning to break under my arms and across my chest. It wasn't a good sweat; I hadn't earned it by using my body. It had come with a growing discomfort in my belly and a chalky taste in the back of my throat.

I looked around somewhat nervously for someone I knew, but all I saw were strange sergeants and lieutenants. Then I saw Captain Kobiyashi, the headquarters company commander, and smiled uneasily at him. I got a noncommittal nod in response, and I felt increasingly uneasy as I walked into the TOC. Across the wide main room inside the bunker, some twenty or twenty-five meters away sat Cottonmouth and Sidewinder talking animatedly, not noticing my arrival. I froze, not sure of what to say to anyone. I was looking around for Red Grizzly when I heard a voice behind me. "Lieutenant Carhart, I'll be with you in just a few minutes. Why don't you wait for me outside?"

I had turned and was confronted with a smiling, gaunt-cheeked forty-year-old face with short-trimmed thinning hair and a sunburn. He seemed genuinely good-humored as he was busily folding maps. A wave of relief washed over me, but as I stepped back out into the bright sunlight, I was uncertain why I could feel calmed by a smiling face. I shied away from thinking about the conversation that awaited me, trying to find something of interest in the surrounding countryside. Birmingham was built on top of the highest hill in sight and dominated the valleys hundreds of meters below it. The view was extensive in most directions, and I was just getting intrigued when I heard Red Grizzly's voice behind me.

"Okay, Lieutenant Carhart, why don't we walk over here where we can talk in private? I've got to go back to Brigade now, and my

slick is going to pick me up in ten or fifteen minutes, but I do want
to talk to you before I go." He was smiling a lot as he led me over to
a tree on one side of the TOC, where we both took off our helmets
and sat on a rock ledge. "What can I do for you, Lieutenant?"

I looked at Red Grizzly's keen stare, then looked down and
cleared my throat. "Sir, I'd like to come back to the battalion again
and go back to the field as a platoon leader and get in line to be a
company commander after I make captain in June."

Red Grizzly had looked down at the ground and was holding his
hand out in mild protest. "Whoa, now wait a minute, let's take one
thing at a time."

He was fiddling with a string that was unraveling from the camouflage canvas cover on his helmet, watching it intently as he spoke.
"Now, as I understand things, you went through a very difficult period while I was on R and R." He lifted his hawk eyes and caught
my dove eyes, gripping them fiercely.

"Well, sir, I think I had some communications problems with
some people, and I'm willing to admit that I may have been hasty
and out of place, but I just want to concede and go back where I
want to be, as an infantry platoon leader on line. I don't want to get
in fights with anyone, sir, and I know you don't have all the lieutenants you're supposed to have, and nobody usually wants to go to the
line, so I could help you out that way, too, because I want to go back
to the line." I was pleading now. Red Grizzly smiled broadly as his
eyes drilled holes through mine.

"Okay, let me tell you what I remember about you before I went
on R and R, Lieutenant Carhart. I remember this big, tall lieutenant
who worked as a duty officer at night in the TOC. You were always
reading books when you were supposed to be on radio watch. You
asked for the Tigers when we happened to have a need for somebody, so I decided to take a chance on you because of your background. I've spoken to my executive officer, Major Green, who was
in command in my absence, at some length about you and what
happened to you and your men. He is of the fixed opinion that you
do not deserve the honor and the privilege of commanding a unit in
this battalion. I know that war is hell; but you just couldn't take it
when the going got tough, and we don't want you back."

My face flushed with shame and anger; a thick knot clogged my
throat. "Sir, you got told one side of the story. We got sent back
down a path we had just traveled, and when we got ambushed, our
own artillery was called in on top of us!"

"I've heard all about what happened. How about the night before? Didn't you cry out on the radio that you all were going to die? Didn't you beg to stop because you were tired? Didn't you try to get out of moving all night to rescue a surrounded C Company? Now answer me those questions if you want to come back."

"Sir, that's not true. None of that stuff is true. We drove on all night!"

"None of that's true, huh? Then tell me this, Lieutenant Carhart, did you cry out on the radio that everyone in the Tiger Force was going to die? Did you use those words?"

"No, sir, I didn't, I never ... well, I did tell the TOC what the situation was like. I did say that if we walked into an ambush, we all might get killed, but I was only trying to describe—"

"Did you say that you and your men were too tired, that you couldn't make it, that you quit?"

"No, sir, I never said that. I said that the men could be run to death, that you could ask too much of them, more than they could do and retain much of their combat effectiveness, but I never said I quit, no, sir!"

"Well, Lieutenant Carhart, that's not what my staff officers tell me. You managed to earn a Purple Heart with this battalion. Now why don't you let it go at that? Because I'll tell you frankly, as long as I'm the battalion commander, I won't allow you to rejoin the battalion. You just don't have what it takes to hold a leadership position under my command. I'm sorry, but that's the way it is. War doesn't give you the leeway to be a nice guy and worry about hurting people's feelings." Red Grizzly stood up and put his helmet on. "I hear my slick coming, and I've got to go. Is there anything else I can do for you?"

My face was afire with shame. "No, sir, I guess there's just no way I can make you understand what happened."

"I understand perfectly well what happened, Lieutenant. You just thank your lucky stars you're alive to talk about it. And don't come back and bother us anymore. We've got a war to fight, you understand?" The red face was smiling broadly.

I stiffly raised my numb right hand in a salute. "Yes, sir. Good afternoon, sir."

Red Grizzly snapped a sharp salute back, spun on his heel, and was gone. I stood outside the TOC for some time, waves of depression cascading over my head. Finally I straggled down to the motor pool far below, where the trucks were still being unloaded.

The motor sergeant told me two more hours and suggested that I get in the mess line that was forming alongside the insulated sealed buckets filled with hot B rations that had been carried out to the fire base on the CO's slick and dropped off just a few minutes ago. But I didn't feel hungry at all and preferred to go off by myself, fifty meters from the nearest group of men. I lay by myself in an empty small bunker and tried to come to grips with the shame I felt. I was composed enough to ride silently in the cab of the truck all the way back to Camp Eagle. By four-thirty, severely depressed, I got back to the S-1 tent and slunk behind my desk. It took me ten minutes before I decided I should tell Major Wallace I was back.

Once again Captain Smith was gone, so I was alone in the tent with Major Wallace. "What happened?"

My cheeks burned furiously as I sat down heavily. "It's no use, sir. Red Grizzly isn't going to let me come back to the battalion while he's the commander." I tried to smile. "Seems that he got his own story from Cottonmouth and Sidewinder."

"Well, whaddya want to do? Want to go to one of the other battalions?"

"I guess that's what I've got to do. I've been thinking about it, and I really do want to get a company."

Major Wallace rocked back on his chair, propping his crossed feet on the corner of his desk, and put his hands behind his head. "Well, it's a pretty important decision, of course. On the one hand, there's no question but that being the company commander of a rifle company of the Hundred and First in combat is a sort of ultimate military experience. In addition, it is an important experience for someone who wants to advance his career. It's a job where we want good men, and I think you'd do a good job as a company commander, in spite of what Cottonmouth or Sidewinder might have said."

"Thank you, sir."

"On the other hand, you have had time as the commander of the Tiger Force, so you know what command of an independent unit in the field is like. I think this war is going to be going on for some time, so you may get a chance to be a company commander on a later tour over here. And then there's the final consideration: You might get killed. Thought about that much?"

I was committed. "Yes, sir, I have, but what it finally comes down to is you've just got to ignore the risks involved, 'cause when your number is up, there's nothing you can do anyway. Besides, I'm not married, and I don't even have a girlfriend anymore, so I'm not going to cause any great traumas back in the World if I get greased."

"Don't give me any of that shit, Carhart. You've got a family just like everybody else, and I know damn well you've got at least one girl back there waiting for you."

"No, sir, no girl. Not anymore." My shattered dreams of Lara spun madly through my head. "And I'm one of five children. The family would get over it. I mean, it's not like I was an only child or something." I laughed out loud. "Besides, sir, they ain't gonna get me, they only get the good guys!"

Wallace smiled lightly. "Okay, Carhart, if that's really what you want, I'll see what I can do. Probably take a couple of weeks, though. Sergeant Connors'll keep you busy till then."

"Yes, sir. Thank you, sir." I went back to my desk, feeling better.

It would be a couple of weeks before I went back to the line, and I was wondering if there might be some excuse for me to go into Hue and see the Imperial Palace. Dick Clark had mentioned it as a possibility on the plane. He also knew an antiques dealer who was selling statuettes and jewelry and ornaments and all sorts of curios that had supposedly come from the palace. I went over to the PIO tent around five, and we made plans to go the next morning as we walked down to the mess hall tents. After supper we both went back to our office tents to clear up work already scheduled for the following day.

By eight o'clock next morning, we were sailing down the narrow highway to Hue in a jeep driven by Jim Parker, my RTO with the Tigers, who had talked his way into writing PIO stories for Clark. By ten o'clock we were crossing a bridge over the Perfume River and entering the Imperial City of Hue. There was one enormous gray stone wall that enclosed a large section of the city, inside which the entire imperial capital had once been located. There were many large stone buildings and tall hardwood trees sprinkled across a pleasant and graceful city. The mark of the French was seen here, just as it had been in Saigon, and Jacqueline had told me there were still five hundred to a thousand Frenchmen living in Hue, while five thousand lived in Saigon and another two thousand in both Da Lat and Nha Trang. The raw wounds of recent combat were all over Hue: shell-torn buildings; uprooted palm trees; piles of brick and mortar rubble along the streets. The North Vietnamese and the Vietcong had captured Hue and held the imperial citadel for several weeks during the Tet offensive, and several battalions of the 101st had helped the marines dig them out. It had been slow and bloody, and the landscape bore silent witness to that. But the Imperial Palace had not been damaged badly, and we told Parker to drive in the main gate so we could get a better look. There was a Vietnamese guard on duty at the gate, and a sign in Vietnamese and English. It said that the palace was off-limits to all personnel, but we just ignored it and drove through the gate. The Vietnamese guard saluted us as we drove by, and we returned the salute.

Inside the citadel a small city of stone was laid out. It included the onetime emperor's palace and administrative seat of the empire. The grounds were meticulously maintained, and we were surprised to see so much of it in such good repair. There was an occasional swath torn through a tall row of hedges or a building with a corner torn off or a roof caved in, but for the most part the palace seemed largely intact. There were very few people around—some ARVN (Army of the Republic of Vietnam) soldiers doing masonry work, but not too much, and two American military policemen, who showed us where the main throne room was. We got into the palace through an open door in the side of a building we were directed to, then wound down a long corridor and up two flights of stairs. And there could be no mistake: This was the main throne room. The high walls were ornately painted and gilded, but everything within arm's reach had been stripped, leaving the palace naked but still noble. The throne was atop a dais, two high steps above the floor, nestled between two enormous green and pink marble columns, shaded by a swooping gilt canopy. Clark and I stood on the dais for several minutes, hands on hips and mouths agape. Then I leisurely seated myself on the imperial throne. I looked down across a wide high-ceilinged room, then out open doorways and window spaces to the private gardens below. It was a stunning sight. I casually motioned to Clark with one hand: "Send four of my legions into Cambodia. Punish the curs." We laughed and jostled each other, then were out in the sunlit garden, looking for our jeep.

After a good luncheon we headed back to camp and I readily slipped back into the tedium that was my life in the rear, signing boarding passes, issuing military driver's licenses to anyone Sergeant Connors said should have one, yawning, sending replacement requests to the division rear at Bien Hoa, reading recommendations for Silver Stars written by REMFs (". . . upon the impact of the enemy mortar round near his tent, Major Johnson, with complete disregard for his own safety, quickly pulled Major Smith into the trench that had been dug outside his tent . . ."), yawning, signing meaningless papers, reading meaningless reports, reading short stories, dime novels, whatever I could get my hands on. There seemed to be a dearth of reading matter in the 101st rear, but considering the mission and the nature of the ideal paratrooper, it was obvious that the literary void went largely unnoticed.

Days were indistinguishable in the S-1 tent, the only variation coming with the weather. We were supposed to be at the end of the rainy season, or maybe it was the beginning. You could never be sure, since the rainy season came at different times of the year in different parts of the country. The 101st never seemed to stay anywhere for more than a few weeks, and then, just as the rain was finally letting up, we'd move to an area where God would piss all over us again. It was an accepted part of the never-ending misery that was the Nam. It only took me a few weeks at S-1 to understand why so many people kept track of the number of days they had left in their one-year tours.

I was half dozing through another dreary morning when I raised my head to a stir at the entrance to the tent. There stood three Tigers, looking nervously around as they talked to Sergeant Connors. I was on my feet and moving toward them when I recognized Uncle Jimmy Haugh, the first sergeant of the Tiger Force, then Bad Ass Brown and Razor Williams, a point man-slack man team. I waved them down to my desk, we shook hands, and I slapped their backs. My ego swelled as I sat back down and put a new cigar in my mouth, then passed around the pack, which they all waved away. "Long time no see, how's tricks with the Tigers?" I could tell something was wrong as the Tigers shifted nervously in place.

Sergeant Haugh answered. "Okay, sir. Well, we got some problems, which is why we came up here to see you."

"What's the problem?"

"Well, sir, we had a meeting of all NCOs in the Tigers last night, before they went out to the field this morning."

"What happened?"

"Well, sir, Lieutenant Blank told us, first thing off, that he didn't want no more niggers in the Tigers, and he wanted to get rid of the ones we had."

"What?"

"That's right, sir. And then he made me drop Williams and Brown here from the roster, leave 'em back in the rear with headquarters company as some kinda cooks or somethin'."

Brown leaned over my desk and glared at me. "An' I ain't no muthafuckin' cook, suh. You rememba me goin' up that Tiger Ridge wit' you, me 'n' Razor, we pulled our parta the load."

I tried to retreat behind an officer's analysis.

"Did he use those words, Sergeant Haugh? Did he say the word 'nigger'?"

He nodded solemnly. "Yes, sir, that's his word, not mine." I steamed inside, not knowing what to do, how to react. I knew it wasn't a crime to say "nigger," but anyone in the 101st who used it marked himself as being out of touch with the reality of combat. Didn't Blank understand that on line, color didn't matter? It was Us against Them. Hell, we *all* were "niggers" in the eyes of the people back in the World. Those of us who went to the field with the 101st were automatically expendable, nobody gave a shit whether we lived or we died, and that's what being a "nigger" was about. How could Blank be so dumb?

"Jesus Christ! What else did he say?"

"Well, he said he'd get rid of the rest of 'em whenever he could, graduallike, the ones that didn't get killed. That's what he said!"

"Goddamn! And so you didn't go out to the field with him in protest, or what?"

"Yes, sir, well, this morning I told him I wouldn't do what he said about Brown 'n' Williams, said they were one of our best point teams, 'n' so he just relieved me, made this new E-seven, Sergeant Erving, the first sergeant, and then he had Brown and Williams dropped from the rolls."

I was stunned by this. Goddamn Blank! "So what are you now, just excess in the headquarters company?"

"Well, no, sir, I went to see the battalion sergeant major, and he went and told Major Green, who came back and told me I had to go to the line with C Company this afternoon or else he'd court-martial me."

I was shocked and confused, but by God, Blank wasn't going to get away with this bunch of shit.

"All right, I'll take care of things. You guys just go back to your units. I'll talk to Snake Eater about this; he'll know what to do." Brown and Williams broke into wide grins, grateful that they had come to the right man. But Sergeant Haugh still wore a quizzical look.

"What about me, sir? Should I go out to the field with C Company, or do I get to go back to the Tigers, too?"

I hesitated for a moment. "Shit, Sergeant Haugh, I know it must be just illegal as hell, what Blank did, but I can't tell you to disobey Major Green; he's still the battalion executive officer. You'd better do what he tells you, or you might get fried."

"Okay, sir, I'll do it, but I sure hope you can take care of Brown 'n' Williams here. They're good men."

"You don't have to tell me that, Sergeant Haugh, I remember. You guys just let me take care of things, okay?"

Suddenly all three seemed relieved. "Thank you, sir, we knew we could count on you! Above the Rest!"

I nodded, smiling, to all of them as they stood in front of my desk and saluted, then filed out the front of the tent. I wasn't sure what to do, so I explained the situation to Major Wallace. He gave me permission to talk to a lawyer on the division staff. I called for an appointment in the judge advocate general's office, was told I'd have to wait three days.

Three days droned by. My appointment was for 1000 hours. At 9:30 A.M. I had Reed, one of the S-1 clerks, drive me down to the division area. I sat in the jeep with Reed for fifteen minutes, then strode across the street and down the timber steps that had been stuffed into the red clay embankment. I was allowed to sit for another ten minutes in one of those ubiquitous gray metal folding chairs that littered the reception tent. Finally I was called and spoke to a slightly balding, slightly fat captain. My story was spilled out rather quickly, and he looked at me impassively. "Well, Lieutenant, if what you tell me is correct, then it would seem your Lieutenant Blank was out of line. But it's pretty important that that's the whole story. If these men, this sergeant and the two other enlisted men, are as upset as you say, then maybe you'd better send them down to see me."

Now we're cookin'! I saluted, sprang back up the hill, and leaped into the front seat as Reed cranked the beast back to life. I was really turned on. Now we'll show Blank something! I had Reed take me directly down to the 1st/327. I found Brown behind the mess tent, smoking a joint in the bushes with two or three other cooks. He was slightly spaced out as I told him what had happened, but he managed to tell me that Williams had been evacuated to Cam Ranh Bay with malaria that morning, and he wasn't sure he wanted to go back to the Tigers without his buddy. I told him I'd be back that evening, for him to straighten out because I wanted to talk to him.

When I walked back down the battalion street to the C Company tents, I found the first sergeant in the supply tent. "Morning, Top. I'm Lieutenant Carhart from Brigade S-one, used to be with Abu; then I had the Tigers for a while."

"Yes, sir, I remember you. How's Brigade?"

"Ah, it's okay. Say, listen, Top, I want to get in touch with Sergeant Haugh, but I think he went to the line with your company a couple of days ago, that right?"

"Yes, sir, that's right, he went out to be the field first sergeant three days ago. Haven't you heard?"

"Heard what, Top?"

"He was a Dogwood six yesterday, sir. Got hit in the head by the first round of a big firefight right at nightfall. We didn't get him out till this morning. We got hit pretty bad, eight other Dogwood sixes."

I said nothing but grabbed the tent pole to steady myself. "I'm sorry, sir. He never felt nothing. It was over for him right away."

I looked down, my eyes suddenly clouded over. I muttered, almost to myself, "Fuck."

"Sorry, sir. You want a shot o' whiskey?"

I shook my head silently. "Fuck."

"Sorry, sir."

I waved my hand and nodded my head in thanks, still looking down, then backed out into the sunlight. I lifted my head as I walked back down the dusty dirt street. I dragged my wrist across my eyes to wipe away the tears, then hawked deeply and spit into the bushes. Uncle Jimmy Haugh. What a hell of a man! If that goddamn Blank hadn't been such a dumb shit, he never would have been out there with C Company, and then he never would have—

Ah, that's no good. When your number's up, it's up. Ain't nothin' you can do. But what a hell of a man. When I swung into the front seat, I was composed again but much subdued. "D'ja find Sergeant Haugh, sir?"

"He got greased yesterday."

"Oh, sorry, sir."

I shrugged.

"How'd it happen, sir?"

"Got hit in the head in a firefight. I don't want to talk about it. Let's get back to Brigade."

"Yes, sir."

We bumped back to the main road, then up to our trench behind the S-1 tent. It was lunchtime, and I didn't even bother to go in the

S-1 tent. Pulling my baseball cap lower over my eyes, I trudged over to the mess tent.

As I walked back to the S-1 tent after lunch, it started to rain, but I barely noticed. I responded to the greetings from Sergeant Connors and Specialist Potter, but offered none of the normal repartee. Ten minutes later Major Wallace came back in and stopped in front of my desk. "How'd it go at JAG?"

I looked up at him. "Okay, sir. I have to send the complaining EM [enlisted men] down to talk to them, though, and then I found out that Sergeant Haugh got killed yesterday with C Company, and Williams got medevacked to Cam Ranh with malaria."

"Oh, sorry to hear that. Well, take it easy, things'll clear up."

I dragged through the rest of the day. After supper I decided to put off seeing Brown for another day, and when my old buddy T.K. showed up at eight-thirty, we got drunk at the officers' club. When I got to my bunk late that night, I cried a little for Uncle Jimmy, but by the next morning I was able to put on a straight face. I was wondering what to do about Brown when suddenly he was in front of my desk.

"Mornin', sir."

"Oh, morning, Brown. I was just thinking about you. We got to talk."

"Right, sir. Well, listen. Lieutenant Blank got his arm blowed off last night, and they're fixin' to send me back to Bien Hoa to be a supply clerk, 'n' I ain't got but eighty-two days left, so if it's all the same with you, sir, I'd just as soon not mess with Mistah Charles no mo'."

"Blank lost an arm, huh?"

"Yes, suh, part of his shoulder, too, I got told. He like to bled to death."

"Hunh."

"That's right, suh, 'n' the only reason he's alive is 'cause he had ol' Davis, you know, that ol' *nigger* medic, out there to keep his young ass alive."

It all seemed too much to me. "You gettin' a ride back to Bien Hoa, too, huh?"

"Yes, suh, 'n' I ain't got but eighty-two days 'n' a wake-up to go, so let's just let things ride, okay, suh?"

"Yeah, okay, Brown. D'ja hear about Uncle Jimmy?"

"Yes, suh, Ah heerd yestiday. He was a hell of a man."

"Yeah, that he was, that he was." I snapped out of my brief melancholy reverie. "Okay, Brown, keep your ass down."

"Yes, suh. Above the Rest, suh."

"Above the Rest."

Then he was gone, and I tried to sort it all out in my mind. At first I thought that Blank had paid a price for his racism. But he had lost only an arm, while Uncle Jimmy had lost his life, and none of it made sense. I knew Major Wallace was alone so I walked into his tent. "Above the Rest, sir."

"Above the Rest, Goat, whatcha got?"

"Sir, I've been thinking about it a lot, and I want to go back to the line."

"Well, okay. If that's what you want. The O-Deuce [502d Infantry] got hit pretty bad a couple days ago, lost a bunch of lieutenants. I'll call the S-three down there; they can probably take you out to the field this afternoon."

"Thank you, sir."

He shrugged. "I'll call you once I've set it up."

I walked back to my desk, slipped into my gray folding chair, and started turning pages, thinking about Uncle Jimmy. A feeling of stepping out the door of an airplane in flight crept over my neck and spilled down my chest, tightening my nipples.

A short eternity later Snake Eater's voice snapped me out of my reverie. "Hey, Goat!"

I jumped to my feet and strode into the adjoining tent. "Sir?"

"After lunch get Reed to drive you down to the O-Deuce with your bag. I just talked to Major Murphy, the S-three, he says they'll fly you out to Bastogne this afternoon, you can meet Colonel Sharp, and then he'll decide where you'll go from there."

A sudden gust of elation swept through my chest. "Hey, that's great, sir!"

"Well, you just make sure you keep your shit straight, and if you need anything from personnel in the next few months, just come see me." He stood up, winked at me, and held out his hand. We squeezed hard. "Above the Rest, Goat."

"Above the Rest, Snake Eater."

After lunch I picked up a couple of paperback books and my desk was clean. I shook hands around the tent and then had Potter get the jeep out while I walked up to the billet tent. I packed my few possessions in my duffel bag, picked up my helmet and my rifle, and a few minutes later Potter dropped me at the O-Deuce.

O-Deuce

I LEFT MY DUFFEL BAG with the supply sergeant and drew the equipment I would need for the field: rucksack; canteens; two fresh bandoliers of ten magazines each; grenades; smoke; albumin; compass; map; a case of C rations to pick over; a pack of five Wolf Brothers cigars; as many packs of Chuckles as I wanted.

I was soon strapped down tight and ready to go. My adrenaline began to churn as I stooped over to run under the whirling blade of the C&C slick that had just arrived and was making a milk run back to Bastogne. I crawled in the open door of the slick, then flipped onto my back and shoved my rucksack into the middle of the craft, my weapon across my thighs. I gave a thumbs-up sign to the Flash Gordon goggled figure watching me from the front seat, and he returned it before he turned away. The craft tipped forward, and we clawed our way up into the sky.

Ten minutes later we began to float down out of the clouds, and then the bare dark chocolate hilltop landing zone at Bastogne, slickened by the morning rain, started to suck us out of the sky. We leveled off our steep descent very abruptly; the pilot honked the slick back hard and lightly kissed the mud with his rails. I was out the side as they touched.

Bastogne was situated on the top of three very steep hills, or perhaps it might better be described as an outcropping from a ridge with three summits that towered above the Song Bo River in the valley directly below. One of the summits was the helipad. The TOC was in a bunker on top of a second. The artillery battery attached to the 2d/502 was dug in on top of the third. The defensive perimeter was a ring of four-man bunkers with overhead covers that had been dug every twenty or thirty meters around the three summits. Most of these bunkers were in commanding positions, with steep slopes falling away in front of them. It looked like an extremely secure position.

I strode up to the TOC and in the front door; the dark cool was welcome on my face. "Hey, Sergeant, where's Colonel Sharp?"

"Over there in the corner, sir, talking to Lieutenant Hayes."

I started to walk over somewhat tentatively, but then Mac saw me and smiled widely. "He-e-e-y-y-y, Tom, heard you're comin' to the Strike Force, welcome aboard!" I hadn't seen Mac Hayes since I had been in Vietnam. He stood up, and we shook hands warmly. Then I turned and saluted Colonel Sharp.

"Sir, Lieutenant Carhart reports to Lieutenant Colonel Sharp for duty."

"Welcome aboard, Lieutenant Carhart," he said as he returned my salute, his West Point ring glinting on his finger. "Lieutenant Hayes has to catch a slick out to C Company, which he's taking over, in about ten minutes. I know you two were roommates at West Point, so I think I'll let you visit until the slick arrives. Then we'll have a talk. Again, welcome aboard!" He smiled widely as he squeezed my hand, and I was moved.

"Thank you, sir, I'm glad to be here."

Mac and I went outside and leaned against the side of the TOC as we shot the shit. He had recently been to Sydney on R&R with T. K. Kinane and was just as full of stories about round-eyed women with long blond hair and legs up to the ceiling as T.K. I saw the slick when it was still two or three clicks away down the valley, just a dark, droning dot in the distance. As the slick drew nearer, I heard Mac's laughter through a cloud of anguish. This was it. I suddenly knew it. I'd never see Mac again.

As the slick honked back and began to alight, I reached into my pocket and pulled out the only thing I carried that meant anything: the brass "327" coin that all the officers in the 1st/ and 2d/327 had been given as unit esprit charms. As Mac crawled into the slick, he flipped his rucksack over and flopped onto his back, facing me, wide smile, and held out his hand. "Keep your ass down!"

"You, too, buddy." I grabbed his hand, holding the coin in my palm, squeezed, and left it with him. He looked at it openmouthed, smiled at me, and waved as I backed away. The slick tilted forward and leaped away. I watched it as it dropped off the hilltop and soared over the valley, quickly building up speed. It disappeared over a ridgeline.

I walked back into the TOC. Colonel Sharp was leaning over the big maps by the bank of radios, but he heard me coming and turned around as I walked up. "Lieutenant Carhart, get a chance to catch up on things a little with your roommate there?"

"Yes, sir, thank you very much; he's a hell of a man."

"Yeah, we think a lot of him here. As for you, do you know Scotty McGurk, class of 'sixty-two?"

"No, sir, I don't think so. 'Sixty-two graduated just before we started our Beast Barracks."

"Hunh! Well, he's going to be your new company commander with A Company. You make captain on eight June, right?"

"Yes, sir."

"Okay, well, you've got about five weeks of lieutenancy left, and that's just what we need. A Company has been getting hit pretty hard lately, and Captain McGurk has got only about eighty-five people in the field right now and only one other infantry lieutenant out there with him as a platoon leader. He's got two junior sergeants running two other platoons, and they can sure use you."

"That's what I'm here for, sir."

"Good. Soon as that slick comes back from C Company, we'll have him take you out to Captain McGurk. That sound okay?"

"Strike Force, sir." He smiled. I had already replaced the 1st/327 greeting ("Above the Rest") with that of the O-Deuce ("Strike Force"), and I felt right at home.

"Well, it'll be back directly. We'll get him up on the horn here; you can go wait on the LZ if you want to. You just make sure you keep your ass down and take care of your men."

"Yes, sir." I locked my heels and saluted again. "Strike Force, sir!"

"Strike Force!"

I wheeled and strode out into the suddenly blinding sunshine, then over to the LZ hilltop. Soon the C&C slick arrived for me. As the craft started to alight, I was running under the flared blade, then clambering into the beast, flipping over, thumb up, and the craft sailed out over the jungle.

Ten minutes later we dropped out of a cloud, and I saw a high ridge crested with a wood line on our right. I saw no one until we were twenty or so meters off the ground. Then four gaunt troopers in filthy fatigues and several weeks' growth of beards moved out of the trees as we alighted. Only then did I realize how much I'd gotten used to the rear, shaving every day, sleeping on a cot, eating in the mess hall. . . . Well, it was good to be back! I was smiling broadly as I slipped out of the slick and into the trees, where a lean, hungry-looking Scotty McGurk was waiting for me.

A Company was down to eighty-five men, but it had been down to fifty-two a few weeks earlier, when it got chewed up by an NVA battalion. There had been thirty-three replacements fresh from the World, cherries every one, within the last week or so, and Scotty was leery about getting into anything big too fast. They had really been chewed up by that battalion: One platoon had been overrun, and two infantry platoon leaders had been wounded, the third killed. The only other lieutenant he had when I arrived was a cherry who had arrived three days ago, Lieutenant Doaks. He was gravely aware of the tight position he had been thrust into, but he still had that most important survival lesson to learn. We could empathize with him and coach and encourage him, but it was something he had to go through by himself.

I was given the second platoon. Bob Doaks had the first platoon, and Scotty the third. It was agreed that my platoon would walk point for a few days or until it looked as if Bob would be able to handle a contact. We were patrolling the highlands above the Song Bo River that fed into the eastern side of the A Shau Valley.

We moved three or four clicks down a ridge from where I had arrived, along with supplies for five days, then set up in a night position, more than an hour before full dark. I talked to each man in the platoon once the perimeter had been established, asking name, age (mostly teenagers), hometown, how long he had been in the Nam (twelve cherries), whether he was married (only bachelors walked point and slack), and why he was there. One guy said that he had been arrested for assault and battery, and the Florida judge had given him a choice: the 101st or jail. Several laughingly admitted they had come for the adventure, but most very simply and humbly acknowledged their patriotism: They had come to fight for their country.

I made sure that everyone understood that I was in command and would take care of them, that they could depend on me absolutely, but that they also had to depend on and take care of each other. We were all one big team, and if we went under, then we went under *together*—*no one* would be left, dead or alive. I told them my two major rules on line: Nobody was to mutilate bodies, and nobody was to smoke grass. I told the cherries that the best way for them to survive was to do *exactly* what their squad leaders told them to do. They all nodded to me gravely, now confronted for the first time with a real life-and-death game in which they were the main players.

I felt a little more at ease after I had spoken to everyone. My platoon sergeant was Sergeant Johnstone, a rocky young E-5 who was on his second tour in the Nam with the 101st. He was a good man, one I knew right away I would be able to depend on in the shit. My radio was carried by Lou Lopez, a Chicano who went by the nickname of Speedy Gonzales. He seemed small but swore he was tough as a burro, which he proved. And he, too, had been in the shit. But somehow, I was still uneasy. I felt, deep in the pit of my stomach, that my number was coming up, that somehow my life had gotten sidetracked, and that it would all end suddenly and messily and nonheroically.

There was no sign of gooks for the next few days, and we naturally began to relax. I realized this and started to get a little antsy. I made all the cherries crawl out and watch as the ambush was set up that night, made sure they understood about claymores and their backblast and about how an ambush was tripped: how everyone in position first was silently alerted, then threw hand grenades, and only when things were getting very bad would they fire personal weapons that marked positions. The cherries all were eager learners, and I wasn't too worried about them.

We droned through weeks of intermittent contact, receiving a steady trickle of reinforcements brought forward when the resupply helicopter came every fifth day. As a rule, our days were tediously boring: a hundred men carrying heavy loads silently through the steaming jungle. But every few days the tedium would be broken by moments of stark terror when we would bump into enemy forces; the noise of bullets screaming by kept that survival instinct alive and well oiled. The cherries seemed to be learning fast. One day we trapped a ten-man North Vietnamese patrol as they arrived on an intersecting trail. We saw their movement first, got down, and waited for them. Then we gave them the surprise of their lives, leaping up and blowing them away in a sudden gust of fury. Forty or so of us opened up at once, killing nine of them right there on the trail, getting the tenth in the bushes, where he crawled in desperation. It was all over in a few seconds. No one got away, and they got off only a few bursts in response, hitting none of our men.

I was as high that day as I had ever been. What a magnificent coup! We had blooded all our cherries painlessly, as if in a shooting gallery! And they all had seen and even tasted the reality of blood-lust, the indescribable flood of emotions that came over us that day and carried us away. What a triumphant moment!

We were high and loose after that for several days, but eventually the tedium of our situation crept back in.

One particularly sun-splashed day the lead platoon was stopped by three RPDs atop a crest in a jungle clearing. The platoon leader was Doaks, and his inexperience and insecurity flooded over, with him finally hiding at the base of a big tree at the edge of the clearing while trying to urge his men up the hill over the radio. They wouldn't move without their leader, of course.

I had my platoon ground their rucksacks. Then we edged our way forward. I was the only other officer serving as a platoon leader, and I simply had to move to the front.

I lined my men up abreast at the edge of the tree line, then passed the order to fix bayonets. The reality of my death was suddenly with me again like an old friend, and he hugged me close. I stepped out of the trees with my men, yelled, "Follow me!" as loud as I could, and started pumping bullets uphill as I strode into the open. A fury of gunfire poured out of us as we climbed the ridge through knee-deep undergrowth. I was on the narrow trail, and as I moved forward, I realized that my head would loom over the crest before my weapon, directly into the sights of one of the RPDs that were covering the trail. Suddenly I knew that my brains would be sprayed over the hillside behind me before I could shoot back. But I couldn't stop, couldn't slow down, couldn't even duck, for I was the platoon leader, and my leadership image was crucial to the success of our assault.

Then, as we neared the crest, Speedy burst by me with the radio, running the last few meters roaring like a man possessed, his weapon spraying a full magazine out on automatic. I was stunned but quickly recovered and followed him. Atop the ridge the RPD was long gone, of course, and Speedy stood there, spraying bullets into the jungle beyond.

I yelled at him in misdirected rage for breaking ranks, then checked on our three wounded and coordinated the dustoff. Later, when the slicks had gone, I felt sheepish when I saw him hide his tears of bewilderment. He had, after all, offered his life to save mine. I apologized, thanked him, and squeezed his arm. He grabbed my hand on his arm, held it for a few seconds, and smiled. There were no words, but we both understood. Thank you, Speedy. Thank you.

Over the next few days we saw no more action. On May 28, Paul Kimberling, who had just made captain, arrived in the field to take over command of the company when Scotty left on June 1. He was short and wore glasses, but as Mac Hayes had told me back at Bastogne, looks can be deceiving. Kimberling's call sign was Mad Dog, a name he had earned as a platoon leader. Mac told me that when Kimberling first arrived in the field as a green platoon leader, his appearance had led his company commander to think that he was timid. At the first firefight his platoon had been told to "guard the rucksacks" of the other platoons, which had been thrown into the fight. But all of a sudden there was Kimberling, carrying two rucksacks, with his platoon strung out behind him similarly laden, going up the back side of the hill the rest of the company was attacking. He and his platoon got there before anyone else, trapping and killing a handful of NVA soldiers as they were trying to slip away. Everyone thought he was a little bit crazy when he did that—hence the name. Apparently nobody could believe that he hadn't been killed! I looked forward to serving under a fire-eater like that, but I was still a little bit uneasy about following someone named Mad Dog up a hill.

On the first of June, when Scotty was scheduled to be extracted, we were also supposed to be resupplied. That morning we found ourselves in the middle of the thick jungle, and after a futile search for a clearing we finally had to clear one by hand with machetes—backbreaking work that took several hours.

Before noon the resupply slick was settling in on the newly cleared LZ, and soon the handshakes and backslaps with Scotty had been exchanged. One welcome surprise was that Jim Parker from Brigade PIO had ferried out to spend a few weeks on line with our company. I didn't have long left in the field, but I made sure he came to my platoon. We had built up a full trust long ago with the Tigers, and it was good to have a known friend join me in the jungle. Then the slicks were only a rattling in the distance, soon swallowed up by the jungle. We were left in the hushed silence, hearing only birds and monkeys as we jammed rounds into magazines, ripped through cardboard boxes, piled and burned the refuse we always had to destroy at every resupply.

Over the next few days Mad Dog ran us hard. But while he always wanted to be near the front of the column, where any action would likely occur, he seemed to have acquired a sense of caution for the company that made us all feel better. The stories about him as a platoon leader were making the rounds; he had served with this company and had come off line some four months ago, so there were a number of men who remembered him. No doubt the stories were exaggerated—he wasn't quite as crazy or bloodthirsty as the legends would have us believe—but he showed himself to be an excellent company commander, and we all respected him. I knew from the way he reacted to sniper fire and brushes with trail watchers that he would be a good commander if we ever got into the shit.

We didn't have long to wait.

The Longest Day

THAT NIGHT Mad Dog is informed of some changes by Battalion. Our company has to move to its initial point (IP) for descent into the A Shau Valley. I look at the map with Doaks and Mad Dog. We have about sixteen clicks to our IP and three days to make it. It doesn't seem to present any problems. Mad Dog wants to avoid any contact that may slow us down, so he outlines roughly the ridgelines he wants to stay on top of. He casually mentions that he wants my platoon to take point for this movement, and I nod.

The next day we move eight or nine clicks by about two-thirty in the afternoon and set up camp on the crest of a thickly jungled ridge.

The following morning, the third of June, one of the ridges on the map tails off into a swamp, and we find ourselves cautiously edging through brackish knee-deep water and rotting undergrowth. The map shows us high on a ridge, and I am starting to get pissed-off. Mad Dog tells me to move directly west, and within about two clicks it looks as if there is another north-south ridge we can get on that would take us toward our IP. We slog through another hour's worth of swamp. Then suddenly we're mounting a gradual slope.

We move some four or five hundred meters up this slope, our speed slowing as the grade steepens. Then all the undergrowth disappears, leaving us scrambling up a steep slope dotted with great gray boulders amid the light brown carpet of dead vegetation.

After a few hundred meters we reach a crest. As I climb over the last boulders, the ground suddenly flattens out, and lush green undergrowth is again all around us. I exhale a pleased, relieved breath, then stage-whisper to Sergeant Johnstone, twenty feet away from me and breathing as hard as I was, "Sergeant Johnstone! Hasty perimeter!" I know everybody's going to want to catch his breath as he comes up. I survey the area. We aren't really on a ridge; rather, we seem to have climbed a single steep hill. Off to my left, it looks as if the hill peaks eight or ten meters higher than we are, thirty or forty meters away, but the vegetation is too thick to see that far. I walk back to the edge and look down. I see twenty or thirty men strung out below me, and the tail of that snake disappears into the jungle some two or three hundred meters down the hill. They are moving very slowly.

"Hey, sir, there's a gook shitter over here!" I turn around at this hissed warning from Parker, some thirty meters from the edge of the steep slope, my skin suddenly clammy, and take long strides in his direction. There, another ten meters from the crest, is a small clearing. In the center of this open space four bamboo poles are embedded in the bare dirt to form the corners of a small latrine. A woven palm-frond roof rests on the four bamboo poles. Squarely in the center of this small, protected plot two small mounds rise six or eight inches from the carefully groomed dirt floor, with holes in the center. No question about it, this *is* a gook shitter! I look quickly around like some frightened bird, then stride over to the latrine and get down on my knees, stick my face directly over one of the mounds and inhale strongly through my nose. A strong odor of fish and shit hits my nostrils, and I know instantly that this is an active latrine.

I stand up and start to turn back when a series of explosions rip the air all around me. I am down on my chest instantly, shaking and scared. Twenty meters away I see the eight or ten men who have made it to the top of the crest scrambling around, shouting at each other or screaming in agony. The fear of God is in my heart now. I look at the top of the hill and see muzzle flashes through the thick vegetation. I hear Sergeant Johnstone screaming, "Up the hill! Get some fire out there!"

I turn and look uphill again. A well-worn footpath leads up the hill from the latrine. Like a zombie, I race up it in a deep crouch, hands sweaty as they grip the rifle stock. I automatically clear the round in the chamber as I run, allowing the heavy metal clunking as the chamber swallows the new bullet to still my heart. Then there is a fork in the path. The path to the left leads directly up the hill, while the path to the right leads around to the right and seems to meander to the top through thicker vegetation. I am only half thinking about anything now, but my heart is leaping inside me.

I take the trail to the right, bending my body low now as I slow my pace. A sudden noise behind me jerks me around. There, close on my heels, is Specialist Fourth Class Kirby Wilson, a sharpshooter from the Carolina hills. I nod to him, and we began to creep forward again. Off to our left and behind us we hear the muffled agony of the men huddling just over the crest of the hill. Then two RPDs open up from the top of the hill, in front of us and off to the left. We hear cries and shouts from down the hill now, and it is clear that the men climbing through the cleared area are getting chopped up. Wilson and I keep creeping anxiously forward. I take the heavy white phosphorus grenade off my web gear and straighten the pin so that it can be thrown quickly and easily. As I peer around the edge of a bush, I see two large overhead-cover bunkers some twenty meters away. We are slightly off to one side of them, the firing slits facing toward the company coming up the hill. Behind the nearest bunker three gooks are huddled in animated discussion. I turn and signal Wilson to come up on my left, then ease out from behind the bush on my belly and forearms. Wilson comes into the clear next to me. As we lay there, bringing our weapons up to our shoulders, two more gooks appear with AKs, then a third. Now there are six gooks in the clearing, four of them quite close together. My weapon is on semiautomatic, and I don't dare switch to automatic, sure they'll hear the click such an adjustment would require. I open fire, watching the enemy's dark shirts soak up my tracers. I get six or seven rounds off before they are able to get out of sight. I have hit only two of them, maybe three.

My adrenaline is really pumping now. I roll onto my left side, pull the pin of my Willie Peter grenade with my left hand as I heft it in my right, then heave it up toward the rear of those bunkers with all my strength. No gooks in sight. Wilson throws an M-48 hand grenade and is pulling the pin on another one. I grab one off the side of one of the ammunition pouches on my web belt and pull on the pin. The spoon that arms the grenade is held on with a heavy-gauge cotter pin that normally has to be straightened before it can be pulled. I look down in terror at what can be keeping the pin from coming out, then instantly recall the important cotter-pin-straightening exercise you are supposed to go through before you throw a grenade in combat. I have completely forgotten! I grunt, close my eyes, and strain on the pin. Fear gives me the strength of ten men, and the pin slowly slips out. I roll over again and heave the grenade blindly uphill with all I have. When it leaves my hand, I hear a loud thunk as it hits the heavy branch of a vine and ricochets. Where did it go? A chill of terror is rushing through me when suddenly another RPD opens up, this time spraying dirt all over us as the bullets chew the ground. Wilson and I scramble back behind the clump of bushes. There are three sharp consecutive explosions very near us. The last one picks me up off my belly, snaps my head back, and blows my helmet out of sight down the hill. Now that they know where we are, we will do no more good here, and I have to get back to my men.

We start to scramble back the way we had come, and soon we are back at the juncture of the two trails. Then we race back down the single trail to the latrine and the crumpled knot of my men. No one sees us coming until we are among them.

"Sergeant Johnstone! Get a couple of men over here to cover this trail, right now! Where's Speedy?"

"I don't know where he is, sir. Jaune, Waldorf! Get over by Lieutenant Carhart and cover that trail. Move!"

I look around madly. It looks as if we have twelve or fourteen men on top of the hill, many or most of them hit. I need two warm bodies to cover that trail in case the gooks get smart and use it. "Jaune, get over there, right now!" I look quickly over in Sergeant Johnstone's direction. He is yelling at a man huddled on his side in a fetal position. I quickly crawl-scramble over to him. "What's the matter, Jaune, are you hit?"

"It's my knee, sir, an old basketball injury, I can't move it."

"Jesus! A fucking *basketball* injury?"

"Yes, sir, happened in high school, I can't move it." I look into his earnestly pleading face, trembling ever so slightly, terror creeping unwanted up through the cow's lick of milk-white peach fuzz that dusts his throat and jaw. He is frozen with fear, and I suddenly, unreasonably, feel sorry for him. Men are dying all around us, and I need him. But as I look into the cold fright that glazes his eyes, I know that he is absolutely worthless to me this day.

"Fuck! All right, stay where you are. Waldorf, get over there, and cover that trail. Sergeant Johnstone, send somebody else over there with him! Where the fuck is Speedy?"

"He's over here, sir. He's hit; I don't know if he's dead or not."

"Fuck! Sergeant Johnstone, gimme a sitrep. How many men we got up here?"

"Fifteen, sir. The rest of 'em either got back down the hill or else got holed up behind rocks on the hill."

"We got any medics up here?"

"One, sir, but he got hit in the arm. They said Doc Gertsch got caught on the hill, and him and another medic is tryin' to make it up here to us."

"How many Dogwoods?"

"One Dogwood six and seven or eight eights, sir."

"You hit?"

"No, sir, not yet."

"Okay, how many M-sixties we got?"

"Two, sir, but one of 'em got hit, and it don't work no more."

I crawl over to Speedy's body where it lies slumped in a small clearing on the uphill edge of our hasty perimeter. Wilson crawls with me, having hooked on to me. Speedy is lying on his side with his belly toward us. His eyes are closed, and I can see only two large splotches of blood, one on his right calf, the other on the inside of his left thigh.

The gooks are firing RPG bazooka-type weapons into our positions and even throwing hand grenades downhill the thirty or forty meters that lie between us. We are slowly being chopped to pieces, and I have to get on a radio to get some artillery or maybe even some air support. As I approach Speedy, I grab his shoulder and shake him gently. "Speedy, you're okay now, we're gonna take care of you. Where are you hit?"

He opens his bleary eyes and stares vacantly at me. "My legs, sir, my legs."

I look down at his legs, then pull him over onto his belly. The splotches on his legs are large, but I can't even see any big holes in his pants legs. I am sure the medics will be able to take care of him. Shouts inform me that Doc Gertsch, the senior medic in the company, and another medic have made it to the top of the hill. "Relax, Speedy, you're gonna be okay. Doc Gertsch is on his way over to take care of you." I start to wrestle with his rucksack and try to strip it and the all-important radio from his shoulders. Wilson helps me, and then it breaks free from Speedy's limp body. Inside, I secretly feel good for Speedy. He got hit in the legs, but he is going to be all right. He'll probably even be going home, especially if any bones were broken by the bullets. Lucky guy.

I then begin talking to Mad Dog, who tells me he has sent the first platoon, under Sergeant Harris, around to the left to try to go up the hill from the other side. He has no word from them except that they walked into a real hornets' nest and were stopped, but he doesn't know how far up the hill they got.

As I am listening to this, a medic crawls over my legs and, pulling up Speedy's sleeve, starts to insert the needle attached to a bottle of albumin. Thank God, I think, he's gonna be all right now. But even as those thoughts are flashing through my mind, Doc Gertsch crawls over my legs and up next to Speedy. He puts his fingers on his throat and lays his ear on his chest. Then his voice tears me apart and leaves me stunned. "Never mind this one," he says to the medic inserting the albumin needle. "He's already dead; let's get to the next one."

I turn away from the radio in horror, looking blankly at Speedy as the medics crawl away from him. Dead? Speedy? Christ, I was just talking to him; he got hit in the legs; he can't be dead! I lurch over to him, pick up his limp arm, then thrust my hand around his throat, squeezing hard, desperately looking for a pulse. At first I feel nothing; then I sense a faint, irregular twitching deep in his throat. He's alive! "Doc Gertsch, wait, he's alive, I got a pulse, he's alive, come save him!"

Doc Gertsch is beside me in an instant, his hand quickly replacing mine on Speedy's throat. Silence for a few seconds as I wait expectantly, certain that Speedy will live now. "That's just nerves, sir; that ain't his pulse. He's dead. I'm sorry, sir, but we got other people to keep alive."

I nod blindly, then turn back to the radio, numb and shaken. Speedy dead. I can't believe it. I try to snap out of it and talk to Mad Dog, but I have problems. Only the very real threat of death all around us helps me forget Speedy for the moment. Mad Dog is telling me that we can't get artillery right away because one of the other companies is in a world of shit and in danger of being overrun, but that tactical air support will soon be overhead. I tell him we need some help and am asking whether the rest of my platoon will be able to get up the hill to support us when a sudden explosion lifts Wilson and me off the ground and rips the handset out of my hands. The fear of God churns through my body. Then I open my eyes and realize I am still alive. I look at Wilson, who is also stunned but looks unhurt. The radio is ripped wide open in the center. I depress the key on the handset I still hold. Nothing. Great, now we have no radio. I hear two or three men screaming behind me and to our right. A gook apparently jumped around a tree by the latrine, fired an RPG round at us, then disappeared. One piece of shrapnel from the shellburst hit the radio, but the explosion, some ten meters away, also seriously wounded three men—already hit once and laid behind a big rock to protect them. The RPG round hit right in their midst. At this moment there are three or four enemy soldiers firing AKs from over there.

Now I am mad, and I start yelling to my men to come up and cover our right flank, which is wide open. "Sergeant Johnstone! Where the fuck is Waldorf? I told him to cover that area!"

"He's a Dogwood, sir."

"We'll get some warm bodies over here now."

Suddenly Sergeant Gamel is beside me, just arrived up the hill. "We got two Dogwood eights down there, and I sent 'em down the hill; but I brought eight more men up here with me, including a machine gun. Where d'you want it?"

"Right over there by that gook shitter, they're maneuvering around us there. We've got to stop them."

"Right away, sir!" Then he is yelling and scrambling over me with three or four other men.

"Sergeant Gamel! We need another radio. This one got blown. Can you send somebody down the hill for one?"

"Yes, sir!"

There is a lot of fire coming from our right now, and it looks as if the gooks are massing for a final assault. The RPDs on the top of the hill are no longer firing down the hill; they have directed their fire on us. Screams from my rear tell me they are finding their mark. Suddenly it is all clear to me: I'm never going to get off this messy little hilltop. This is where it all comes to an end, in an ugly, dirty, grime-encrusted lack of poetry. But even as I recognize this reality of the immediate future, it all seems so unreal, so removed, so anticlimactic. No great thoughts come to me, only the painful regret that I still have half a canteen of lime Kool-Aid, that delicacy of jungle delicacies, and now I'll never get to drink it. Well, they won't get me easily, and I add the fury of my M-16 to the feeble fire being pumped toward the NVA circling to our right. We survivors are all but surrounded now, having only, it seems, the open hillside behind us. We can die here, or we can get pushed over the edge and get killed by the RPDs still raking the open slope.

My naked head feels suddenly bare in the thickening storm of bullets. I reach back over Speedy's body, grab his helmet, and clap it on my head. A sharp explosion directly in front of me lifts my shoulders off the ground, snaps my head back, and pitches Speedy's helmet backward onto my legs. I am stunned and feel only my ears ringing. Then, through a cloud, I hear Jim Parker's voice: "Sir! Sir! Are ya hit, sir?"

"I don't know, I can't—"

"You got hit in the chin, sir, and it's bleedin' a lot; but if you can talk, it doesn't sound like you broke your jaw." I start feeling my jaw with my fingers, reassured as I gingerly move my fingertips, feeling no break. Wilson is fumbling with the bandage he carries on his web gear as Parker examines my chin. I am still numb as he places the bandage Wilson gives him squarely on my chin and wraps the gauze streamers around my neck. "There, sir, it's bleedin' quite a bit, but head 'n' face wounds do that, often look worse 'n they are. That too tight?"

I can only grunt in response. Then a man crawls up and extends a handset to me. "New radio from down the hill, sir. Mad Dog is waitin' to hear from you." A radio! Maybe it isn't all over yet! I press the key.

"Mad Dog, Billy Goat, over."

"This is Mad Dog, what's your situation? Over."

"Billy Goat, our shit is very weak. Do we have any tac air yet? Over."

"This is Mad Dog, roger that. Blue Leader is upstairs right now; he's on the tac air push. Over." I madly twist the dials to the new frequency. "Blue Leader, this is Billy Goat, I am marking my position with smoke at this time. Please identify. Over."

I roll over onto my back, and pull the smoke canister off my LBE [load-bearing equipment]. I pop the ring and toss the can behind me. The yellow smoke seems to be moving in slow motion as it coils slowly upward, then begins to pour out of the can in great volume, wreathing up through the trees to the sky above.

"Billy Goat, this is Blue Leader, I see two yellow smokes and one purple. Over."

Fuck! We have four colors of smoke—yellow, purple, green, and red. Green is rarely used because it is difficult to pick out against the jungle, and it is very difficult to find red smoke; that means yellow and purple are the most commonly used. The gooks seem to monitor our radio transmission whenever things are tight, like right now, and they just toss their own smoke, stolen from American supply channels, to confuse things. But I have an ace in the hole. "Roger that, Blue Leader, we are one of the yellows. I am popping smoke again, at this time, please identify. Over." I pull the other canister of smoke from my LBE, pop it, and toss it where the other one was just running out. Soon clouds of bright red balloon out and up through the scrawny trees.

"This is Blue Leader, I see one yellow, one purple, and one red. Over."

"This is Billy Goat. We are the red; other smoke is the bad guys. From our position enemy forces are concentrated some forty meters to our west, azimuth of two seven zero degrees, on the very top of the hill, and some twenty to thirty meters to our north and east azimuth of zero degrees running to ninety degrees. We are in a tight spot. Anything you can put on them will help. Over."

"This is Blue Leader, roger that, Billy Goat, I am now inserting one flight of HE [high explosives]. Where do you want the first strike? Over."

"This is Billy Goat. Put the first one in to our north. Over."

I crawl toward Sergeant Gamel's position. I am just approaching his men when an F-4 goes over like Zeus, close enough to make us all flinch. A second after he has passed, the thunderous explosion rolls over our heads, making me want to crawl inside Speedy's too-tight helmet. I crawl up beside Sergeant Gamel, dragging my radio with one arm. "Whaddya think, Sergeant Gamel?"

"Bring it in another twenty meters, sir."

"Blue Leader, this is Billy Goat, request you move the next one in another twenty meters closer to us. Over."

"This is Blue Leader, roger, wilco, over."

We all bury our heads and hold our breaths as the next F-4 sweeps in. The explosion seems to wash over us, the energy ballooning our shirts around our bodies. Sergeant Gamel is grinning as I looked at him. "That's the one, sir. Couple more strikes there oughta wipe out that assault they were thinkin' about."

I grin back at him, then get back on the radio. "This is Billy Goat, Blue Leader, that last one is on the money. Can you put more strikes in and arc them around to ninety degrees? Over."

"This is Blue Leader, roger that, but how 'bout your other target on top of the hill? Over."

"This is Billy Goat, roger, if you can put anything in there, we'd appreciate it. Over."

"This is Blue Leader. I've got two more strikes of HE, then eight strikes of napalm. Want me to put some burn on top of the hill? Over."

"This is Billy Goat, roger that, torch those fuckers. Over."

"This is Blue Leader, get your men down. Over."

I turn and start to crawl quickly back to my original position. Then to my right a great orange fury blossoms and roars through the jungle, up by the gook bunkers. But as I get on the radio to adjust the napalm, the RPDs on top of the hill seem to open again with a renewed fury. Fuck me! Where the hell are the gooks hiding?

"Sergeant Johnstone, how was that strike?"

"Too far away, sir, gotta move it in."

"How far should I move it in?"

"Another twenty meters at least, sir. But before we move that shit any closer, somebody oughta go get Lesley. He's right up there, and I don't think he's dead."

He is pointing to our front, directly up the hill. Private First Class Lesley was the point man and somehow got about twenty meters uphill from the hasty perimeter when the shit hit the fan. He was hit in the first burst. I see his motionless legs and butt slumped in front of us, and I start to sweat again. I can't ask anyone else to go get him; that is part of my job. I suddenly start tasting acid deep in my throat. "You say he's still alive?"

A voice beyond Sergeant Johnstone answers me. "Yes, suh, Ah heard 'im yellin' two, three minutes ago." I nod grimly, then cup my hands over my mouth and yell in Lesley's direction. "Lesley, I'm comin' to get you, hang tight." I see his shoulder jerk to the side over his hip. I turn to Sergeant Johnstone and murmur the useless "Cover me."

He nods grimly back to me. "We'll cover you, sir."

I lay my weapon down and wipe my soaking, grimy hands on my soaking, grimy shirt. I have two or three dry heaves before I can control my body. I jam Gonzales's too-tight helmet down over my ears, take a deep breath, and burst out over the small rise I have been behind, crawling like a mad fiend for everything I am worth. The underbrush is very light here, and I feel as if I am crawling across an open stage. Gunfire erupts with renewed fury on both sides; but I am unhit, and soon I am reaching out, then touch Lesley's foot with my right hand. I pull myself up over his body, edging up toward his head. Suddenly RPD fire starts to rip through the air and bushes all around us. I mash my weight down on Lesley's body, and he screams in agony. I am rattled and unsure what to do. "Sorry, sorry," I murmur as I try gently to raise my body a few microinches, yet not high enough to get hit.

"Mah helmet," he screams, "gimme mah helmet!"

I glance hurriedly around and see no helmet. Blood is pouring freely out his collar, and his neck is bathed in it, the bright scarlet shining on dark ebony skin. I take Speedy's helmet off my own head and clap it onto his. He immediately seems to relax and drifts into deep moaning. "Okay, Lesley, we gotta get back now. I want you to put your arms around my neck and hang on." I wrench his limp, moaning body over onto his back, then drape inert arms over my shoulders. "Now hang on, Lesley. If you wanna live, hang on!" I feel him weakly clutch me, and I begin to crawl backward the way I had come. Our movement is deathly slow. Then a bullet hits my right forearm and hammers it back against my side. I am frozen in terror for a heartbeat or two but then force my shaking body to start moving again. I can hear automatic bursts from Sergeant Johnstone and several of his men now, and it is a reassuring sound. C'mon, God, I think, just this once get me back. Then I am belted in the butt with a shocking force that slams me down on Lesley and causes us both to yelp in pain. For a moment I lie immobilized, then start the agonizing backward crawl. Lesley falls silent, and his hands fall away from my neck. I drag him with me as I crawl, low and slow and scared. Then Sergeant Johnstone is pulling me and Lesley, other arms are helping, and we are back over the rise.

"You okay, sir?"

"Fuck, I don't know. How's Lesley?"

Doc Gertsch suddenly appears, crawls over us, and starts to open Lesley's shirt. Another medic is there beside me and quickly runs his hands and eyes over my butt. "You're not bleedin' too bad, sir, but I'll have to rip your pants off to be sure."

"No, let's hold off on that for now. We got stuff to do, and it doesn't hurt so bad now. Let me get the air in." I grab the handset from Parker, who has taken over as my RTO, just as he had been with the Tiger Force, with no need for spoken direction. "Blue Leader, this is Billy Goat, over."

"Billy Goat, this is Blue Leader, waiting for adjustment. Over."

"This is Billy Goat, roger that, we had to clear the stage a little. Request you put another strike in twenty meters closer to our position. Over."

"This is Blue Leader, roger, wilco, over."

There is a sudden roar to our right that throws everyone's face into the ground. I jerk my head quickly back up and look around. I can't tell whether anyone has been hit by this explosion, but as I turn back to the radio, I see there is now a hole in the middle of it big enough to stuff with an orange. I depress the key on the handset, but it is just as dead as I knew it would be. "Hey, Steele!"

"Sir?"

"We need another radio. Can you help us out?"

"On the way, sir."

"When you get down there, tell somebody to tell Blue Leader to repeat that last strike. Do you roger?"

"Roger that, sir."

I turn and edge back over to Speedy's body with Parker. We lie next to him and begin firing uphill on semiautomatic again. I go through two magazines. Then stop and look at what we have left: twelve magazines from Gonzales's bandoliers. After that, we'll have to scrounge from the other Dogwoods. I turn to my right and yell as loudly as I can over the din, "Sergeant Gamel, how you holdin' up?"

His cry comes back instantly: "Okay, sir. Could we get another air strike?" A booming roar to my left and a wave of intense heat tell me as I wince that Steele has reached the bottom and gotten my message through.

"We got no radio. We're waitin' on one. Then we'll get more air strikes."

A sharp outburst of sustained gunfire on the far side of the hill, off to our left and below us, tells me that Mad Dog is at least trying to relieve some of the pressure on us, but without a radio I can't tell what is happening. I turn and begin to squeeze off rounds slowly up hill. With all the Dogwoods we are suffering, every rifle is needed. I am inserting another magazine into my weapon when a band of ten or twelve of our men appears out of the woods to our right rear, racing forward in a deep crouch. One of them sees me, comes streaking over to me, and throws himself flat on his chest next to me. "Sergeant Harold from Lieutenant Doaks's platoon, sir. I brung a squad of men with me. We come around the long way an' up the ridge."

I am elated. "Christ, that's great. D'ja bring a radio?" He shrugs resignedly. "Yes, sir, but it crapped out on us comin' up the hill."

"Shit! All right. Sergeant Gamel is over there on the right. Send half your men over there with him. D'ja bring any M-sixties?"

"Two, sir."

"Good, send one over there; then put the other one over on the left there. Sergeant Johnstone'll show you where."

"Strike Force, sir," and he is gone.

I breathe a heavy sigh of relief; then I hear a plaintive "Sir!" to my left rear. I roll my shoulders over and see Steele on his chest, leaning on his forearms, a radio by his side, the handset in his extended hand. I streak the twenty meters to his side.

"Way to go, Steele, are you hit?"

"Yes, sir, I got hit in the left leg jes' as Ah started back up, 'n' then Ah got one in the right foot jes afo' Ah got here."

"Shit, let's get a medic to look at you. Doc Gertsch! Over here!" I depress the key on the handset. "Blue Leader, this is Billy Goat. Appreciate the last strike. Now we're having some problems back where you put in that first strike. Think we could get some bad stuff in there again? Over."

"This is Blue Leader, roger that, please be advised all I've got is napalm. Do you still want it? Over."

The firefight from Sergeant Gamel's position is reaching a roar now, and both M-60s are hammering full force.

"This is Billy Goat, roger that, we need some help fast. Over."

"This is Blue Leader, roger that. Tell your men to get down; strike going in now. Over."

I raise my head a foot off the ground and yell at the top of my lungs, "Sergeant Gamel, get your men down, napalm going in now!" I hear him echo the warning, then two or three other voices echo his, to be drowned by the all-consuming roar of the huge, ugly F-4 that is suddenly with us, seemingly down in the treetops, its ear-shattering soul-shaking roar paralyzing us. Then as it passes, the second explosion rolls over and through us, the wave of intense heat tightening and burning the skin on my face as I seek desperately to return to earth and feel cool dirt against my belly again. As the roar of the inferno dissipates, Sergeant Gamel is yelling at me, "Tell 'em to drop the next strike back twenty meters, sir; that was too close."

My stomach gnaws at me as I relay the message to Blue Leader and more napalm goes in. Sweat beads unnoticed all over my body, only in part from the heat. The gunfire from the top of the hill is starting to heat up again, but by now everyone has found a position of some refuge, and with the new men Sergeant Harold brought with him, we are answering the fire with more punch. I forgot to call Mad Dog, preoccupied as I was with putting in air strikes, but he hasn't forgotten me. Soon after I put Blue Leader on hold, he comes up on the radio. "Billy Goat, Mad Dog, over."

"This is Billy Goat, over."

"This is Mad Dog. How bad are you hurt? Over."

I glance around, trying to sort my thoughts out. "This is Billy

Goat, I think we've got four Dogwood sixes, maybe a couple more, ten or twelve Dogwood eights, maybe more, all kinds of wounds, and we're kinda locked into one small position, can't move around much. Over."

"This is Mad Dog, roger that. Have you seen Pepper Dog and the squad I sent up there with him? We have lost radio contact with him. Over."

Hmph. Pepper Dog must be Sergeant Harold.

"This is Billy Goat, affirmative on that. He arrived in our position about one-five ago. Over."

Sergeant Gamel's yell takes over. "We're ready for another strike, sir, and we need it bad."

I turn and yell to Sergeant Gamel, "Everybody down, Sergeant Gamel, here it comes!" I hear him start to echo the warning to his men, but then he is drowned out by that great ugly, roaring green and black winged beast that thunders through the trees and leaves behind another billowing fire egg. This time it is just a touch farther away. "Sergeant Gamel, want another one?"

"Yes, sir, make this one another twenty meters farther away. We'll get 'em in the trees."

"On the way!" I depress the key again. "Blue Leader, Billy Goat, that was beautiful. Can you put another one in twenty meters farther down the hill? Over."

"This is Blue Leader, roger that. Be advised that I only have two strikes left. If I put one in where you requested it, that will leave us only one. Over."

"This is Billy Goat, roger that, request you put the last one in squarely on the top of the hill, where you were putting in the first napalm strikes. Over."

"This is Blue Leader, roger that, both on the way at this time. Over."

I yell to Sergeant Gamel again, "Sergeant Gamel, here comes the last strike, get your asses down!" Again the great ugly roar of death streaks in from the sky.

Mad Dog is back on the horn. "Billy Goat, Mad Dog, over."

"Billy Goat, over."

"This is Mad Dog, we've got to get clear of this mess. Can you break contact and come down the way Pepper Dog went up? Over."

"This is Billy Goat, negative, we're hurt too bad to move until we get some help. Over."

"This is Mad Dog, roger that. I just sent about twenty men; they should reach you soon. Are you in any danger of being overrun? Over."

"This is Billy Goat, I don't know. I don't think so since those air strikes, but our shit is very weak. Over."

"This is Mad Dog, roger that, help is on the way. As soon as you can, break contact and come down the hill the way Pepper Dog went up, out."

Noise behind me turns me over. Forty meters away I see green forms loping toward us from the long end of the hill where Sergeant Harold appeared. Thank God! I raise my arm and wave. "Up here! Up here!" I turn over toward Sergeant Johnstone's position. "Sergeant Johnstone, how many Dogwoods you got over there?"

"I think we got two Dogwood sixes, sir, and about twelve Dogwood eights. Some of 'em bad."

"Okay, help on the way; then we've got to break contact and get back down the hill." I pass the same word to Sergeant Gamel.

Doc Gertsch is working on men right next to me, and I hear a couple of muffled moans. Then the reinforcements are among us and edging uphill past us, forming a protective umbrella that will allow us to lick our wounds and struggle back down hill. I am confused and stunned, mired in guilt and self-pity and numbness. I roll over onto my back and see that men who were over with Sergeant Gamel are being guided, at a slow crawl, by some of the men who came up with Sergeant Harold. I turn and grab Speedy by his shoulders, then firmly grab the middle of his shirt with my left hand and begin to snake my way along the gentle downgrade. Parker moves silently with us, helping the body along. After a short eternity and sixty or eighty meters, the steep slope blocks the top of the hill and we are in defilade, now protected from the still-active gunfire. Men begin to stand up.

I stop, soaked with sweat, and stretch my back as I stand up. I lean down and slip my right arm under Speedy's left shoulder, then gradually wedge my left arm under his thighs. With a lurch I lean sharply back, heft his dead weight off the ground, and clasp his limp body firmly to my chest. As I do so, his body seems somehow, mysteriously, to break in half at the waist, and his knees are suddenly jammed into his face as his body starts to collapse in my arms. I grasp desperately at his legs, stumbling off-balance and fall heavily forward onto my face and Speedy's uncaring body. I release Speedy's body and turn to my right, trying to pull my feet free. Speedy's body slumps slowly away from me, his shirt riding up over his back. Where the bottom of his rib cage should have been on the left is an ugly red hole. Out of it ooze pink, red, and yellow glistening tubes and entrails. They cascade down indiscriminately, steaming and slowly uncoiling. I stand up again and bend over Speedy reverently. I pull his shirt back down over this unsuspected death wound and again slip my right arm under his back, lower this time. His head lolls back limply on my shoulder. I slip my left arm under his butt and again lurch to my feet, clasping his body to my chest.

I stumble numbly downhill, following the green figure in front of me. The tears that fill my eyes run down and mix with the snot sprayed over my lower face. I felt a hot, fresh trickle running over my chin and down my throat onto my chest, and I realized that the bandage has slipped off my chin and now hangs cold and stiff around my neck like an outlaw's bandanna after the stickup. I feel a hot spot on my belly and my crotch and realize that Speedy is passing his life's blood down the front of my body.

Soon there is no more gunfire behind us, then we move down a steeper stretch, and link up with more filthy, bearded green monsters that drift out of the weeds. No one speaks. I see people gesticulating up in front of me, but I just keep walking, looking neither right nor left, sobbing softly over the dead body of the son of America I carry in my arms. My blood runs over my chin, down my body, mixes with his somewhere on my chest, runs in rivulets down my legs, into and over my squishing boots, and leaves bloody tracks in the Vietnamese jungle floor. We stumble what seems to be ten thousand endless miles, then stop.

I lay Speedy on an open poncho next to other poncho-wrapped bodies, then stand back up, my aching back screaming unheeded. I look down at his slack, openmouthed innocent face. His eyes are closed. Then, before I can say good-bye, the poncho is quickly and neatly folded over his face, and he is gone. I look down unthinking as I move away. After ten or fifteen steps I stop and lean against a tree. I don't know where I am or what is happening. I close my eyes and breathe deeply. Gradually order begins to seep back into my mind.

I open my eyes and stand up straight, lean back and arch my back, blink hard, and take slow, deep breaths. Off to my right some twenty meters I see ten or fifteen wounded men stretched out on their backs. Twenty meters beyond them an LZ is being chopped out of the jungle for a dustoff. I walk slowly over to the group. I see Sergeant Johnstone bending over one of the bodies as I approach.

Then I remember. "Sergeant Johnstone, did Jaune get hit back there?"

"No, sir, I don't think so."

"Find him and get him over here to me."

He stands up and moves off silently. I slowly cast my gaze back at the bodies wrapped in ponchos. Only three Dogwood sixes. The medics are amazing at keeping men alive. Then I begin to count the wounded stretched on the jungle floor before me. I get to twenty-two when I hear someone behind me. I whirl around and stare into Jaune's ashen, shaking face.

"Well, good job, Jaune, see what you done?" I don't know what I am going to say to Jaune, but I want to chew him out good, humiliate him in front of the wounded. Then a storm of rage comes over me, and I suddenly hit him in the face with my right fist with every ounce of strength in my body. He goes down like a sack of wheat, and I am after him, yelling like thunder. "You killed Speedy, you sorry motherfucker, because you weren't man enough to do your job, and by God, you're gonna pay!" Through my fury I hear Doc Gertsch yelling. As he wedges his body between mine and Jaune's, I swing at Jaune again, around Gertsch, and hit his shoulder. Then I suddenly stop pressing and back off. As I turn to my right, there, thirty meters away in the jungle, is Mad Dog, staring at me in shocked, openmouthed disbelief. Then, quickly, he lowers his gaze and turns away. My fury is still coursing through my body, although I know that I have just broken every rule in the army by striking an enlisted man. I am worse even than George Patton when he slapped that enlisted man in the hospital in World War II. I will probably end up court-martialed for my actions. Mad Dog saw the whole thing, but I don't care. Jaune was a coward and shirked his duty, and I blame all the casualties we suffered, especially Speedy's death, on him. I steam with fury as I walk around. I stop and lean against a tree, gritting and grinding my teeth.

Suddenly I see Sergeant Johnstone's face. "Sergeant Johnstone, how many men we gonna have left in the platoon that didn't get hit bad enough to get evacuated?"

"I don't know, sir, but I'll find out. The guys that was strung out on the hill and never made it up to our position got chopped up pretty bad, too."

"Okay, let me know ASAP." I turn and start to walk away, then stop, trying to breathe slowly and recover my bearings.

Sergeant Johnstone is back before I expect him. "Five, sir."

"Huh?"

"Five men will be left in the field, including me, unless you stay, sir, then we got six, but you got it in the chin."

"Hunh. Yeah, but I'm goin' in a couple days anyhow, and I don't wanna leave Mad Dog out here with just Doaks." The thought of Doaks makes me seethe with anger again. I wonder where his candy-ass was when his platoon came up to rescue us. "Besides, Mad Dog saw me hittin' Jaune, and I gotta show him I'm on his side so he doesn't court-martial me."

"Shit, sir, we're gonna get you a medal of honor for what you did on that hill, savin' Lesley 'n' all. Mad Dog ain't gonna do nothin' about this, 'n' besides, Jaune had it comin', we all know that."

"Yeah, well, I don't wanna take any chances. I don't really know him, and I think he could really hang my ass now if he wants to."

"Well, if you're gonna stay out here, you oughta let Doc Gertsch take a look at your chin, sir."

"Yeah, I will. Thanks, Sergeant Johnstone."

"Strike Force, sir."

I move back over toward the wounded now, see Specialist Gertsch bent over one of them. There are four or five other medics working with him, but he is the senior medic in the company and the one I trust the most. "Hey, Doc Gertsch."

"Sir?"

"When you got a minute, I wanta talk to you."

"Be right with you, sir." I walk back into the trees, and he is there behind me. "Sir?"

"Hey, listen, Doc, I'm not hit too bad, and I can't afford to go to the rear now, so could you take a look at my chin?"

"Sure, sir, lemme get my stuff."

I sit down and lean against a tree, and he is back. He starts poking at my chin with his fingers. Suddenly it hurts. "Unh!"

"Sorry, sir. Looks like you need some stitches there, and I'll have to give you a couple shots; but it won't take long. Whyn't you lay your head back on the ground so's I can work on you?" I lie down and close my eyes, and then he is sewing my chin together. I am amazed that it doesn't hurt as much as I expected. Doc Gertsch cleans the wound on my right forearm and bandages it up, then checks my ass. Some cooling salve is all I get on a thousand tiny wounds.

The dustoff slicks are now hammering in and out, and I see all the wounded have been evacuated; it is time for the dead to be taken out. I walk over to Speedy's body wrapped in a poncho, bend down, and heave him up.

The poncho starts to slip off, and I feel it drag between my legs as I walk. I wrestle with it, kick at it, and it finally falls clear. I step into the knee-deep swampy area that has been cleared for an LZ and begin to wade unencumbered, holding Speedy close. His calmly sleeping face softly nuzzles my shoulder.

Oh, Speedy, Speedy, Speedy, you son of a bitch, I hardly even know you, but I know you too well. Just a few days ago you stepped in front of me as we neared the crest of that hill, so that you'd get hit by the expected RPD burst instead of me—to give your life that I, your platoon leader, might live. And now you really are dead.

You should never have been carrying my radio, you dumb shit, with that heavy Mexican accent. Why the hell did I let you stay on? I should have gotten somebody else, you'd still be alive....

I hug him to me as I wade. Wise guy. Smart ass. Kid. The tears well up as his blood resoaks my chest and stomach.

I look up at the dustoff slick dropping from the sky in a blur, the rotor wash ballooning my shirt. I lean back and lift Speedy up, my arms aching.

I am just an American soldier lifting the body of a fallen brother-in-arms up into a helicopter. But at another level I am offering him back to America for all of us over here, as evidence of our selfless commitment. This is, finally and undeniably, the Offering of those in my generation of Americans serving in Vietnam: our lives offered for our country. Speedy's offer has been accepted.

More bodies are being loaded into the other side of the hovering helicopter, and I strain to lift Speedy up to the reaching hands. Then, suddenly, his weight is taken from me, and the dustoff rises, leaving me cold and shaken, a shiver stirring my legs. Good-bye, Speedy. Good-bye.

I stare after the dustoff until it disappears.

Mission Impossible

AFTER THE EVACUATION and resupply were completed, we moved a few clicks and set up for the night. The next day we moved down the ridge slowly, my platoon on point, but we made no contact. Two days later another lieutenant was ferried to the field to take my place, and I climbed onto the slick with a deep sigh of relief. I hadn't said anything to Mad Dog about hitting Jaune; but then he hadn't said anything to me either, and I was a little bit uneasy. I don't know what he thought, but I never heard about it or any Medal of Honor, again. Fair trade, I guess.

When I got off the slick in the rear, I immediately walked over to the battalion aid station tent right next to the landing zone. A couple of medics were on duty, and I handed them the card I had gotten from Doc Gertsch, which specified the shots I had received. They took my stitches out, and I moved up to the Brigade S-1 tent, where I set up my R&R with Sergeant Connors. He put me on a trip to Tokyo on June 18, which was the earliest he could manage, but that was fine with me. Another couple of weeks, and I'd be going home, or at least to the mobile location of my family hearth. This was summer, and I had heard from my mother that my two brothers in college would be home, and my older sister, married to an air force officer herself, would also be visiting. My baby sister was still in high school and living in Tokyo with my parents, so a complete family reunion was expected. I was really excited by the prospect, and the assurance of a ride home on R&R was enough to lift me off the ground.

On June 7, the day before I was to be promoted to captain, my company first sergeant told me we had some problems. The men would be coming to the rear on June 12 for a five-day "stand-down," which would be their periodic chance to relax in a secure area for a few days. They would be able to sleep on foldout cots rather than on the ground, to eat hot B rations out of a mess-hall tent rather than cold Cs out of a can, to get drunk pretty much at will. They could forget the strain of constantly being shot at, the drudgery of having to pull leeches off their legs each morning, the unspoken terror of worrying about getting their dicks blown off by a Bouncing Betty land mine that sprang up two feet before detonating. If they were lucky, depending on what local queens the first sergeant could line up, they might even get laid. A stand-down, in short, was a good deal for a line doggie.

But there was bad news in the wind: The first sergeant had been unable to locate any beer or Cokes in bulk, the first requirement for a stand-down. The nearest access point was Da Nang, some fifty miles of Indian country away. We had no truck available, so my "Mission Impossible" was to go to Da Nang, purchase a pallet (144 cases) of beer and a pallet of Cokes with a check from the unit fund, then somehow hustle them back to Camp Eagle before June 12. The prime candidate for a return trip, of course, was the U.S. Air Force. It was against regulations to fly alcohol in bulk by air, but I was assured that it was done all the time—all I needed was the right "war booty" bribe.

I was delighted by the prospect: go to a strange city and free-form solve a transportation problem, by hook or by crook. I didn't really want to bribe air-traffic controllers or pilots or anybody else, but I finally accepted an AK-47 Communist submachine gun from the first sergeant for "trading purposes."

Next day, I climbed aboard a slick for Da Nang, the second-largest city in South Vietnam after Saigon. It was the in-country headquarters for the U.S. Marine Corps and it really was their town: American marines were everywhere.

As soon as I got off the slick, tension automatically set in. The traditional interservice army-navy rivalry was brought to a somewhat keener edge between these services' most elite units, the paratroopers and the marines. I had to be very careful.

I made a few investigative calls on likely-sounding U.S. Air Force and Marine Corps offices, but I never mentioned the AK-47 slung over my shoulder, and I readily accepted formal refusals to bend the rules. Then I headed for the Da Nang airport, where I hoped to pick up a few men from the 101st to assist me in my plan.

The opportunity now before me was splendid: With the help of recruited paratroopers, I would steal a truck from the marines, and we would use it to carry our beer and Cokes back to Camp Eagle. The mechanics would be easy: Military vehicles in Vietnam had a simple on-off ignition switch with no key required for operation. In theory, drivers in the rear were supposed to lock a chain between the steering wheel and the brake pedal before they left their vehicles, but in practice, this step was sometimes ignored. It looked simple enough, but what a tremendous coup it would be!

I scooped up five guys with the 101st eagle patch on their shoulders from a line waiting to board a flight to Phu Bai. Their only baggage was their weapons, and once outside, I laid my plan out for them, especially the unknown. The road north to Phu Bai was an asphalt strip some ten meters wide, and once outside of town, the countryside was "contested." Our greatest danger would probably come when we drove through the Hai Van pass, a traditional Communist ambush site where much Western blood, first French, then American, had been spilled. American vehicles always traveled in convoys between cities, and we would be running solo. But I told them a single truck barreling north would be unanticipated, and I expected us to blow right through without raising a single slanted eyebrow.

Whoops of enthusiasm reassured me, and we danced off toward the China Beach PX, a holy mission to perform for the Great Paratrooper in the Sky! I was brimming over with self-confidence, much of it caused by the fact that this wasn't the first time I had stolen something from the marines. It was only a few years ago that I had carried off an even bigger feat, and had then been anointed by my peers with the psychic chrism of Jason and the Golden Fleece in the twentieth century....

... Sometime around 1961, when I was still in high school and trying to get into West Point, I read a story in a national magazine that moved me deeply. It was the account of the 1954 theft by West Point cadets of the Navy goat, the Naval Academy mascot, one week before the annual Army-Navy football game. It was heady stuff to an eager young aspirant—the almost mythological tale of West Pointers creeping down out of their mountain fastness one night, clambering over the wall at a slumbering Annapolis, and spiriting away that most-prized mascot! I decided then and there that, if I ever did get into West Point, one day I, too, would steal the Navy goat.

In the fall of 1965, during my senior year at the academy, it was time to act. I began to talk to some of my rowdier classmates and was pleased to find wide support for the idea. Soon we held our first meeting of potential goat thieves: I had recruited Art Mosley, Deme Clainos, Mike Brennan, Mike Mewhinney, Bob Lowry, Mac Hayes, and Bob Kesmodel.

Kesmodel's parents lived in Severna Park, Maryland, and we planned to use their house as our base of operations. We agreed to leave West Point on a weekend pass one week before the game (an "open" weekend for both teams), steal the goat on Saturday night, and take it to my grandmother's farm in Eagle Mills, New York, some hundred miles north of West Point. Since the 1954 theft by West Point cadets, the Navy goat had been kept at the Severna Park Naval Security Station across the river from Annapolis for the two weeks before the Army-Navy game. The superintendents of both academies made gentlemen's agreements each year not to steal each other's mascots and directed their cadets and midshipmen not to violate this agreement. But we felt that the word of some general did not constitute our word.

We met regularly through the fall as we gathered our skimpy intelligence. Captain Slinky, veterinarian in charge of the Army mule—a mascot never successfully stolen by midshipmen—told us a few things about goats. The most important thing I remember was that the goat, once approached, would probably not make any noise but might well attack. This was not comforting.

As the day grew near, we learned from Bob Kesmodel's father that the Navy goat, Billy XV, was indeed housed at the Severna Park Naval Security Station. But we learned more as well. The station, he said, housed a number of 250-foot towers used for communication with the Atlantic fleet, as well as some classified research laboratories. He said he had taken his daughter to the front gate and asked to see the goat, whereupon he was escorted several hundred yards to another fenced-in area, well inside the first fence, where he was shown the animal in a pen immediately behind a guardhouse. The theft looked impossible, he said, and he was concerned for our safety.

We were a bit discouraged at this news, but decided any marine could be distracted by a girl, and we recruited some female allies. We also borrowed a fast new Chevy with a big engine from a Chevrolet dealer who would soon be selling literally hundreds of cars to our class. Mike Brennan's girl, Helen, brought her father's

Ford station wagon, and on Friday, November 20, the first group left for Severna Park to do some preliminary reconnaissance. I left the next day with the rest of the team, and we arrived around eight-thirty that night to meet the other three girls who would act as decoys. And more warnings. Mr. Kesmodel had played golf at a course next to the station a few days earlier, and had sliced his ball over the fence. A loudspeaker had warned him that his ball had violated a federal security area, and under no circumstances to try to enter the area and recover it. He was shaken by this incident, and warned us to be careful.

Those who had come down on Friday took us to the station to check things out. We first drove through a gate into a military housing area, but in the dark, our green military ID cards from West Point got us waved in without a second glance; to the marine guard at that gate, we were probably just other marines like him.

After a few hundred yards, we came to the main gate of the security station, reputedly the highest-security naval installation on the East Coast. The whole area was brightly floodlit with many signs warning intruders away. The actual gate—a small guardhouse and raisable barrier—blocked a two-lane road leading toward the communication towers in the distance, eerily studded with red lights. We pulled onto a side street and parked where we could see two beefy marines inside the guardhouse and a fenced-in pen attached to the back of the small building. Things did not look good.

When we got back to the Kesmodel house, some of us were no longer quite so sanguine about the task. But Deme Clainos and I were determined.

·Leaving the others in a nearby bar, we went back to the station, parked in the housing area inside the first gate, and walked toward the second fence. It was a Cyclone fence ten feet high, topped with barbed wire, and it looked impregnable. Its whole length was brightly lit and bordered by a fifty-foot-wide strip of closely mown grass. We walked along it, staying just beyond the reach of the light. After we had gone a half mile or so, we approached what looked like a small pedestrian gate through the fence. We stopped, still in the shadows, as we saw a man approach that gate from inside the fence, then walk through it without even slowing down. He walked away from us, and soon disappeared. Deme and I walked over to the gate, and sure enough, it was open about two feet, apparently as some sort of convenience for people who lived in the housing area! Just to be sure of our fabulous good fortune, we walked through the gate ourselves and stopped. No problem. With adrenaline pumping, we raced back to our classmates in the bar.

Our excitement reignited the team, and soon we were back at the Kesmodels' making our final plans. The backseat had been taken out of the fast Chevy and replaced with straw. Bob Lowry would wait with this car in the housing area a hundred yards from the pedestrian gate. We smeared our hands and faces with burnt cork and, in our black turtlenecks and Levis, were soon dark from head to toe. At 11:30 P.M., I would creep through the pedestrian gate with Deme Clainos, Art Mosley, Mike Brennan, Mike Mewhinney, and some tools. Mike would hide with a crowbar in a clump of bushes just inside the gate, in case someone closed and locked it before we got back out. We gave ourselves fifty minutes to cross the half mile to the goat pen. Mac Hayes and Bob Kesmodel would stay with the four girls at the bar, but would leave in time to get through the outer gate by 12:20 A.M., according to our synchronized watches. Once inside the first gate, Mac and Bob would get out and wait in the housing area while the girls approached the second gate. There they would get out of the car and approach the marine guards, flirt like crazy, and keep them busy with some cock-and-bull story while we stole the Navy goat.

We got back to the still-open pedestrian gate by 11:30, and walked in. Mike Mewhinney quickly disappeared into a nearby clump of bushes, and we could see the faint shadow of our fast Chevy just beyond the reach of the lights a hundred yards away. Pulses pounding, we edged through the darkened buildings toward the main gate, dodging a marine jeep patrol that seemed to be checking for unlocked doors. By midnight, we were in position behind a row of bushes near the gate. We watched as the guard was changed, and by 12:10 A.M., were left alone with the goat and two big, fresh marines.

At 12:20 A.M., right on schedule, the girls drove up to the gate in their station wagon. We saw one guard walk up to the car, and then the other emerged from the guardhouse as the girls started to get out. We instantly went into action, creeping to the goat-pen gate. Both marines were standing with their backs to us no more than twenty yards away, talking animatedly to the girls. The pen was a twenty-foot square of the same ten-foot Cyclone fence topped with barbed wire, and the gate was secured with a huge padlock. As I pulled out a small crowbar and slipped the end through the hasp of the padlock, we could plainly hear Helen break into tears. Mike

Brennan wrapped a black towel around the lock, and the rest of us jerked down on the crowbar on signal. There was a loud metallic snap as the lock broke, and we froze. But Helen was really getting into her act, and now the marines were trying to help the other girls console her.

We slowly edged the gate open. At the center of the pen was a small hut, where Billy XV slept. He was standing on the other side of it, shaking his horns at us silently. He looked enormous, and his horns, painted Navy blue and gold, were immense. Art and I each had a lasso to slip over his head, but frankly, we were terrified.

We were slinking around either side of the hut when suddenly we were bathed in light. Everyone hit the dirt, which for Art and me was equal parts dirt and goat droppings. We froze in the headlights of a car stopped entering the station. The marines checked the driver's pass, then raised the barrier, and the car drove by. Art and I were quickly back up, but now Billy was pawing the ground. We didn't know what to do, so we rushed him, each grabbing a horn. To our surprise, Billy was calm, almost docile. We started to slip our lassos over his huge horns, and Art quickly had his around Billy's neck. But I watched Billy step through my loop as I tried to get it over his horns.

With mounting panic, I tried to lift his leg out, but Art suddenly hit my shoulder, and we were back down in the goat droppings. Someone was walking in the gate. It looked like a young marine in civilian clothes. He showed his ID, then walked by the floodlit cage no more than three feet from my prostrate, blackened form. We had stopped breathing, and my heart was going like a triphammer, but he walked by kicking rocks and looking back at those pretty girls. We waited a short eternity until he was gone, then I got Billy's foot out of the loop and the loop around his neck. Art and I led him out of the pen, waved Deme Clainos out in front of us, and started back toward the pedestrian gate. We had been uncertain how Billy would react, but he wanted to run, and we ran with him—just like Navy cheerleaders running him into a stadium in front of their football team before a game. Deme Clainos and Mike Mewhinney held the pedestrian gate open for us as we ran Billy through it. Bob Lowry saw us coming and the monster engine roared to life as we approached. We ran Billy into the backseat area filled with straw, piled in after him, and took off.

Back at the Kesmodels', the girls arrived, and we marshaled our forces for the trip north. We left around 2 A.M., two men leading in the fast car with the goat, the rest following in the station wagon. We soon discovered that we had been well-advised to replace the back-seat in the getaway car with straw: Billy had an upset stomach, and riding with him became a duty, if not a punishment. We stopped every few hours to change goatherds, and laughed at looks we got from tollbooths on the New Jersey Turnpike.

Around 6:30 A.M., headed north on the New York State Thru-way some thirty miles west of West Point, the station wagon threw a rod and ground to a halt. We blew the horn desperately at the get-away car ahead. But Clainos and Brennan, goatmen of the hour, never heard us and kept driving north. Neither knew the way to my grandmother's farm in Eagle Mills.

Mike Mewhinney and I walked through several fields to a nearby road where we were able to hitch a ride back to West Point. It was around 7:30 A.M. when we got there, and my regiment was forming up in full-dress uniforms to march to chapel. We did some dancing, in blackened faces, to get back into the barracks without being seen. We found a classmate, John Ford, who had a girlfriend visiting with a car, and were soon headed back to our broken-down station wagon. We piled everyone in there as a wrecker arrived to tow the car, then headed north again. The goatmobile turned up at the next rest area, with Billy contentedly grazing beside the freeway. Within hours, we had him safely stabled in my grandmother's barn and were back at West Point. That evening, I called ABC sportscas-ter Mel Allen in New York City and told him—anonymously—the whole story. He later broadcast the interview over ABC radio, and the word was out—Army had gotten Navy's goat!

The next day, West Point denounced the Mel Allen interview as a hoax. We had told no others of the theft, but wanted the Corps of Cadets to know the goat was in Army hands. So, Monday morning, I used the West Point band's sheet-music mimeograph machine to print up several hundred flyers, which I left on tables in the mess hall. At lunch, the Corps of Cadets erupted in roars of celebration.

But enormous pressure was brought to bear on the Corps of Cadets as the West Point staff tried to find out who had the goat. We thieves met several times each day to plot our next moves. But by Wednesday, when the staff began grilling cadets individually, the time had come to give up our prize.

That night, after taps, six of us slipped away and drove to Eagle Mills. We took pictures of our crew with the goat, then took him back to West Point. We arrived around 5 A.M. and slipped him into the mule barn, where we hid him in a private lavatory off Captain Slinky's office. We intended to retrieve him a few hours later and take him to lunch where we would present him to Sonny Stowers, the captain of the football team. But a janitor cleaning the office discovered the goat, thought it had been put there by the cheerleaders for some sort of rally, and told the Tactical Department they'd have to remove this surrogate goat before Captain Slinky came to work. Alerted by our contacts in the chain of command, Art and I roared up to the mule barn in our fast Chevy but found the place swarming with military police. We decided the only thing left was to have a massive rally before lunch and fall on our swords, just to ensure the corps knew of our coup.

We set up a loudspeaker in an area everyone passed on the way back from class, and we stood on top of a dumpster and told the cheering corps what had happened. They carried us into the mess hall in triumph, as a three-vehicle caravan commanded by a colonel returned Billy XV to Annapolis.

Nothing really happened to us until after the Army-Navy game, which ended in a dismal 7–7 tie. Over the next few weeks, we met three times with a board of five colonels, to whom we described our feat in great detail. The colonels submitted a report to the commandant of cadets, Brigadier General Richard P. Scott, who later saw each of us individually. I was the last man he saw, and he told me that I had done well, and he would be proud to have me serve under him in the army. But we had broken the rules and must be punished. Our punishment, he said, would be loss of our senior privileges for two months—a slap on the wrist we accepted with relief. And later, with a wide smile. In fact, we all smiled hard after that for some time....

. . . So it was with the vivid memory—and now revived spirit—of that episode from my West Point years that I strode off with eager paratroopers to steal a truck from the marines.

When we got to the China Beach PX some ten minutes later, we took some time out to sit down and savor the delicacy of an ice-cream sundae—oh, the heavenly delights available to REMFs!

We walked back out front and waited only a few minutes before a fresh USMC five-ton truck cruised into the parking lot across the street from us and stopped, two young studs popping out of the cab so fast they barely had time to shut the engine down, let alone chain it up in accordance with regulations. My crew passed wide grins around as the driver and his companion shouldered by us into the snack bar.

By prearrangement, two of my men followed them in, to start a fight in the unlikely event that either of them started back outside. The rest of us crossed the street and swung up onto the truck just as if we owned it. My designated driver cranked it up as I swung into the other side of the cab, the rest of the men vaulting into the truck bed as we lurched forward. We turned wide and drove back in front of the snack bar, the two potential fight provokers running out and leaping aboard as we passed the door, both convulsed in laughter. The marine driver, it seems, was in the process of chewing his companion out for some imagined slight with a bar girl the night before—boy, did he have a surprise waiting for him in the parking lot!

We made our way across town and down to the correct dock with the help of directions elicited from passing marines—none of whom seemed to think anything strange about a crew from the 101st in a marine truck. Once there, I gave the unit-fund check to a navy petty officer, and within an hour, a forklift loaded a pallet of Budweiser and a pallet of Coca-Cola into the bed of our truck. Again, not even a funny look, and my arrogance grew—it seemed you could get away with most anything in Vietnam, just so you wore captain's bars on your collar and looked righteous in the execution!

Soon enough, more directions from passing marines got us across town to the gate that opened onto Highway 1 north. It was a huge sandbagged edifice, and I felt antsy as we pulled up to the barrier that blocked the road. A marine in a flak jacket and helmet came out of the guardhouse on our left and approached, but I was able to bullshit my way by him, and he raised the barrier and waved us through.

We soared out that gate on wings of eagles, yea, verily, the wings of those 101st eagles we all wore on our shoulders! As we drove north, we headed up a long escarpment, and Da Nang and its vast harbor fell below us and behind us, resplendent in the bright after-noon sun. The plastic window in the back of the canvas cab had been left open, and one of the riflemen in the truck bed had tuned a portable radio to the Armed Forces Network, which was playing a new Beatles song. I had him turn the volume up all the way as my heart flew with the almost wordless song of "Hey, Jude." Man, I was high!

The Hai Van pass could have been Golden Gate Park in San Francisco, although the guys in back kept their weapons at the ready and shut the portable radio off. A couple of hours later, we drove into the rear area of the 2nd/502nd, where eager hands off-loaded the beer and Cokes. Then the first sergeant had some men take the truck over to the Third Marine Amphibious Force in Phu Bai, where it was abandoned near a motor pool. Mission accomplished.

A lot of different people bought me beer that night, and I got pretty drunk. But I stayed naturally high for days.

R&R

TWO DAYS AFTER I came back to Camp Eagle with the marine truck and the beer and Coke, Sergeant Connors got me a slot on an R&R flight to Tokyo on the fifteenth. It was already the eleventh—only four days to spend in Saigon. Hmm. I fairly danced down to the Phu Bai airstrip, walked over to the trailer where Clark had taken me so many months ago, and quickly got lined up on a T-28 flight to Bien Hoa. I didn't take much with me; as usual, a toothbrush in my pocket was the only baggage other than my weapon. But the division base camp had been moved to Bien Hoa from Phan Rang a few months ago, and our duffel bags of personal gear had been moved with it. If I ever located it, I intended to dig into my duffel bag when I got there and pull out my class A uniform, as well as some civilian clothes. I got high thinking about what lay ahead of me, and when I got to Bien Hoa, I was soon directed to the correct storehouse. Within an hour I had checked my weapon and rummaged through my bag of personal gear. I hustled a jeep from the HHC first sergeant and was soon steaming down the highway to Saigon, the private who was driving glad for the free trip to town. I carried a song in my heart that kept trying to tumble out my mouth as we soared south. Soon we were in metropolitan Saigon, and the dust, noxious fumes, and impatient Honda snarls that filled the air only diluted my high a little.

I had no idea whether Jacqueline would be home but just played that blind. If she weren't home, I could walk around the block and stay at the Majestic Hotel, which had been taken over by Uncle Sam and was being used as a BOQ. I waved thanks to the driver as I carried my small bag into the apartment building at 95 Rue Pasteur, and I ran up the back stairs, two at a time, until I got to Jacqueline's door on the fourth floor. I knocked hard as I rang the bell. Thi Teu answered the door, but Jacqueline's delicate face appeared over her shoulder even as I walked in. We rushed into each other's arms. *"Oh, chéri, je ne savais pas croire. Pourquoi m'as tu pas écrit un mot?"*

"Eh, bien, c'est la guerre, n'est-ce pas?"

"Ah, oui, chéri, tu as bien raison, serres moi, là, là, ah, oui!"

The shrieks of joy announced Kinou's presence even before I felt him pulling on my pants leg. Then I had to bend and scoop him up to our level, again enfolding Jacqueline into my arms. I was squeezed tightly, then eased gently into the living room, Kinou now excitedly telling me about his day on the playground. I sat down on the sprawling couch and turned my full attention to him. The air conditioning was welcome bliss, and Jacques Brel was crooning softly in the corner. Thi Teu brought me a cold "33" brand of French beer, unbidden, and as I took a first swallow, I glanced at Jacqueline, softly glowing on the couch next to me. Kinou was still babbling excitedly, as only five-year-olds can do, but contentment was welling up deep in my breast. We might have been in Paris. . . .

After a few minutes with Kinou, Jacqueline shooed him away, and I went into the spare bedroom and changed into my civilian clothes, then was back in the living room. Jean-Michel had been calmed down by his grandmother by this time, but his bubbling laughter welcomed me back. It was close to seven o'clock, and after one more beer we went into the dining room and sat at the table, where the three of us were served by Thi Teu. After a leisurely meal, with good French wine, we returned to the living room. Jacqueline and I sat and sipped Grand Marnier while Thi Teu took Jean-Michel into his bedroom and changed him into pajamas. Within a few minutes he appeared again, shyly clutching his teddy bear, as the strains of Offenbach's *Gaîté Parisienne* soothed my tenseness or what was left of it. Then Jacqueline and I were left alone, the touch of her fingertips on my brow weaving that magical spell. We had another drink, then repaired to her bedroom, where the mysteries of the world were silently explained to me in velvet song.

I arrived on a Friday night, and my flight to Tokyo wasn't until Tuesday morning. I spent a magnificent weekend in Saigon with Jacqueline and Kinou, delighting in walking the streets in my disguise of civilian clothes—almost magically removed from the war. But the best times were at night in Jacqueline's arms, and I found myself willingly becoming heavily involved. It was a wonderful, delicious time.

Monday morning Jacqueline left me in bed but promised to be home at noon with Christophe and a free afternoon. I got out of bed and the apartment around nine and, wearing my fatigues, walked around to the Majestic, where I was able to use a military phone. I had received a letter from an old high school friend, Tom Barnett, a few weeks after I had gotten out of the hospital. Tom had lived a few doors away from me in Arlington, Virginia, but we had gone to rival high schools. When we had graduated, he had gone to the U.S. Naval Academy while I had gone to West Point. I had seen him only a few times in college, but we remained good friends from the early days of neighborhood sandlot baseball. In his letter he had mentioned that he was near Saigon, at a place called Nha Be, and said that if I was ever in Saigon to try to call him and we might be able to get together. I had no idea where Nha Be was, but what the hell. It only took me a few minutes with the Signal Corps operator to get hooked into Nha Be, and, wonder of wonders, to get connected with Lieutenant Barnett. Tom was commanding a flotilla or a squadron or some such organization made up of six PT boats. They weren't really PT boats in the World War II sense, he hastened to tell me, but their modern counterparts, PBRs. I assured him that I didn't know a PT boat from a bathtub but wanted to know if we could get together. Much to my surprise, he suggested that very afternoon. It turned out that Jacqueline had to stay at school, but Kinou was ready for some fun. In a few hours, Tom brought one of his PT boats and its crew up the Saigon River, and met me and Kinou at a floating restaurant.

We spent a delightful time on the Saigon River, a truly joyful interlude in an often ugly year for both Tom and me. We did all sorts of silly things, like making hard turns at full speed and letting Kinou steer. What a delight it must have been for a five-year-old! After several hours of play on the river we finally called it quits, and Tom took us back to the base of Tu Do Street. I was leaving for Tokyo the next morning and had to go report in at Tan Son Nhut. I promised to give his greetings to my family and to get in touch again next time I was in Saigon.

It was a five-hour ride to Tokyo, but I could have flown under my own power. When we arrived at Yokota Air Force Base, I just went around the R&R processing lines and got on a base phone. My older sister, Sally answered. She was a nurse in Boston and was married to Joe Scifers, a captain in the air force who was going to graduate school in Boston. They were in Tokyo with my parents on vacation. My father was in Korea, at Osan Air Force Base, where one of the squadrons of his tactical fighter wing was assigned; but my mother was down at the staging unit, and we agreed to meet there. Seriously wounded casualties arrived here continuously on C-141 jet transports. When they were taken off the planes, they would be held briefly in the staging unit while they were assigned to different hospitals in Japan or simply transferred to a flight back to the World, depending on their wounds. My mother was a nurse and worked there four or five times a week.

I fairly skipped over to the staging unit, getting there just as Sally and Joe did. There was a lot of hugging and kissing and laughter, and then my mother was there and her arms were around me. For the first time, I felt *safe*!

We drove home and found Judd, a junior in college, Thad, a freshman, and Brita, baby-sister-sixteen-year-old-cheerleader, were also there. Again, hugging, rejoicing, laughing. We were a tight family, and we had learned long ago that as a military family that moved regularly, the children had to be each other's best friends. But what a life we had experienced—from the heavy heat of rural Alabama to Washington, D.C., to the noblesse of Fontainebleau, France, to the frigid warmth of Minnesota; then a three-year reprise in the nation's capital, on to the ethereal intellectual climate of Amherst, Massachusetts, and finally to the land of the Rising Sun.

Now, in Japan, we were united once again, and it was one of those experiences that stay with you forever. I drank a lot, spending the days draped around the officers' club pool in the company of members of my family and/or stewardesses from World Airlines and fighter jocks who flew for my father. There was usually some sort of more or less formal evening meal at home, but just as often we'd have something at the club and then get into the evening's entertainment, followed by a party or two at the bachelor officers' quarters. I was deliriously happy.

The last twenty-four hours were spent with my family. I could feel the war beckoning, leering its blue-steel teeth as it reached for me, and I shuddered. I was uneasy, antsy, breathing shallowly. I didn't want to accept the reality fast approaching, and then it arrived.

The whole family accompanied me down to the flight line that night. As we walked into the terminal, Sally pulled me off to one side. "Listen, Tommy, I know this is gonna sound funny to you, but

I've had this really funny dream about you twice since you've been home. I had it again last night, and I want to tell you about it."

My curiosity was slightly piqued. "What kind of dream was it?"

"Well, it was really weird, but you are in Vietnam, and you are walking alone with some Vietnamese, and it's nighttime. All of a sudden you come to some dead dogs in the middle of the road, and you pass them, and then pretty soon some guys point their guns at you, and you are a prisoner with your hands up, and you look really unhappy, and then everything sort of disappears."

I stepped back for a moment and suppressed my laughter, then looked into her frightened eyes. "Sally, I really do appreciate your warning me, but that's just not gonna happen. I'm with American troops in the field all the time. The only Vietnamese I see are the enemy, and I'm shootin' at them."

Sally was smiling now but impatiently dancing along beside me as I started to walk toward the gate to the flight line. "Yes, I know, Tommy, but promise me, if you ever see dead doggies like I said, promise me you'll stop what you're doing and go back. Promise me, please!"

As I walked, I had been laughing at Sally's little dream; but now her tone was becoming insistent, and she was tugging hard on my sleeve. I stopped again and looked at her, cold and serious now. "Okay, Sally, I promise you, if I ever come across dead doggies, while I'm walking with Vietnamese at night, I promise you I'll stop and go back to some place safe. How's that sound?"

Sally was smiling at me now, and she suddenly threw her arms around my neck and squeezed me against her. "Oh, Tommy, I know that sounds silly, but you really make me happy, just by promising me that."

Joe and my mother were suddenly with us. Then my whole family was surrounding me. "Hey, what's going on, you two getting into another fight?"

"Yeah, Sally's beating Tommy up again."

Sally, two years older than I was, had been my constant childhood sparring partner.

"Nah, Sally just had this freaky dream about me killing Vietnamese doggies, or something, and she made me promise not to be mean to doggies."

"Or else she'll report you to the ASPCA." Judd chimed in.

"That's the *V*SPCA." Joe corrected him. We all laughed, not really at Joe's line, but rather in an effort to ward off the cloud that threatened our family group.

Then we were at the gate. I turned to my family, a wide smile frozen to my face, but something was beginning to crawl around the pit of my stomach. I hugged them all, accepted their warm embraces and bits of verbal bravado. Sally and Brita and finally my mother had started to cry softly. "Hey, c'mon now, this is the good-bye family. We leave often, but we always get together again. Now don't make me feel like you're sending me to my doom!" That brought on a second wave of hugging. Everyone was smiling as I stepped back. Then I waved a last good-bye and strode off toward the waiting C-141 jet cargo plane that would carry me back.

When I got off the plane at Tan Son Nhut in Saigon, the oppressive heat enfolded me like an old friend. I begrudgingly accepted my fate but was not quite ready to step so precipitously back into the jungle as I climbed into a cyclo-cab. "Ninety-five Rue Pasteur." It was seven o'clock when I arrived; supper had already been served, and Thi Teu had cleared the table and washed the dishes. However, Jacqueline had her fix me a couple of sandwiches, and I ate them along with a 33 beer on ice. The next day was Wednesday, but it was also some kind of holiday for the French schools, so Jacqueline begged me to stay. That wasn't hard to agree to. The next morning I dressed in civilian clothes, and Jacqueline, Kinou, and I walked across a resplendent Saigon that was just stretching in the cool breezes off the river before noon. Eventually we stopped a cab and made our way to the Cercle Sportif, the private club that had formerly been the exclusive province of the French but that was now slowly being taken over by the Vietnamese. In my civilian clothes I might have been one of the wealthy Europeans who clustered there.

Or perhaps one of the American correspondents who reported the war from the confines of the club, writing lyrically and poetically of the savagery of the war that they could only re-create from scattered conversations with REMFs. I had read the stories that were printed in *Time* and *Newsweek* by correspondents assigned to cover the war, and for the most part the authors really had little idea what was going on. I found it hard to blame them for the sometimes unrealistic stories that they filed. After all, their job was not to close with and destroy the enemy; it was only to report such action. And I could understand their reluctance to take a closer look. We never saw correspondents at the front, even in areas as protected as Camp Eagle. If you didn't have to go to the line, if you could hang out in Saigon, amusing yourself with unlimited liquor and drugs and women, and get by with only occasional one-day trips to "safe" fire bases, where there was very rarely any real danger, why tempt fate? Why stick your ass out in the wind and risk getting greased if you didn't have to?

The only thing that really galled me, and other line doggies as well, was that in print the war correspondents often seemed to be genuine heroes when in fact they were in less danger, in Saigon and even on the fire bases, than they would have been cruising down the Santa Monica Freeway.

This led to another strange fact about the war, little understood in the World: Out of the more than half a million U.S. troops in Vietnam, no more than about sixty thousand, including the artillery batteries located on the fire bases, were actually fighting. There were Saigon Warriors all over the place, wearing flashy uniforms, carrying flashy guns, telling flashy stories, but they were the American version of the White Mice, those show-troop police in white uniforms who patrolled the streets of Saigon. They had no more idea of what war was like than the man in the moon. The line doggies who were actually out in the weeds killing and dying were generally scared shitless and grateful for every second they lived. Unfortunately the correspondents got their stories from the Saigon Warriors who abounded everywhere rather than risk their lives to talk to a grunt in the field. Besides, the Saigon Warriors were generally better educated and smarter (as evidenced by their having been able to filter themselves out before they fell into the dirty field).

And more articulate: Their war stories were well thought out, literate, and even romantic. The sad result was that the American public got, and was satisfied to hear, a fantasy story that might more appropriately have dealt with Disneyland or Errol Flynn than with the real war being fought in the jungles and the rice paddies. After Tet, when there had actually been gunfire in downtown Saigon, there was just no way to slow the REMFs down; everyone in-country was automatically an expert on the war.

At the Cercle Sportif that day I walked around rather freely, incognito in my civilian clothes. I saw only one U.S. officer in fatigues there, a major general who was clearly someone's guest. Beside the swimming pool lay ten or fifteen women in bikinis, about half of them Westerners. Jacqueline and I sat on the veranda and had sandwiches and beer. It was a restful moment, but one could see how the war had impacted, even here, in a seemingly protected island. Guns were everywhere, mostly pistols in hand-wrought snakeskin shoulder holsters. In the context of Saigon it was barely even noticeable, but when I thought about the Yokota Air Force Base officers' club, where I had been only the day before, there was really no comparison. And although I was enjoying myself because of the company, I felt wistful for the physical comfort I had so recently left behind.

Jacqueline could tell there were ghosts in my heart, and we left soon after we had eaten, not even staying to walk through the protected park. We went back to her apartment and locked ourselves in. After half an hour or so of listening to Jacques Brel I started to soften up somewhat, but I was still possessed by unknown spirits. One of them was clearly fear. I didn't want to die, of course, but that was a fear that I could carry comfortably, a known passenger on my voyage. There was more, however, and I wasn't sure what it was. Certainly it had to do with the joyful interlude I had had with my family and the fact that I was now, once again, going back to dance with the enemy, never sure if or when death might cut in on me.

I got back to Camp Eagle the next day and reported in to my battalion. While I was in Tokyo, the assault on the A Shau Valley had been made. The units that went in on slicks had drawn a lot of heavy ground fire, and many helicopters had been shot down. But once the units had gotten on the ground, they had met very little resistance. For whatever reason, it seemed that Charley didn't want to square off and duke it out. The result had been that our troops were uncovering enormous caches of weapons, ammunition, explosives, matériel, and rice, all seemingly destined for the war in areas of the country far to the south. We seemed to have hit an enormous supply and marshaling area, but there was no big fight being put up to protect it.

The following morning the battalion XO, who ran the rear area at Camp Eagle, informed me that I would be the new assistant S-4 for the battalion, meaning I would be in charge of the motor pool. Ugh! That sounded like as bad an assignment as I could get; but then I was the junior captain around, and I couldn't expect a good job right away. I'd just have to see if I could breathe some life into an otherwise dreadfully boring job.

A few days later I saw the battalion S-1, Captain Grady, in the mess tent. While we were eating B ration mystery meat, he informed me that my name had come down that day on a brigade levy: to go to Military Assistance Command, Vietnam (MACV) as an adviser.

I went over to his tent with him after lunch, and he showed me the orders. General Creighton Abrams had recently taken command of the U.S. Army in Vietnam from General Westmoreland, and he had embarked on an effort to Vietnamize the war. As part of that effort he was increasing the number of advisers by drawing officers and sergeants from the U.S. units in Vietnam and converting them into advisers. My name was on the list; that seemed normal, since I was a brand-new captain fresh off the line. I thought about that for a few minutes. I knew that if I went and saw Major Wallace, the brigade personnel officer, whom I had worked for and counted as a friend, I could probably get my name taken off the list. But that meant I would stay with the O-Deuce and would, at least for a while, remain the assistant S-4, or motor pool officer. That sounded pretty grim. But if I just kept my mouth shut and went along with the orders, I could be an adviser, probably go to the delta, and see an entirely different part of the war. That sounded intriguing, almost an adventure. And I knew that as an adviser, my ass wouldn't be nearly as much on the line. Oh, I would miss the opportunity to be a company commander in combat, but this war looked big and open-ended enough that I could expect to be back later on another tour, when I would very definitely get the chance to command a company.

Fuck it, I thought, I think I'll see what life is like in the delta! Also, I could take this chance to travel around the Nam a little more and check out other possibilities for jobs that I knew about but that had only seemed like fantasies until now. It didn't take me long at all to stuff my toothbrush in my shirt pocket, throw a bandolier over my shoulder, and round up a ride to the Phu Bai airport. I had to go through the brigade rear in Bien Hoa to pick up my duffel bag of personal possessions and sign out, then on to the new adviser training school at Di An. I cleared the round out of the chamber of my weapon, since I was now headed for the Deep Rear, hopped into the jeep that picked me up, and we headed out.

I looked back at the row of tents as we pulled out onto the main dirt road, and I felt a little wistful to be leaving the Eagle. But not too much. I leaned back in the jeep seat and laughed out loud, somewhat alarming the driver. "What's the matter, sir?"

I turned and looked at the driver, my face erupting into an uncontrollable smile. "Ain't nothin' the matter. I'm just leaving on" —I turned and looked back at Camp Eagle, then shouted—"AD-VEN-TURE!"

He smiled with me in spite of himself. "Okay, sir, if you can call anything in this shitpot country an adventure, good for you!"

BOOK · II
ADVISER

And the end of the fight is a tombstone
white with the name of the late deceased,
And the epitaph drear:
"A fool lies here who tried to hustle the East."
　　　　　　　　　—RUDYARD KIPLING

Mat 85

I WAS ABLE to catch a flight to Bien Hoa that day, then a short jeep ride got me to the Mobile Advisory Team (MAT) center in Di An. When I arrived, I found an intensive effort being made to create a relaxed atmosphere. The MAT school was using some of the buildings that constituted the rear area for the 1st Division. I was told that I would be the commander of a MAT, which would consist of myself, a first lieutenant, and three sergeants, one of whom would be a medic, I hoped. I was shown to a small "clubhouse," which meant a cement floor under a tin roof, metal chairs and tables, a free jukebox filled with music fresh from the World, and a bar that sold cans of U.S. beer for a dime. I was introduced to two members of my team who had reported in just before me, a Sergeant E-7 Jesse Horner from Baton Rouge and a Sergeant E-6 Norman Stiles, from Buffalo, New York. Sergeant Horner had been assigned to the American Division up in I Corps, the northernmost section of South Vietnam, and Sergeant Stiles was a medic who had been assigned to the 8th Field Evacuation Hospital in Saigon. We had nothing to do until the next day, when classes would begin, so I had a ten-cent can of Pabst Blue Ribbon with these, the first members of my new team.

I had taken no more than two or three swallows when the last two members arrived: Lieutenant Jerry Carmack, from Honolulu, and Sergeant E-6 Dick Lightner, from Rushville, Indiana. Lieutenant Carmack had been with the 9th Infantry Division in the delta, and Sergeant Lightner had been with the 2d Brigade of the 101st. We moved over to the mess hall for chow, and afterward, we went back to the barracks building, where we rearranged our bunks so that we were together. Then we went back to the club and started to drink again, getting to know each other better.

Jerry was half Hawaiian, six feet three inches tall, and had a constant smile on his lips. He had gone to the University of Hawaii, then been drafted and had gone through officer candidate school at Fort Benning, Georgia. He had been married when he had gotten out of OCS, and his wife was waiting for him back in Columbus, Georgia.

Jesse was a short, skinny guy with thin sandy hair and an easy smile. He was a true southerner by any definition of the word and was in his mid-forties. He had three children in high school, was rather soft-spoken and quiet, but seemed like a dependable guy.

Norman was bright and couldn't have been more than twenty, yet he had risen quickly to his present rank, obviously because he was good. He wore thick glasses, and his hair was neatly styled, insofar as you could style the two or three inches of hair the army allowed. He wanted only to get this year over with and then go home, where he spoke eagerly of eventually becoming a veterinarian.

Dick had been in a different brigade of the 101st, so our paths had never crossed. But this was his second tour in the Nam; he had come over with the 1st Brigade in the summer of '65 and had been on line with the O-Deuce for eight months. He was about five feet ten and heavily muscled, and he was twenty-three, Jerry's age and only one year younger than I was. He laughed easily also, but I could sense the killer instinct lurking just beneath his skin. He had been in the shit. Jerry had been also, but Jesse and Norm readily admitted they hadn't been and, thank you very much, didn't really care to be. That was okay with me, just so I knew where everybody was in his mind.

Later that afternoon we went back to the orderly room and asked if we had been given a team number, as many of the other teams in the club had. The clerk shuffled through some papers, then informed us that we were Mobile Advisory Team 85. We went back to the club, greatly enthused by this recognition of our existence, and drank to 85. The song on the jukebox when we hoisted our beers in celebration of our newly discovered existence was "The Dock of the Bay" by Otis Redding, and became our instant team song. It was a big hit at the time, and was played often during our two-week sojourn in school.

Classes started the next morning, and we got a broad-brush exposure to Vietnamese history. I learned a lot, for example, that the French had first started trading with Vietnamese hundreds of years earlier. The trade had been so profitable that the French had arrived in force, building great houses in the cities and eventually in the countryside, on enormous, labor-intensive plantations. In 1887, the French had formerly declared Indochina, which included North and South Vietnam as well as Laos and Cambodia, part of their national territory. The colonial administration had been strengthened considerably, and wealth had been sucked out of Indochina. The great Michelin rubber plantations became one of the major segments of the French economy, and Saigon bloomed and flourished, justifiably acquiring the name of Paris of the Orient. Then, in World War II, the Japanese had run the French out of Indochina, and under their rule the communist Vietminh, led by Ho Chi Minh, a Vietnamese from Phan Thiet who had been partly educated in France, began to acquire power. When the Japanese were driven out of Indochina in 1945, they left Vietnam completely in the hands of the Vietminh, who refused to allow the French to return. Within less than a year, however, a newly liberated France was able to barge in and wrest back control of its former colony. The Vietminh went underground. The war continued and reached a crescendo in 1954, when a French unit was massively defeated at Dien Bien Phu.

After that the French had withdrawn, and pursuant to the Geneva Convention, Vietnam was divided in half. The northern half was given to the Vietminh; a million Vietnamese who feared communism fled south, while only around twenty thousand moved north to live under communist rule. Elections had been promised within a few years, but agreement could never be reached between North and South Vietnamese on how they would be held, so they weren't. Dreading the eventual triumph of communism, the United States had supported the Ngo Dinh Diem government in South Vietnam, hoping for the eventual emergence of a stable, capitalistic economy. If that could be accompanied by the success of a democratic form of government, so much the better. But even a dictatorship, however marginally benevolent, was seen as preferable to the success of communism.

And so, nearly fifteen years later, we found ourselves, the sons of America, offering our lives for the success of a questionable-at-best government. But I still didn't understand this war. Then I reminded myself that I was only an agent, a simple weapon being used by my older, wiser leaders. . . .

We found ourselves going through this schooling experience with fifty or sixty other men, with the size of the student body increasing every day as newly levied officers and NCOs arrived, were formed into five-man mobile advisory teams like ours, and shuffled into the classroom. In addition to Vietnamese history, our schooling consisted of some exposure to the political realities of the moment at different echelons of command in the Vietnamese military; training with the World War II weapons with which the troops we'd be advising were armed (we all would be going to Regional Forces or Popular Forces, units comparable to the U.S. National Guard, which were uniformly dubbed "Ruff Puffs" by American advisers); and three hours every day of Vietnamese language and social customs.

We quickly learned that our formal duties would be minimal. One officer and one NCO would accompany each Vietnamese unit we were assigned to on operations, generally search and destroy. The NCO would carry a radio, and we were to provide liaison with U.S. air support, medevac helicopters, and artillery, when it was available. In addition, we were to provide tactical advice when it was needed, but generally we were just representatives of the United States accompanying the Vietnamese on operations. It was emphasized that we were at no time to give commands. But since we were the connection for U.S. support, both in the field at an immediate level and in a larger sense as representatives of the enormous American logistical creature that lay sprawled across the entire country, it was simply noted in passing that rarely would our Vietnamese ally ignore whatever advice we might offer. We were taught to advise our units strictly by the book, the way we had learned to operate in army schools back in the World. And we were warned that we would probably see some Vietnamese commanders doing things much differently—often seemingly flying by the seat of their pants. Our job was to try to standardize things, to get the Popular and Regional Forces squared away to the point that they could operate effectively in the field and put some pressure on the Vietcong units throughout much of the delta.

With three days of schooling left, we learned that MAT 85 would be going to a small province in the Mekong delta south of Saigon, the name of which I will change to Kien Hoa for reasons that will become apparent. Kien Hoa was reputed to be one of the three safest provinces in the Nam. We were kind of charged by this; the imminent death of any of us seemed less likely now. We were crammed with a few more days of adviser crap, most of it repetitive, and most of it slipping away with the same speed it was fed to us. I did remember that I was a *Dai Uy,* pronounced "die we," or captain, and that I was a *Co Van My,* or American adviser. I retained some other basic words and phrases, but that was probably the most they could hope for.

On the last day Jerry and Jesse went to pick up our jeep and a trailer full of equipment. We got a heavy squad tent, two small refrigerators, a gasoline generator, an M-60 machine gun with two thousand rounds of ammunition, an M-79 grenade launcher, two PRC 25 radios, batteries, ten cases of C rations, a four-burner gas stove, pots and pans, stainless steel mess trays and utensils, five cots with poncho liners, air mattresses, pillows, and mosquito netting.

We left Di An, around nine o'clock that morning and drove down Highway 1 to Saigon, then continued south some hundred miles to Can Tho. There we left the main road and turned east on little more than a dirt road. A few miles outside Can Tho we came to a ferry, where trucks and three-wheeled Lambretta scooter-buses were lined up for more than half a mile. Since we were Americans, we just drove to the front of the line and, as soon as the rope-guided barge ferry arrived, drove right on board. No one said anything, of course, nor were we asked to pay.

The only formal contact we had had with any Vietnamese so far was with civil servants such as the ferrymen, who dealt with us by giving a sigh, shrugging their shoulders resignedly, usually looking down, and turning away. Whatever we wanted, we got. This was beginning to have an impact on me, and even after only two weeks of hurry-up schooling, I felt genuine concern for the plight of the Vietnamese. I wanted to understand, to help, but I didn't even know how to approach them, let alone do anything to support them.

Now, for the first time, I was immersing myself in Vietnamese society, and it was strange. From the time we left the main highway in Can Tho, I had seen no more indications of American presence. The countryside was heavily cultivated, and we were surrounded by rice fields. This was the dry season in the delta, there were no crops in the field, and there were no more than a few inches of water in some of the paddies, none in others. The dirt roadway had a number of pedestrians on it, each usually carrying over one shoulder a stick from both ends of which heavy loads were suspended. The bearers, usually women or old men, moved forward at an accelerated walk, bouncing along and almost running. That pace must be brutal, I thought, but everywhere I looked, it was the norm. There were quite a few bicycles on the road, and occasionally we would pass a motorbike. The children seemed especially friendly; they smiled happily, waving and dancing about, their gleeful shouts welcome on our ears. The only Vietnamese children any of us had really seen before had been in Saigon, the street-wise kids, old far beyond their years. Their normal greeting had been an extended hand as they grappled with each other to reach us, and the plaintive cry "Okay, Sa-lem, okay, Sa-lem!" was how these skinny, little, undernourished street orphans begged for a mentholated cigarette. Considering the common American memory of what it was like to be an eight- or ten-year-old, the Saigon youth scene was like a bucket of cold water thrown in your face. It was refreshing and invigorating to see happy fat babies and young children, all well fed, greeting us with laughter.

We had learned in adviser school that the Mekong River delta was one of the most bountiful land areas in the world, and something like sixty percent of the population lived there, cultivating the soil and living in the countryside that made up less than one-sixth of the geographical territory of South Vietnam. The rest of the population was clustered in Saigon and coastal cities, farming the thin strip of arable land that ran along the edge of the sea but generally avoiding the mountainous, jungled hinterland, an area where the 101st had operated without making contact with any indigenous civilians other than nomadic Montagnard tribesmen.

We cruised along some twenty or thirty kilometers, basking in the warm morning sun. We passed a road on our left that led to a cluster of huge houses—estates would be a better word—unmarked on the map. I was suddenly intrigued. These had obviously been built long ago by French colonials, and I wondered how they were being used now. Even from the several thousand meter distance that separated us from them, they looked enormous. I made a mental note to check on them one day. Soon enough we passed another road on our right that led down a dike between rice paddies, and a kilometer away we could see the huge metal gate that marked the edge of the village of Hoa Dong, a district headquarters in Kien Hoa province on our map. Beyond it we could see the dark tops of tall coconut trees fluttering softly in the light breeze. The map showed this as a large forest, and it looked seductive. Dick was the first to comment on this. "Goddamn, sir, look at them palm trees. Don't that look great?"

The road was lined with huge poplar trees, planted by the French long ago, but straight ahead a few kilometers away, a dark green island rose out of the paddies, with red and yellow brick and plaster splotches clearly showing this to be a large town. We were approaching Kien Hoa city, capital of Kien Hoa province. As we grew closer, we could see a few buildings, three or four stories tall, emerging above the treetops, and the spire of a church. It truly looked idyllic from our vantage point. I turned to the NCOs in the back seat. "Goddamn! It don't look too bad from here, whaddya think?" I was answered by a chorus of approval, including a hoot from Jerry, who was driving. I stretched involuntarily, suddenly exulting in the prospect of spending time in what looked like a small jewel in the fertile span of farmland that surrounded it. The sun warmed my shoulders and chest as it sparkled through the trees. I took off my helmet, and it felt as if I were driving through the colorful pages of an issue of *National Geographic*. I felt safe and warm and cozy and *chez moi*. I knew that this would be a truly delightful experience.

I turned and wordlessly grinned this news to Jerry, and then to the sergeants uncomfortably crammed into the back seat. Dick clapped me on the shoulder. "It's gonna be okay, sir, I can tell already. We're gonna straighten these people out, and they're gonna win this war, by God!" Wide smiles all around. I noticed that for perhaps the first time, he hadn't referred to our allies as gooks, though they were still the same people they had been the day before. Somehow, now it was different. We were involved and wanted to help. And by God, we *would* help, too! Suddenly nothing seemed impossible. Where there's a will, there's a way, and with genuine effort, and a shovelful of American ingenuity, we'd show those sorry-ass Vietcong what this war was about! We were fresh, eager, dedicated, and nothing could stop us!

All this because a Vietnamese town looked attractive from a distance. In truth, the prospect of sleeping in a bed each night was seductive to me, and the sun on my face had done quite a trick. I subconsciously flashed back to the rain and the exhaustion and the agony of that ridge climb with the Tigers, and I shuddered. That was all a mirage, but this was the real world. With the 101st I had been little more than an expendable jungle rat, but now I would be able to live life the way it was supposed to be lived. This was going to be a war as the French had known it, where an officer was respected as such, not dealt with as an animal. I realized that the French had lost the war in this country, fighting the same enemy. But I refused to accept that their attitude had had anything to do with their defeat. No, we had learned in MAT school that the French at Dien Bien Phu had been outnumbered on the order of nine to one. And now we had the miracles of modern technology they'd never had access to. There was nothing to fear; the war was as good as won, and we were just mopping up the last, most recalcitrant Vietcong and their North Vietnamese allies. Confidence rode high in my heart as we drove through the open metal gate and down the shaded main street of Kien Hoa city.

After a few kilometers we drove across a small bridge that spanned a canal choked with sampans. On the far side of the bridge was a heavily sandbagged guardpost, and we stopped to ask directions. A small Vietnamese soldier in fatigues, a flak vest, and a helmet came out and saluted. I returned his salute and launched into my new language. *"Chau, ong, toi la co van My, dau la* American headquarters?" He unleashed a spiel of incomprehensible Vietnamese but was pointing down a street to the left. I saluted him, smiling broadly.

It was a huge French mansion inside a high stone wall. A number of American soliders milled around the courtyard. We pulled in through the open gate and parked next to three or four other jeeps, then went up the main steps and into the building, where I met a captain in the Adjutant General Corps behind a desk. He stuck out his hand as he stood up. "Hi, I'm Jim Claiborne, the general S-one ash-and-trash administrative officer for the province. I got a message about your team a couple of days ago. Welcome aboard!" We shook hands warmly.

"Thanks!"

"Colonel White is the senior province adviser, and he's the guy in command, so c'mon, I'll introduce you. The rest of your team can stand by."

I walked into the office, and saluted my tall, thin new commander, his red face smiling brightly. "Sir, Captain Carhart reports in with Mobile Advisory Team Eighty-five as ordered."

He returned my salute, then waved me to a chair. "Welcome aboard, Captain. Here, sit down, sit down. We're glad to have you."

"We're glad to be here, sir. Looks like a great little town."

"It is, it is. I think you're all gonna like it here. How big is your team?"

"There's myself, a first lieutenant, an E-seven, and two E-sixes, one of whom is a medic."

"Well, that's great, you'll be a welcome addition here, believe me. This province is one of the most loyal provinces in-country.

Loyal to the government, I mean. We've pretty well got Charley on the run here, but you'll find that out for yourself. It said on that message that you'd arrive with a tent, that right?"

My heart dropped. I had hoped we'd be put inside a building. I didn't want to live in a goddamn tent, and neither did anyone else on the team! "Yes, sir."

"Well, we're a little tight on space right now, so we're gonna have to ask you to set the tent up for now. But there's a small warehouse you can use once we fix the roof—got torn up in a mortar attack during Tet. Once we do that, you can fix it up, live indoors, sound okay to you?"

"Yes, sir, that's no problem."

"Okay, now why don't you and your team go downstairs and get some lunch? Then Captain Claiborne'll show you around and where we want you to set your stuff up, and you can get a little more comfortable. How's that?"

"Fine, sir."

He stood up and stuck out his hand. "Welcome aboard, Captain Carhart."

"Thank you, sir, we're genuinely glad to be here."

I turned and walked back out into the outer room, where my men were waiting. Claiborne came around from behind his desk.

"He said we should eat," I told him. "Then you'd show us where to set up."

"Right, follow me."

He led us back out into the hallway and down a narrow staircase to the basement, which had been converted into a mess hall, except that the cooks were Vietnamese women. We took trays and went down the line. The food was reconstituted B rations, but there was also plenty of fresh fruit, apparently obtained locally. Captain Claiborne ate lunch with us and filled us in on a lot about the province. Colonel White, ran the military aspect of things, but he also had a lot of other domestic "pacification" work to do. There were about fifty other American advisers, both officers and enlisted, assigned to Kien Hoa province. We learned that the forest of palm trees we had seen behind Hoa Dong as we were arriving was known as the Coconut Grove, that it was about twenty-five square kilometers in area, and that it was the VC R&R center for the delta; anywhere from two to eight main force battalions could be found in there relaxing from the war at any given time.

"Shit, why don't they bomb it or send part of the U.S. Ninth Infantry in there, catch 'em with their pants down?"

" 'Cause the province chief won't let us, and in fact, he's a very gung ho guy, Colonel Tran, you'll see that. He wants to bomb it or go in there, but Saigon won't let him." Reality began to dawn on me now. Yes, this was one of the most pacified provinces in-country, but there was an important quid pro quo: Kien Hoa was also the site of a dependable R&R base for the VC. You don't fuck with us, they were saying, in our R&R base, and we won't fuck with you in this province. That was a rather shattering discovery to make on the day we arrived. In other words, we would be doing little more than playing finger games here, while the bribes were paid and decisions made by the Vietnamese at a much higher level.

I stood up and stretched. "All right, let's go set up our tent and get our shit in order." We all left the mess hall and followed Jim's jeep toward town until he turned down a short, quiet street that fronted on a closed-off canal. It would have seemed like a peaceful reflecting pool were it not for the green scum that choked its edges and covered half its surface. We instantly named it the Jade Pool. Then Jim turned inside another gate in a stone wall, and we found ourselves in the yard of a huge stone French house. When we drove in, there were six or eight Vietnamese men milling around the yard, wearing bits and pieces of military uniforms, an olive drab khaki shirt over blue jeans there, black pajama tops over khaki pants there. I was surprised but not about to say anything.

We began to unload the crap out of the trailer, none too happy about having to look forward to life in a tent but willing to accept it as inevitable. Soon enough we got the tent up, then got our cots unfolded and set up. It looked pretty dismal, but we had arranged as much as we could, which was precious little. I stepped back outside and walked out the gate, crossed the road, and flopped down next to a tree at the edge of the slime-choked Jade Pool. Well, it wasn't that bad. So we had to live in a tent for a while. The warehouse with the holes in the roof was in back of the house, and all we really needed was roofing material. I was sure I'd be able to work something out. Besides, a tent beat the hell out of sleeping in the open air, as I had for so long in the jungle with the 101st. It wasn't bad at all really. Claiborne's voice returned me to present reality.

"Okay, let's get one of your sergeants, and I'll show you where the other American house is. We've got our own little club over there with beer and Cokes, and we show movies there a couple times a week, and play half-court basketball, in case anybody's interested."

"Great! Lemme get somebody."

I soon enlisted Dick, and he hopped into the back seat as I slipped into the front. We pulled back out onto the main drag. A few blocks away, we pulled through a gate and drove around another huge stone house. The house itself housed thirty Americans, and a building in back served as a clubhouse.

"Well, this is it. May not be much by Hollywood standards, but then we're quite a ways from Hollywood."

"Looks pretty nice to me, better'n anything we had in the Hundred and First." Jim smiled broadly, happy to know that Kien Hoa measured up.

"Every week or so, we get a movie here from Can Tho. We usually have movies showin' two or three nights a week in the clubhouse. We've got lights out on the basketball court there, and there's usually a game goin' on every night. You'll see, this can be a pretty fun place. You'll meet all the Americans in province here pretty quick."

"No worry about getting back to where you live at night?"

"Nah, this is a pretty safe town. The gates are closed at sunset, and there's only good guys inside the town walls—it's only a city in name. There's no need to carry a weapon around at night or anything like that."

"So if the gates are closed at sunset, I guess that means the VC control everything outside the walls during the night?"

"Oh no, some of the other towns have walls too; it isn't *that* bad!"

"No, no, what I mean is that the VC have pretty free run of the countryside—the villages and hamlets where the farmers live. You know, outside the fortified areas."

"Well, basically that's right, and those are sort of the ground rules pretty much everywhere in the delta right now, but we're workin' on it. Just imagine you're back in the World a hundred years ago: This is Fort Apache and outside the walls is Indian country."

"Any of our troops ever operate out there at night?"

He shook his head. "We're not ready for that yet. Although Operation Phoenix here in province has a really good platoon of

LRRPs who go out at night and run ambushes and things. But that's highly specialized stuff, mostly intelligence missions, and it won't affect you."

I turned, grinning to Jim as I slipped into the jeep. "Well, I reckon you're gonna see a lot of us over here at night. That right, Sergeant Lightner?"

"I reckon so, sir. Hell, movies 'n' beer, that's *livin'*!"

The Province

THE NEXT MORNING early Jerry and Jesse left in the jeep with the trailer to scrounge some roofing materials from the 9th Infantry Division. Dick and Norm and I got buckets of whitewash and put a couple of coats on the inside of the little warehouse that day. We were walking back to our tent from supper at the compound when the trading party pulled in, overflowing with tin sheets, lumber, screening, all sorts of extras like wooden shelves and a couple of flower pots. We were gonna turn that warehouse into a by-God home! The next morning we became busy-bee housebuilders, and two days later we were ready to christen our new home. We drank a lot of beer to that end and really whooped it up when we heard "The Dock of the Bay" on the radio. We were a team, and this was our home. The next morning Dick carefully affixed to the side of the doorway a black wooden plaque, that bore the name of our new homestead in bright, freshly painted infantry blue letters: "The Ponderosa."

"Whaddya think, sir?"

"Shit hot, Dick, Airborne!"

"Thought we could dress the place up a little, you know, make it kinda homey."

We spent the rest of the morning puttering around the house, finishing off the screen porch. Then the five of us drove down to the main compound for lunch, after which I stopped by Jim Claiborne's desk and told him we were all set. I was ready to get back to the war, and I eagerly awaited my first exposure to it in the delta.

I went in and saw Colonel White, who told me we would be going out the next day or the day after, depending on the operations schedule, with the 44th Popular Forces Battalion on a search-and-destroy operation.

Jim had already filled me in briefly on operations in the province, and it looked as if the upcoming operations would be through a highly pacified area where there was little actual probability of enemy contact. The decision on whether it would go the next day or the day after wouldn't be made by the province chief, a sort of miniwarlord, until 1800 hours, or six o'clock, that night. I took maps back for the rest of the team and gave them the same overview I had gotten from Jim. We needed only one officer and one sergeant to go on each operation; that meant three of us would be sitting at home. I quickly decided to go on the first operation myself and to take Dick with me. I had him drive us down to the compound, where we learned that we were on for the next day. Our interpreter would report to us at the Ponderosa that night around eight-thirty, and we were to take him with us to the province chief's house for a tactical briefing at nine o'clock. This was the norm on the night before an operation, I was told: A briefing on the area to be swept and the responsibility of different units on the following day's operations would be given at nine o'clock the night before.

We went back to Ponderosa and listened to the latest tunes from the World on AFN as we sat on our bunks triple-checking our equipment. I spent a long time fine-polishing the receiver and bolt face of my M-16, a close and almost sacred friend that could always be counted on so long as you took good care of it.

We had our first team supper at home in the Ponderosa that night. Even though it was only beans and franks, the sweetness of freedom from the compound and its invisible controls was worth the difference in food. Jesse and Norm took it on as their responsibility that our cupboard would never be bare. I don't know (and didn't want to know) how they did it, but we started to eat quite well and only on rare occasions would ever eat at the compound again.

Around eight that night Ha, our interpreter, showed up at our door. He was a teenager and was initially quite frightened. Truly, the Ponderosa must have been a real lions' den to him. We tried to get him to relax and discovered that his English was really limited. But we found that we could get our thoughts over to him with frequent sign language assistance and hoped it would do the trick.

Ha hopped into the jeep with Dick and me, and we soon arrived at the province chief's house to hear the briefing for the next day's operation. In the dark all I could see was that the province chief lived in what was clearly the largest house in town, with grounds about one hundred meters square inside the usual high stone wall. The house was impressive in its size, and I had been told that the yard was filled with flower gardens, though I could see nothing. But I noted as we approached the house that a large trailer tank of gasoline was parked in the grass, ten or fifteen meters off the driveway, and the area in front of it had been rudely ripped up by the wheels of tactical vehicles gassing up. I half wondered what the Frenchmen who had built this house or lived in it later would have said if they could have seen how the present tenant maintained the entrance. We pulled up to the front of the house and parked among twenty or so other vehicles. Ha hopped out of the back and ran into the house, after telling us that he was going to get the Vietnamese battalion commander we would be advising.

We walked up the wide flagstone steps and stepped inside the enormous doorway. The ceilings were very high, and the scale of the house was immense; but I immediately noted that there was virtually no furniture in evidence, at least not in the entryway or in the next room. There were many Vietnamese, all in olive drab fatigue uniforms, bustling to and fro, and we could see two or three familiar American faces moving around as well. As we entered the next room, our interpreter reappeared, nearly running into me when he rounded a corner. He turned sideways and made way for the Vietnamese officer who followed him.

"Dai Uy Ca-ter, this Dai Uy Trung, is commanding foty-foth Battayon, Populah Foces. We go with him to fight." I stuck out my hand, which was quickly grasped by a very tall Vietnamese. He must have been five-ten or so but was excruciatingly skinny, and although his hair was jet black, his face looked old and somewhat grizzled. As he smiled, I noted two gaps in his front teeth.

"*Chau, Dai Uy.*"

"*Chau, Dai Uy.* This Sergeant Lightner, he go with me tomorrow." Dick reached out and shook hands, shifting his plug of chewing tobacco high in his cheek so that he could talk as he extended his hand. "*Chau, Dai Uy.*"

Dai Uy Trung said something to Ha as he extended his hand, and Ha turned to me. "He say he happy you come. Now we listen to province chief tell plan."

We entered a large room, empty of furniture save for two or three wooden benches and thirty or forty government issue gray folding metal chairs. We followed Trung and Ha to the far side of the room and sat down in the chairs indicated to us. I looked around the room and saw Jim Claiborne standing before the front row of the chairs, which had been arranged in rows. Behind him was a small raised dais, on which was a bare wooden lectern. Behind that was a large blackboard, covered by a white sheet. Jim waved to me, and I waved back.

Colonel White was sitting in the front row, talking animatedly with a Vietnamese officer who had his back turned to me. White was smiling a lot as he talked, and I could see that he was speaking English, but I couldn't make out what he was saying. I turned in my chair and looked around the room. I saw most of the Americans, officers and enlisted, who were generally to be found around the American compound during the day. There was the first sergeant, an old grunt with a lot of time in the army under his belt. There were two of the captains who sat behind desks in some sort of administrative capacity and several of the enlisted clerks. Their faces were reassuring in this unfamiliar setting.

A voice from the front of the room silenced everyone. The province chief, a handsome man in tailored fatigues, lectured the audience of some forty men in Vietnamese from the lectern. After two or three minutes of gibberish unintelligible to Americans, he turned, took two long steps to the blackboard, and dramatically flipped the sheet over the back. A large map of the province was on the blackboard, and an overlay was highlighted in red, showing a sweep operation in the northwestern corner of the province. He had a pointer now, and he stabbed at the map as he talked, showing the way the operation would be conducted. I had pulled out my own map of the province and could tell that the 44th would be landing in boats from a small river, then sweeping north in conjunction with the 52d. The rest of the province forces would be attacking from the west, and we would sweep an area to the edge of a major river that marked the northern edge of the province.

The province chief droned on for another ten minutes, then curtly ended his talk, and the room was immediately alive with scurrying Vietnamese, some rushing out of the room, others pressing forward to talk to the province chief, apparently to curry favor. I turned and asked Ha what was going on. "We go on boat tomorrow, suh. I come you house six o'clock, then show you where we go."

"Well, shit, Dick, here we go, guess we'll just have to wait and see how things develop."

We were quickly back at the Ponderosa, where we both fiddled around with our equipment for five or ten minutes, checking our weapons for the last redundant time, although redundancy never even occurred to us, for we were going back to the life-and-death shit, or so it seemed. We were soon satisfied that we were as ready as we'd ever be. No sign of Jerry, Jesse, and Norm, but they were big boys. Dick and I hit the sack before ten-thirty.

Ruff Puffs

I HEARD DICK hit the floor in the dark, and a quick glance at my luminous dial told me it was five-thirty. Time to roll. I was tying my boots when I first smelled coffee. We chowed down, our silence broken only by grunts. It was a few minutes before six when we finished, and a noise outside told us someone else was about. I stood up and moved toward the door, hearing a tentative "Suh" from twenty meters away even as I did. I stepped out into the dark confidently, perhaps stupidly, but what the hell, this was a safe town, right? "That you, Ha?"

"Yes, suh, me Ha."

I saw his form in the shadows and, smiling now, turned back in the door. "Okay, c'mon in." As I reentered the kitchen, I saw that Jesse, a steaming mug of coffee in his hand, had joined Dick at the table.

"Mornin', sir."

"Mornin', Jess, how's your head?"

"Aw, it's okay, sir, but I don't know 'bout Lieutenant Carmack 'n' Norm. They was doin' some pretty heavy singin' there for a while."

We all laughed at this. Dick was strapping his LBE on, and I turned, realizing that Ha was still out in the dark. I went back to the door and pushed it open. The sky was light gray now, and Ha stood at parade rest twenty meters away. "Hey, Ha, I said to c'mon in. You no hear me?" He stood quickly at attention, bolt upright and clearly scared. I waved my hand in the strange Vietnamese overhand beckoning gesture that looked almost like waving good-bye. *"La day, Ha, la day."* He strode quickly up to me, than as I held the door open, he strode by me and into our brightly lit kitchen, taking

189

his hat off as he entered. He was shaking, frightened at this venture into the devils' lair. "Relax, Ha, you friend, we no hurt Ha, Ha very beaucoup important, *bief?*"

He quickly nodded up and down. "Oh yes, suh, I unnastan."

"Okay, you want some coffee?"

He shook his head vigorously from side to side as he spoke. "No, suh, Ha okay, no coffee."

I was strapping on my LBE now and looking around for my helmet. "Okay, it's what, oh-six-ten. Let's get down to the boats. You takin' us, Jess?"

"Yes, sir, just say the word."

"Okay, *vamos.* You got some piasters on ya, Dick?"

"Yes, sir, I got about thirty in change, plus a couple hundred in bills."

"All right, so do I, but I don't know how much good they'll do us."

Jesse cranked up the jeep as I stepped into the front seat and Dick and Ha scrambled into the rear. Then we were out the gate and moving through the predawn shadowed streets and buildings of Kien Hoa.

Soon enough we arrived at the docks. The street was blocked by six or eight large army trucks of varying sorts, empty and silent in the middle of the road. "I guess this is it. Wait for us here, Jess, just in case there's been a fuck-up."

Dick and I got out and walked around the trucks, Ha bobbing eagerly behind me. We could see the river on our left, and as we moved toward the front of the string of trucks, we could see several hundred Vietnamese troops bustling about fifty or a hundred meters to our left front. Beyond them were four or five longboats tied up. These weren't military landing craft, but gaily painted boats that must also serve as ferries or some kind of tour boats. Jesus! But hell, I guessed that this was just one of the limitations we had to face. There was a stirring among the troops some thirty meters away from us. Then I saw a widely smiling Dai Uy Trung making his way toward us, a cloud of subordinates fluttering at his sides and in his wake. I stuck out my hand as he approached.

"*Chau, Dai Uy.*"

"*Chau, Dai Uy.*" Then a cloud of unintelligible Vietnamese.

Ha took up my slack. "He say come wif him, get on boat, we go soon."

"Okay, tell him we come soon. Dick, go release Jess, and tell him to make sure somebody is here to pick us up when the operation is over; that can be coordinated through the compound."

"Okay, sir."

Dick left in a lope, and I turned back, smiling, to Trung, talking to him through Ha. "I must wait for my sergeant; then we go, two minutes." After Ha had translated this, Trung told me through him that he had some things to take care of and asked that we make our own way to the boats. I nodded my agreement, and he turned and walked away, his cloud of aides and battalion satraps faithfully hovering behind him. It was a strange sight indeed, but it wasn't really dangerous to me, at least not yet, so I just shrugged mentally and accepted it as one more difference in this society.

Dick was soon back, and we made our way to the boats, with Ha's occasional queries keeping us on track. Soon we were standing beside a long red boat with high two-man seats lining the gunwales. We stopped to wait for Trung while noisy, bustling Vietnamese troops boarded. Then we were standing alone on the quay while the troops settled into place.

"Ha, where's Dai Uy Trung?"

"He up front, suh."

"Okay, go ask him if everybody's on board. Let's get out of here." I waited as Ha snaked forward.

He was quickly back at my side. "Suh, Dai Uy Trung asleep. Trung Uy [First Lieutenant] Bac say you come now, we go." Dick and I stepped aboard, and the boat cast off, slowly moving into midstream.

"Hey, Ha, ask Bac if he knows where we're supposed to go."

"Oh, yes, suh, he know, we go here many time."

"Many time? How many time you go here?"

"Oh, mebbe every week, mebbe every two week, we go dis place."

Every week or two? Fuck me, this was just a big game. I wondered. . . . "Hey, Ha, you ever see VC this place?"

"Oh, yes, suh, mebbe two time, we find VC sleep, but mos' time not find."

"Okay, thanks."

I walked back to where Dick was standing, working on a fresh chaw. "Well, it looks like this is gonna be nothin' but a walk in the sun."

"May just be a walk in the sun, sir, but I'm ready for anything."

Trung Uy Bac yelled something back at us from three or four

rows of seats away, and Ha was quickly interpreting from behind me. "Suh, he say fif mo mints, we get down boat."

"Okay, Ha, thanks."

Before long the boat was making a wide, sweeping turn to the right; then the heavy roar of the motor told us we would be accelerating. I turned to Ha, mystery written on my face. "Is okay, suh, you see." I looked around me at the Vietnamese troops, who were beginning to stand up and strap their gear back onto their shoulders and backs. Then a warning was issued, and they all grabbed seats or uprights and braced themselves. I mimicked them, expecting that we were about to run into the bank. We soon did, but the boat was only slowed dramatically in its forward momentum. We could feel the bottom of the boat sliding over the dirt of the shallows, and the engines roared with an increased fury. Soon all forward movement stopped, and the engines were quickly cut. The Vietnamese began to climb out onto the gunwales and move forward. After a few minutes the boat had pretty well emptied out. Dick and I stood up and walked down the center aisle and then up the four or five stairs onto the narrow walkway along the outside of the boat.

Some thirty meters in front of the prow of the boat, a strip of thick green grass demarcated the crest of the riverbank. I had expected that we would just jump off the front of the boat and walk up to the edge of the rice paddies that covered the landscape. But I soon discovered that things were never that simple in the Nam. The area between the boat and the vegetation was a dark brown riverbank. Even that didn't seem to present too much problem to me. You just run across the bank to the grass, then deploy—a typical tactical amphibious landing, right? Wrong! To my great amazement, only two or three Vietnamese soldiers had reached the grass and firm ground so far, some ten minutes after the boat had halted. The rest were strung out in a bank of mud, sunk up to their knees or higher, laughing and shouting like children as they struggled to move ahead. I couldn't believe it! I looked off to my right and saw the other two boats carrying our battalion. They were similarly beached, high up on the mud flats, but still thirty or so meters from hard ground, and their human cargo was also struggling madly, pulling legs free and stumbling forward at an incredibly slow pace, all with peals of inappropriate laughter.

I turned and looked at Dick, stunned. "What the fuck, over."

"Jesus, are we gonna have to do that shit, too?"

"I don't see any other way of gettin' in. I can't believe this shit."

"Can you imagine what would happen now if a couple of RPDs opened up from the tree line? They'd fuckin' murder those poor bastards!"

"Makin' enough noise, aren't they?"

"Fuckin' Boy Scouts, sir. C'mon, let's get to it. Bet I can jump farther'n you can."

Dick eased by me, walked up to the prow, looked over deliberately, then came back five or six steps. He grinned broadly at me, yelled "Airborne!," then turned and bolted, leaping off the front end as far out as his legs would take him. I followed him a few steps, just to watch him land, and saw him go in up over his knees about five meters in front of the prow.

"Jesus, Dick, you're gonna be in there for another hour!"

I sat down on the prow, eased my ass over the edge, and turned as I gently lowered myself. I still held much of my weight up through my arms as my feet touched the mud, and I gingerly turned my body and took a long stride toward the green bank, releasing my grip on the wooden hull as I did so. The minute I let go, I felt my feet slip quickly down into the mud. I tried to lurch forward, dragging my right foot out of the mud with the weight of my body moving forward, but it was no go. The mud had me in its gushy grip. I had never felt anything like it in my life! In order to free my right foot, I had to put all my weight on my left one, feeling it being driven ever deeper into the trap in accordance with the laws of physics that had been only blackboard games until now. Jesus! Once all my weight was on my left leg, I had to reach back with both hands, grab my right leg, and pull it up out of the thick, congealed slop that imprisoned it. And it was hard work! Once I finally got it above the surface, I stretched it out as far in front of me as I could and tried to shift my weight. But now my left leg was in over the knee! I couldn't believe it! I leaned hard forward and to my right, having shifted my hands back to my left leg, which I pulled desperately on. Slowly, it began to come up, even as I felt my right leg sinking inexorably deeper in the goo.

I was overwhelmed. I stopped pulling, breathing hard from my exertions now, and looked around me. Ha was off to my left a meter or two, having the same sort of problems. Although he was much smaller and lighter than I was, he also was apparently much weaker, and his progress through the mud didn't seem to be much faster than mine. Dick was two full strides in front of me, and about half the Vietnamese soldiers were now on dry land, laughing and chortling, pushing one another around and playfully shouting to their friends.

Finally, after a short eternity, Dick was scrambling up on the grassy bank in front of me. Then he turned and walked two or three meters along the bank to a point where he could reach me and help me get up on dry land.

I told Ha to find out where Dai Uy Trung was, and after a few cursory questions we were pointed down a dike to our right. We made our way through the crowded soldiers milling around and, after fifty meters or so, came to a small hut. As we approached it, Trung and his aides came out the door and walked up on the dike toward us. He was smiling broadly, and as I walked up to him, he clapped me on the shoulder and said something to me in Vietnamese. His face was no more than two feet from mine, and as he spoke, the odor of booze hit my face like a slap. I tried to cover my recoil even as it began and painted a false smile across my teeth, holding my breath as if frozen. Ha's voice came from my left, and I turned gratefully toward him, shifting my shoulder out from beneath Trung's hand. "He say you like Vietnamese riverbank."

"Ya, you tell him me like beaucoup. But now we must go find VC. Ha, ask Dai Uy Trung how he has his unit deployed in front of us. Tell him I want a map check."

"Okay, suh."

After a brief interchange Trung barked a curt order to one of his aides, and a plastic-encased map was unfolded on the ground at my feet. As Trung and I stooped over it, he began to talk, indicating movements on the map with a short stick.

Ha tried to keep up with him. "Suh, he say one company go dis way, on left, one company go on otha side, on right, ova hea, like dis ... den we come, wit otha company dis way, like dat, den we all finish togeda on road by riva, get on trucks, go home."

Trung had the movement down, and it seemed tactically sound, with the companies moving in echelon across open rice paddies and farming country, each within mutually supporting distance of the others. But I wondered how long the same operation had been repeated. "Ha, ask Dai Uy Trung how long he has been going on this same operation."

"Oh, suh, we do dis evy week, two week."

"Okay, Ha, now ask Dai Uy Trung the same question."

"Me not unnastan, suh, me go dis operation evy week, two week."

"Look, Ha, you interpreter, me unnastan you do dis evy week. Now ask Dai Uy Trung same question. I want his reaction, *biet*?"

"Yes, suh." A chastened Ha turned and asked Trung a short question in Vietnamese, to which a smiling Trung quickly spun out a short answer. Ha turned to me. "Suh, he say we do dis evy week, two week."

"Okay, Ha. Me unnastan, now ask him if he doesn't think mebbe VC unnastan, too, *bien*? When VC see boats land on river, they know where Dai Uy Trung will go and where he will not go, *biet*?"

Ha nodded, then turned to Trung and poured out a stream of Vietnamese, to which Trung gave an equally long answer, still smiling widely. Ha turned back to me. "Suh, he say it not make different, because VC already know about operation last night, know everything, so we always do same thing because men know how, not make mistake, sometime catch VC sleep."

I looked at a widely smiling Trung, not clear exactly what to say. "Ask him how VC know night before."

Ha relayed my question, and Trung opened his arms and his mouth at the same time, murmuring to me over suppressed laughter, *"Khong biet, Dai Uy."* Then he grabbed my sleeve and pulled me closer, winking at me, and used his broken English, which I didn't know he spoke. "But VC know, always know." Then he raised his hands again in mystification and broke into a spontaneous peal of laughter, which was quickly echoed by his hangers-on.

I was confused and turned to face Dick, standing at my side poker-faced. "Shit, Dick, whaddya think?"

"I dunno, sir, it seems pretty clear the VC have got an inside man or maybe a whole bunch of 'em."

"Yeah, I'm afraid that's what it looks like. Well, hell, let's finish this one." I glanced at my watch. It was 1015 hours.

"Okay, Dai Uy, let's go." Trung, still smiling, turned and started down the paddy dike with his followers. I continued to scan our flanks as we moved, occasionally catching sight of files of Vietnamese soldiers who were part of the two companies in front of us on either flank. Soon, realizing that we were just going through the motions, I began to daydream.

I was oblivious of all else when a sudden gunshot from thirty or forty meters to my front sent me sprawling on my belly in the dirt, panicked because I had lost touch with what was going on around me and now might pay with my life for my foolishness. Trung and his boys were standing some twenty meters in front of me, where the shot must have been fired. Dick and I moved in long, low strides, ready to melt back into the ground, and crept up behind Trung and followers. They were standing upright, laughing and shouting to each other with incredible abandon. I thought they were asking to die, until, as I approached them, I saw that one of the underlings was scooping the bloody remains of a small gray songbird, no bigger than my fist, from the thin grass under a scrawny sapling.

In my anger I lapsed into my pidgin Vietnamese. "Dai Uy Trung! *Khong ban, khong ban, VC biet chung ta la u day!*" Although I was flustered, I managed to keep from yelling, and as I finished the sentence, it simply sounded as if I were scolding him. But even as I uttered the words, telling Trung not to shoot because it would tell the VC where we were, I knew that I had stepped out of line. Clearly I couldn't correct Trung like that in front of his men, for if he did what I said and changed his actions because I had corrected him, he would lose incredible face. So what if we all got killed? It was still better for him that he not lose face.

He answered me in broken English. "VC look you me now!" He held his thumbtips close to his fingertips over his eyes, simulating binoculars, then fanned his arm in an arc in the front.

Then he spewed a stream of words to Ha, who turned, respectfully frightened, in my direction and spoke in a low voice. "Suh, he say VC watch us alla time from time we get down from boat. VC know where we are. He shoot bud fo suppa, do dis alla time."

I nodded, then turned and started to walk away, fuming. Now it was my turn to swallow my pride, maybe even lose some face; otherwise, I could blow this whole advisory relationship before it even got off the ground.

I was slowly steaming off as I walked. Then I heard Dick behind me. "Hey, don't let this cheap shit get to ya, sir."

"Jesus! Yeah, I know, Dick, just pisses me off, that's all. Here we are, on a supposedly tactical search-and-destroy mission, and that yo-yo is shootin' fucking songbirds for the dinner pot! I just don't fucking believe it, that's all."

Another gunshot rang out behind us, then another, followed by a burst of cheers from Trung's boys. Nothing could be done now. Trung was just showing his men that he wasn't about to take any shit from some dumb American. And if I said anything to him now, it would only be taken as a challenge. Jesus! What a mess!

Dick and I hooked back up with Trung's group. Ha looked at us with fear dancing in his eyes. I slapped him on the back, laughing. Trung, seeing our return, came walking over, joining our laughter, and bubbling something out at me. Ha was right in step. "Suh, he say we have beaucoup good food eat today."

I glanced at my watch: 1145 hours. Hmph. How time flies when you're having fun. "Okay, Ha, you tell Dai Uy Trung we beaucoup happy eat Vietnamese food." Ha blurted that to Trung quickly, who turned smiling toward me, waving his arm in that overhand beckoning gesture that was the least of the mysteries I was exposed to in the Orient. I followed him as he turned and stepped down off the dike, then through a clump of bamboolike vegetation.

Another fifteen or twenty meters we came out of the undergrowth in front of a farmhouse, or the Vietnamese version of one. It was a single-story building, walls made of some kind of tightly woven matting, doors and windows consisting simply of openings. The roof was thatched, and as Ha led the way inside, two middle-aged women bowed to us. The floor was hard-packed dirt, and against one wall was the massive bomb shelter with thick dirt walls found in every farmhouse. I saw two infants playing in a corner. They wore only bib-type dresses, with no underclothes. As I watched, one of them urinated. But since he (I noted that it was a boy) had no diapers or underclothing in the way, it was really a simple administrative matter to take care of. One of the women, alert as a hawk, scooped him up and threw a handful of fresh straw on the wet spot, even as it started to soak into the shiny dirt floor. Hmph. They sure had a handle on the diaper problem, but I guessed that the floor had to get pretty gamy after a while. I noticed that the children, both of whom must have been less than two years old and could barely walk, were playing with a baby pig, shrieking with laughter as they cavorted together. Well, different strokes for different folks.

Trung had seated himself on a low wooden platform that seemed like a table, but then, flashing back to my classroom days in Di An, I realized that it was the bed as well as the place of honor to sit at meals. He was beckoning to me and patting the place next to him. I turned to Dick. "C'mon, Dick, whatever I do, you do with me." I turned then, smiling, and walked over to Trung, seating myself on the wooden bed and directing Dick to sit beside me. Ha and Trung's four or five assistants squatted on the floor below us. I called Ha, who turned to face me.

"Suh?"

"Ha, tell Dai Uy Trung that we have brought piasters. Ask him how much we should pay the *Ba* for our meal."

"Oh, no, suh, you no pay."

"Ha, just ask the fucking question, will ya?"

"Yes, suh." He asked Trung, who turned to me and put his arm around me, smiling. He directed a stream of unintelligible words at me, and I felt uneasy as he leaned his face closer to mine. Ha's voice gave me a justification to turn and lean toward him. "Suh, Dai Uy Trung say you no pay, because he own this house and all land you see around. He beaucoup rich man."

I turned back to Trung, smiling and nodding my head. I was flustered and could not remember how to say "thank you" in Vietnamese, so I just said, "Thank you." He started to lean toward me, his whiskey breath hitting me like a cold slap. For a minute I thought he was going to try to kiss me, and I had already decided that I wouldn't accept that. I was ready to go a long way in trying to help these people out, but that was too much. I turned away toward Dick, who was having trouble controlling his laughter.

"Whatsa matter, sir? He just wants ta give ya a little kiss on the lips, that's all!"

I was forcing myself to smile now but kept my head turned toward Dick as I slowly answered him. "Yeah, maybe that's okay with you, but if this motherfuck tries to kiss me on the lips, he's gonna get the surprise ride of his life!"

"Dai Uy! Dai Uy!" Trung was pulling on my sleeve and calling me. I turned to face him but shifted my hips a bit so that our bodies were facing each other more.

"Ya, Dai Uy?"

He leaned conspiratorially toward me, putting his arm over my shoulder and leaning toward my ear. I let him draw closer; then he whispered, "Whiskey? Whiskey?" I pulled back and looked down in front of his crossed legs. In his right hand he held a clay cup in which he was swirling a large swallow of amber liquid. He held the cup out to me.

I drew back, shaking my head from side to side and holding my hands open toward him defensively. *"Ya khong, Dai Uy, ya khong! Toi muon live, toi khong muon die!"* Trung laughed softly. Although I couldn't remember how to say "live" or "die" in Vietnamese, I had clearly gotten the message across. He mumbled something I didn't catch, then lifted the cup to his lips, tilted his head sharply back, and drained it. I looked away, only mildly miffed that he was drinking openly in front of Dick and me, even inviting me to join him.

He pulled on my sleeve, and I turned to face him again. He was pouring more booze out of a canteen into the cup, then looked up at me. "No VC today. No VC." He was waving his forefinger back and forth as he shook his head softly from side to side.

I made a motion of lifting a utensil into my mouth, then asked, "We eat soon? Ha, ask Dai Uy Trung if we eat soon, *biet*?"

"Yes, suh."

Ha spit out a quick phrase, which caused Trung to turn to me again, smiling slyly. He nodded curtly, then threw the liquor down and started to bawl orders. Two of his underlings quickly slipped away from their positions below us and were as quickly back with rice bowls and chopsticks, which they passed out to the three of us seated on the low wooden table as well as to those squatting below. Then the two women slipped in front of us. One of them carried a large bowl of steaming rice, and the other carried a platter of what looked like some kind of cut-up chicken, cooked with some strange-looking red and green vegetables. Trung had the platters laid at his feet, and after scooping healthy portions, first of rice, then of chicken into his own small bowl, he passed them on to me. I helped myself to what I thought were reasonably sized portions, then passed them to Dick. As I was passing the chicken to Dick, Trung nudged me with his elbow. When I turned, he extended another small bowl with a spoon in it to me. He said, "Nuoc mam." He indicated with motions that I should put it on top of the chicken.

I had heard at Di An about nuoc mam, a strong sauce made from fermented fish innards that the Vietnamese use liberally to add flavor to their foods. I was a little hesitant as I spooned it out; but I enjoyed exotic dishes, and I figured what the hell. As Trung urged me to take more, I scooped as much onto my food as he had. Then, seeing that Trung was already devouring his meal, I took a deep breath and caught a large bite between my chopsticks and lifted it to my mouth. It was hot, very spicy, and very strange, but I had to admit it was quite good. I was really beginning to enjoy myself when I happened to glance over at Dick. He didn't seem to be enjoying himself as much as I was; in fact, he was eating only big chunks of chicken and ignoring the rest. He had passed on the nuoc mam sauce and seemed to be putting in the minimally acceptable job of consuming our allies' food. "Whaddya think of the food, Dick?"

"Shit, sir, I'm glad I've got a B-two unit and a chocolate bar in my pocket."

"Yeah, well you're putting on a good show, anyway. Drink a lot of tea; that isn't so bad."

"Hey, sir, I just figgered out—I thought them red things was peppers, but now I know, they's just chicken tongues, that's all." My choked laughter sputtered out, and I found myself drooling into my little rice bowl. Trung and several others turned expectantly to me; then Trung said something to Ha.

"Suh, he say it good you like Vietnamee food, yes?"

"Yes, Ha, that's exactly right. Trung Si Lightner here just told me a funny joke in a letter from his wife."

"Oh, yes, suh." He rattled this off to Trung, and the meal continued. After a final cup of tea we all filed outside, and the walk in the sun continued.

It soon became apparent that it was just going to be a repeat of the morning's tedium, but this time I refused to let my mind drift off, concentrating on the far wood lines as if I really expected to see enemy soldiers appear out of them. The walk dragged on.

Finally, at about 1430 (2:30 P.M.), we passed through a tree line, and I could see the battalion trucks lined up on a road a few hundred meters away. Behind them I could see our jeep waiting for us, though I couldn't see who was behind the wheel. The other two companies, which had been moving on either flank, were already loading up, and only we, the command group, and the company behind us were still operational. The guys in the trucks had stacked arms and were no more ready for an unexpected attack than the man in the moon. I sighed under my breath. What a bunch of clowns! Here it was, 1430 hours, and everybody's ready to go home. Jesus Christ! What a hell of a way *not* to fight a war! I trudged the last stretch to the jeep blindly, not really giving much of a shit what happened. As we mounted the dike the road was on, I saw Jerry's wide smile as we walked toward our jeep. Then Ha was calling me from my right front, and I turned to see him standing next to a smiling Trung, who had his arm raised in farewell. "Suh, he say you make good fren for fight VC. He hope fight wit you again soon."

I smiled falsely, raising my arm in a similar fashion. "Okay, Ha, you tell Dai Uy Trung it has been fantabulous being in the field with him. Tell him never in my wildest dreams did I think I'd see anything like this, tell him that." Ha started to turn to Trung, then stopped, unsure of what I'd said. "Tell him Ha, beaucoup, beaucoup. Then you ride back with him, ya?"

"Yes, okay, suh."

He turned and started to tell Trung what he thought I had said, and I just walked up to our jeep and plopped into the front seat, throwing my weapon across my knees. Dick jumped in back and Jerry pulled out; but his irrepressible smile came through his voice as he posed the obvious question: "He-e-e-y, wha' hoppen, guys?"

Steam was slowly curling up from the general region of my temples as I turned to him. "It was a bag of shit from start to finish, and something's gotta be done. But I don't wanta say anything until we can all sit down and talk it over together, whole team. So let's just wait until we get back, and then we can talk it out."

"Okay, Dai Uy, you the boss."

An uncomfortable silence settled over the jeep, and I soon had to break it myself. "Hey, listen, Jerry, Dick and I got along great. That's not the problem. Right, Dick?"

I turned in my seat to face Dick, seeing him stuffing a fresh chaw into his cheek as I spoke. "Airborne, sir, I'll follow you anywhere."

"The problem is with our allies, but we'll get to that."

We were driving through open paddy land now, on a dirt road that ran on top of a dike between two fields. We had driven around the trucks of our allies as they were loading up and now were sailing alone. The countryside on either side of us appeared beguiling. The fields were empty, with just a touch of water moistening their dirt bottoms, changing them to dark brown mud that glistened in the sun like so much rich chocolate frosting. Dikes enclosed them in squares of a hundred or so meters, and their irregular interspaces were filled with hedges or trees, all dancing lightly in the afternoon breeze. Again I found it hard to accept that such a beautiful land could be so brutally torn by war. But not this province, I mused. They've got a handle on things, or so they think. It must be reassuring to believe that the sort of truce that seems to exist here between the Vietcong and the government forces can go on indefinitely. But clearly that's not the case.

I snapped out of my reverie as we were turning in by the slime-choked reflecting pool. Another hundred meters, and we passed through the front gate of the big house and around it to our humble abode. Jess and Norm came strolling out the front door as we arrived, smiling widely. Warm handshakes and backslaps met us as we climbed out of the jeep. "Welcome home from the war, sir, Dick. Good ta have ya back safe 'n' sound." I was grinning in spite of myself. As Norm shook my hand, he held out two freshly opened Miller High Lifes in the other. I took one, and he passed the other one to Dick. "Here ya go, guys, this'll do ya some good."

"Mmm, thanks." I took a long swallow that coursed refreshingly through my body, renewing and invigorating it. "Goddamn, that's good! Jesus!"

"How'd it go, sir?"

I looked up at Jesse. "Well, hell, this is as good a time as any. C'mon in the house and we'll get this over with—it's debriefing time!"

I did my best to convey the total unreality of the day's operation. When I finished, I stood up and stretched. "Shit, it's four o'clock, and I feel I've been up for thirty hours today. I'm gonna go down to the compound and see if I can get a little of the real skinny on what's goin' on in this province, if the VC really know about our operations ahead of time or if that's just a bunch of shit Trung is puttin' out. Anybody wanta come?"

Jerry jumped right in. "Yeah, I'd kinda like to come with you, find out whatever I can before I go out on an operation."

Jerry and I drove on over and soon approached Jim Claiborne's desk. We flopped into two chairs as he raised his head from the papers he was pretending to be busy with. A broad smile appeared below his neatly waxed handlebar mustache.

"Hi, Tom, Jerry, what can I do for you?"

I looked nervously around. "I just came in from that operation a little while ago, and we need to talk to you. Is there somewhere we can be alone?"

"Sure, Colonel White is over at the province chief's house; we can use his office." Jim led us into the larger office of the senior military adviser for the province and closed the door behind him. He sat in a large easy chair as he gestured toward the couch with his hand. "What seems to be the problem?"

"Well, I'll tell ya, first of all, I brought Jerry along just to give him some background. I went out with the Forty-fourth myself today with one of our sergeants; but Jerry's gonna be goin' on the next operation, and I want him to learn as much as he can beforehand. Anyway, the battalion commander, Dai Uy Trung, seemed to me, admittedly on the basis of one operation, but still, he seemed to be just a terrible officer. He was drinkin' some kinda booze from the time we first stepped on the boat, seemed half-smashed all day long and seemed just sort of indifferent to fighting a war."

Jim shifted uncomfortably in his seat. "Well, okay, now you've seen him, maybe it's time we told you a little bit about Dai Uy Trung. First of all, as I'm sure you know, the population in general is being drafted into the military service. Now the way things work here, the very rich can get out of the military service; but most of them have left the country anyway, and they're off livin' high in Paris or Switzerland or someplace. Now Trung comes from a sort of moderately wealthy family, they own a lot of farmland in the province, so he was able to keep from having to serve with the regular army. In fact, he could probably keep from serving with the Ruff Puffs, too, if he wanted. For whatever reason, he wants to serve.

"Now one of the things we feel pretty sure about is that he's not a VC agent, mostly because he's sort of rich, at least by these people's standards. Anyway, he wants to serve in the local forces, but he doesn't want to fight, let alone get killed, so the result has been that he goes on 'safe' operations often over land that he owns. Like today. You were up to the northwest of town, right?" I nodded yes. "Well, he owns most of the land you went over today, so he gets a chance to see how the tenants are farming his land. I'm sure that's part of it. Now we know he's an alcoholic, and all sorts of things that wouldn't be acceptable in our army, he treats his men like shit, for one thing. But you've gotta try to remember that this *isn't* our army. This is the army of an ally with a tough war to fight, and we're here to try to help them fight it; but we're not in charge. We've gotta try to do what we can with what we're given; we can't reform the whole thing!"

The door suddenly opened, and Colonel White came in, looking somewhat surprised as the three of us stood up. Claiborne quickly took the mike. "Afternoon, sir. Captain Carhart here just came in from an operation with the Forty-fourth and he's got a couple of bitches about Trung. This is Lieutenant Carmack, Captain Carhart's deputy, who'll be going out on the next operation. I was just giving them some background."

"Good, sit down, sit down. How far d'ya get?"

"Well, sir, I told him that Trung might not be the best officer by our standards, and I was just about to explain why we decided Captain Carhart's team should start by working with the Forty-fourth."

"Okay, good, let me try to pick it up from there. Dai Uy Trung is not only 'not the best' but he's terrible! If he served under me, I'd have him in the stockade within half an hour! But there's the rub: He doesn't serve under me. I'm just here, we all are, as an adviser, and I can only advise the province chief on how to fight the war. Colonal Tran is pretty much of a tiger himself, but most of his men are not. I don't know what you've heard so far, but Trung is absolutely petrified by combat. Unfortunately he's the commander on the ground, and all your team can do is make strong suggestions to him. Now what we've been hoping is that with American advisers along on every operation, maybe we can screw his courage up a little bit, get him to take part in this war. How'd things go today? Any contact?"

"No, sir, no contact, and that's one of the things I want to ask about. He told me, while we were in the field, that the VC know about all our operations the night before, and they were watching us through binoculars all day long."

Colonel White looked at Claiborne, and they both sighed, looking down. "Well, unfortunately, it's true. The VC know about our operations within half an hour after the briefing breaks up at the province chief's house. It used to be a lot worse—the guys in the local forces were actually VC soldiers—but we've cleared that up a lot. Unfortunately there are still a lot of leaks, and that's basically because ... well, hell, the political situation here is just unbelievable. You see, for historical reasons, this province has been a 'safe' province for some time, meaning the government's control has never been seriously challenged for the last eight or ten years for a variety of reasons, and we know only some of them. First of all, several of President Diem's brothers were pretty firmly established here; they've got some pretty splendid mansions north of Hoa Dong that are just shells now. Another thing is that the people in this province were and still are pretty resentful of the way they were treated by the rich people, like Madame Nhu, the Dragon Lady, wife of one of Diem's brothers who ran the secret police. She used to live out there by Hoa Dong in one of those palaces. Anyway, the VC have had a pretty resentful populace to support them. Then you throw in the Coconut Grove—have you heard about that yet?"

"Well, I heard it's an R and R center for main force VC units from all over the delta."

"Yeah, well, that's about all we know, too. Our G-two says there are anywhere from two to eight battalions of main force VC in there at any one time, but I think that's quite an exaggeration. In the first place, if that many men were moving in and out of there, we'd see something. But we don't. All we know is that quite a bit of the rice grown in province and a lot of other food from the main market here in town—fruits, vegetables, fish, meat, you name it—end up going in there."

I couldn't resist asking the obvious question: "Well, why can't we just bomb the fuck out of the place?"

"You forget, Captain, we're guests in this country, and that land is privately owned. Even the province chief's hands are tied. He wants to bomb the place, but if he let us, I suspect he has been warned that he would be financially ruined by VC sympathizers who have a stranglehold on his own finances. You see, like I said, the politics in this country are a real mess. Now do you understand what it's about a little better?"

"Yes, sir, but while we're talkin', let me ask you this: I noticed today that Trung was takin' a shot of booze every so often. The guy's a fuckin' rummy, and he makes a terrible leadership image for his men! For instance, at one point, right in the middle of the sweep, he shot two little birds out of a scrawny little tree, fired four shots out of his M-two carbine, scared the hell outa me 'n' Sergeant Lightner before we knew what was happenin'. Now isn't there some way we can get a better man in there to act as battalion commander?" I had started to laugh as I retold the bird-shooting incident, and the others had briefly joined me.

But Colonel White was looking down and shaking his head even before my question was finished. "No, I'm afraid that's out of the question. You see, this society is still structured in almost feudal ways, and Trung owns a lot of land, and that gives him a certain amount of political power. No, I wish there were something we could do about changing the people in charge here, but there's not. Oh, there are some exceptions, like Colonel Tran, the province chief; he's a real pisser! Wish there were more like him, but since there aren't, well, then our job is to make some, right?"

"I guess so, sir."

"Of course, it is! Look at the South Korean Army! Why, when we went over there fifteen, sixteen years ago, I was still in high school, and I can remember reading about how worthless their army was, even worse than the South Vietnamese army. But we gave 'em some training, helped 'em build up their economy, gave 'em something to be proud of, and look at how their army has come around! All you've got to do, really, is give the people something to fight for, and they'll pull themselves up by their bootstraps. I can't say that the South Vietnamese have come that far yet, but I've got nothing but the utmost admiration and respect for them. But enough of that. How are other things? How's your new house?"

"Great, sir. The roof was full of holes when we moved in, but we were able to do some horse tradin' with the Ninth outside My Tho, and we got all the new tin sheeting we needed. Just about battened down for the rainy season."

"Okay, sounds good. You know there's an operation scheduled for the day after tomorrow, and that'll be your turn, Lieutenant Carmack, right?"

"That's right, sir."

"Okay, I'll see you at the briefing."

I felt strange as the door closed behind me. Now I understood why Trung was the way he was and could get away with it. But that didn't mean I liked it! I pulled my hat on and headed for the door. I turned to Jerry. "Whaddya think of that shit, Jerry?"

He looked back over his shoulder at the closed door, then pulled on his own hat as he softly answered me. "I think one hundred fifty-three days and a wake-up till my DEROs, that's what I think!"

I grinned again as I led the way down the hall.

Local Color

WE ATE AN early supper at the Ponderosa, then were in the club by
six. Since we were among the first arrivals, we greeted the other advisers in province as they arrived.

"Sit down, Tiger, tell me about the war!" I looked to my right in
some surprise, and saw Captain Neon sitting at a card table, beckoning to me. I smiled, remembering that I had liked him when first I
had met him a few nights ago, and I dragged up a chair.

"Wanna hear about how Dai Uy Trung is winnin' the war all by
himself?"

"Is he?"

I gave him a vile look. "That fuckin' clown! He doesn't know
what the word 'war' means!"

"Well, I got to agree with you there. We got some real pretenders
in this province. God knows we're spendin' enough money on it."

"Shit! Hey, you're the guy in charge of Operation Phoenix for
this province, right?" He nodded slowly, smiling. Operation Phoenix was being run from Saigon, and its avowed purpose was to kill,
capture, or drive away the members of the Vietcong shadow government who actually ran much of the country, generally using the
province reconnaissance unit (PRU) mercenaries for the dirty work.
"Well, who do you report to? Are you responsibile to Colonel
White, or what?"

"Fuck, no, I go directly to Saigon. Why?"

"Oh, I'm just interested in that shit, that's all. You must be in the
CIA, then right?"

"Well, actually I'm in military intelligence."

I looked him over with a suitably dubious expression. "It makes no difference to me. We're fightin' the same war. I've just always thought that James Bond shit is neat, that's all."

"Well, I dunno about James Bond shit, but I sure could use a jeep."

"A jeep?"

"Yeah, you wanna sell yours?"

I burst out laughing. "Boy, now I *know* you're not in the army. Do I wanna sell my fucking jeep? My old first sergeant in the Hundred first would love you!"

"Lemme buy ya a beer."

"Sure, James Bond can buy me a beer anytime."

Neon was eight years older than I was and had gone to the University of Oregon, and we were soon telling college stories, getting friendlier with each beer. Finally, he went home for the night, and I joined Dick and Norm at another table. The movie machine had still not been fixed, and about midnight we stumbled out of the club and wandered through the still streets, managing God knows how to find the Jade Pool rather quickly and then the Ponderosa. When we crept in, Jess and Jerry were fast asleep, resting for the next day's operation. I heard their stirrings in the predawn but managed to turn over and stay asleep.

The three of us who stayed behind worked away all day at painting our house. We finished about three in the afternoon, just as a call came on the radio that the 44th was finishing its operation and was ready for a pickup. Norm hopped into the jeep and ran it down to the compound, where he would get more specific directions for picking up Jerry and Jesse. Dick and I stood in the front yard and lit cigars, looking appreciatively at the glint of orange and blue (the only colors of paint we could get) visible through the door and windows, the bright outlines of which foretold the color scheme hiding inside, all set off by the brightly gleaming tin roof. Jerry and Jesse both had bored, exhausted, pissed-off looks on their faces when they arrived home. "Okay, let's hear it. How'd it go today?"

"Well, shit, we went out in trucks, Norm took us to the kickoff point in the jeep this morning, down in Hoa Binh, southeast of town about ten clicks. We got off the trucks okay, then moved down trails for a couple of hours. Again, it looked like the battalion movement, tactically was very good, but the men were making incredible noise, laughing and shouting to each other. I really thought that they were trying to make so much noise just to tell the VC they were coming, so they could clear out and there wouldn't be a firefight. I didn't have much chance to say anything to Trung, and like you said, I saw him sneakin' into little huts with his boys, and I'm sure he was drinkin' in there, but what the fuck do you do? Well, shit, that's all, we just walked along this trail; then, finally, about eleven-thirty, we stopped for lunch—"

Jesse broke in on him. "You forgot 'bout the fishin', sir, when we was crossin' the little river."

"Oh, yeah, we had to cross a river that was only about twenty, thirty meters wide, and when we got there, I'll bet there were ten sampans waiting for us, all manned by young, strong-lookin' guys wearing black pajamas, that scared the shit outa me, and I asked Ha right away who they were, and he said they were farmers; but there just aren't any young farmers around, or there aren't supposed to be. The draft was supposed to get them all but the old men, and these guys were teenagers or in their twenties. So I made Ha ask Trung, and Trung said they were farmers, too, didn't seem to bother him at all. But I'm sure as shit that those guys were VC, scared the fuck outa me. So anyway, we start to cross, and the river looked pretty deep, and Trung had his boys take over one of the sampans, and they went out in the middle and dropped grenades over the side. Couple seconds later there'd be this muffled explosion, and then fifteen or twenty fish, either dead or stunned, would float up to the surface. Trung had five or six guys swimming out there, rounding the fish up, and even after everybody was across, we musta waited half an hour while Trung's boys were killin' fish with hand grenades and then scoopin' 'em up. I didn't know what the rules are about that, but you can bet your ass they're not supposed to be doin' that! Using hand grenades to kill fish while their VC boatmen sort of oversee the whole thing, keeping the government troops amused while their troops are running the countryside. It was unfucking believable!"

I managed a wry smile. "Yeah, I know how you feel, Jerry, but what can we do?"

One night at the club I found myself drinking beer with Red Neon. I casually mentioned to him that I thought half the South Vietnamese officers in province were VC. He looked at me wryly.

"You're not far off, Tiger. We got some real serious political problems in this province, but I'm doin' my best to undercut that."

"Yeah, that's what I thought. You've got special troops for that, right?"

He shrugged. "I'm supposed to, but that hasn't worked out too well."

"Whaddya mean?"

"Well, when I first got here eight months ago, Phoenix was brand new. About twenty Chinese mercenaries were sent down here from Saigon or somewhere to work for me as my 'hit team.' I had two Navy Seals assigned here to run them for me, and they were both good men, but on the second day he was here, one of them broke both legs in a jeep accident, medevaced back to the World. Then about a week later the other one came down with purple syphilis or some God-awful thing, and he was gone too. Colonel White, also new, decided we didn't need any more Navy guys here, so he has the PRU administration handled through the main compound. He told me and one of my sergeants to run them ourselves, but I'm not trained for that. I mean, I went on a couple of field exercises at Benning, but I didn't learn how to lead patrols out to hit targets at night, which is what the PRUs are *supposed* to do."

"How about the PRUs themselves? Can't they handle that?"

"Hell, no. As far as I'm concerned, they're just a lazy, worthless bunch of draft dodgers. All they want to do is lie around town drinkin' beer and chasin' women. I've sent them on some missions, but they just go three or four hundred meters outside the walls and go to sleep; then when they come back the next morning, they tell me either their target wasn't home or they got lost. I gave up on 'em months ago."

"Hunh. Sounds just like the way everybody else in this town fights the war."

"Yeah, it's some sorry shit, but I want to change that. I've got a bunch of Hoi Chans—they're former VC who turned themselves in for amnesty under the Chieu Hoi program—and most of them are damned good soldiers. All I need are some Americans to go out with them. You ever hit any targets at night?"

"Fuck me, that's all we did for nine weeks in Ranger school, and then I had some dicey nights with the Tiger Force in the Hundred first that I remember well."

"Shit, Tiger, you sound like just the kinda guy I'm lookin' for."

"Not so fast, Red. I'm assigned here with MAT Eighty-five as an adviser. And it looks to me like anybody who goes outside the walls

at night is all alone. You get wounded out there, and there ain't nobody comin' to get you. It's all fucking over: You're either dead or
on your way to Hanoi—on foot!"

"I know it's risky, Tiger, but I need some help if we're gonna
turn this province around, get 'em back into the war."

"Well, you're definitely right there. The way the Ruff Puffs are
pretending to be fightin' this war is just shameful. They've got two
fucking battalions in province, the Forty-fourth and the Fifty-
second, and they go on three or four operations a week, but they're
just goin' through the motions. Hell, they go out of their way to
avoid combat. It's almost like they coordinate their operations with
the VC so they won't stumble into each other."

"They do."

I had to laugh. "Aw shit, Red, what a mess."

"So come work with me, and maybe we can change that." He
was serious.

"Well, I'm not ready for that just yet, but if that ever changes, I'd
definitely want one of my sergeants with me, Dick Lightner. He was
on his second tour with the Hundred first when he got levied. He's
good, and I trust him."

"Okay, Tiger, the more the merrier. I may call you on that in a
few weeks."

"Yeah, okay, well, like I said, lemme think about it."

Next day there was no operation, and there was nothing to do.
Jerry had gotten five old issues of *Mechanics Illustrated.* I had never
even picked one up before. But after reading no more than half a
page, I threw it back on his bunk, listening to the AFN rock music
throbbing in the kitchen as I closed my eyes. After five or ten minutes I could take no more. I stood up and pulled my hat on. "I'm
gonna get some fresh air. This little dump makes me antsy. I'll be
back for supper."

I glanced at my watch: twenty to two. A full afternoon free in
town. I trudged out the door into the full heat of the sun, and I was
glad for the bill of my cap, which protected my face. I walked
around the big house, then out onto the street. I started to walk
toward town, then crossed the street and walked in the shade of the
huge hardwood trees, undoubtedly planted by the French, along
the banks of the Jade Pool. The sky was cloudless powder blue,
and the sun was really beating down. Didn't look like rainy season
was even on the schedule, and it was hotter than hell. I had already

broken a sweat just from moving around, but the branches of the trees overhead provided a slight but welcome respite.

When I entered the small business district of town, I slowed my walk to a stroll. There were very few people on the streets now, and even many of the small shops were shuttered up, apparently for siesta time. Hmph.

I walked down by the commercial docks on the small river that ran through town. There was a large, open-air roofed area, with board tables stacked against the roof supports, the cement floor newly hosed down and draining water into the adjacent river. Bits of fish entrails were snagged in the cracks and separations between adjoining cement slabs. Pretty clearly this was the site of a fish market, but it was closed now. Probably it operated only during morning hours. I made a mental note to come back early some morning and check things out. We might even be able to buy something nice for the table at the Ponderosa. I doubted that anyone on the team would be able to whip up anything good with fish, except maybe Jerry; Hawaiians ate a lot of fish, didn't they? At any rate, if we ever hired a Vietnamese cook, that could mean some tasty additions to what might otherwise turn out to be—to *continue* to be—a pretty bland diet. I walked past the market area and saw that there was only a small alleyway in front of me. No sense walking down there, especially with no reassuring weapon under my arm. There were no boats tied up at the wharves next to the marketplace, so I turned and walked back up to the main road, then continued away from the Ponderosa, toward the road to Hoa Dong. I knew that there were perhaps two more kilometers of town over here, and I was curious about what lay below the tall palms, their soft frond tips nodding gently in a light breeze high above me. I approached the small bridge over the river, bunkered on my end with a small sand-bagged guardhouse and a flagpole from which the red and yellow Vietnamese flag hung listlessly. A Vietnamese sentry came scurrying out of the guardhouse and snapped to attention, holding his M-2 carbine smartly at present arms. I saluted, smiling, and nodded to the teenaged sentry. *"Chau, Ong."*

He smiled widely at me. *"Chau, Dai Uy."*

I walked over the bridge, no more than twenty meters long. Funny, I thought, these people are really friendly. That smile from the sentry was natural. They *want* to like you, and they want to be liked. Why is it that we can't make ourselves and our interests understood? We're really not like the French were, ready to bleed their colony of whatever could be had; we really came to fight for the people. Do they understand that? And from whatever I had been able to read, it did seem that we were here helping the Vietnamese people fight an invader from the north. Hell, that's all we had seen in the 101st and all we'd faced, the North Vietnamese regulars. It had never seemed to me that this was a case of a popular uprising, an internal revolution against the government by the people, who felt abused. But was that the truth? It did seem different down here in the delta. Although the delta made up only something like one-sixth of the land area of South Vietnam, it contained well over half the population. It was, what had they said at Di An, the third most productive land area in the world. But now, because of the war, only women and old men were doing the farming. The men were all in either the ARVN or the VC, fighting and killing each other.

I was on the main road now, and the tall palm trees that lined the pavement were beguiling as I moved through the filtered sunlight they allowed to reach me. On the right side of the road were rows of small Vietnamese huts, many of them with thatched roofs, while on the left a number of large Western-style houses were tucked behind high stone walls, complete with the appropriate garages and other outbuildings that their French builders would have installed as a matter of course. I pulled a cigar out of my shirt pocket, wadded the cellophane wrapper up, and stuffed it into one of my pants pockets, then lit it, took a couple of heavy drags, and continued my stroll, trying to absorb the natural beauty that surrounded me. It really was a splendid country—if it wasn't for the goddamn war!

As I walked, I noted that the huts on the right side of the road had given way to a number of long buildings with thatched roofs. Probably some kind of warehouses or storage barns, I thought as I started to pass them, directing most of my interest to the large, more mysterious-looking French houses on the other side of the road. Suddenly my head spun back to the right side of the road as someone hailed me: *"Chau, Dai Uy!"* It was a smiling, hatless Ha, standing expectantly in front of a tall, open gateway.

"Hey, *Chau,* Ha. You live here?"

"No, suh, me live otha place. You come see sojas?"

"What?"

"You come see Vietnamese sojas?"

"Why, is this where they live?"

"Yes, suh, mos' of Foty-fo Battayo live dis place."

"Oh. You mean this is the barracks?" I hadn't really expected all the men from Trung's battalion to live in one cantonment area, somehow just presuming that they had separate residences somewhere in town.

"Me no unnastan, suh."

"Sojas live dis place?"

"Yes, suh."

"Everybody?"

Ha shook his head violently, grinning hard, but nervous as a cat. "No, suh, maybe half dis place, also . . ." He made a wide, circular gesture with his hand, conveying to me that half the battalion lived here, the rest spread through town.

"Okay, yeah, I'd like to take a look, see how the men are getting along."

Shit, this was rare good fortune, I had stumbled onto the cantonment area for the troops I advised, and now I could casually visit them, showing my interest in their welfare. I crossed the road to Ha, and he led me through the open gate. There were four of the large, long buildings, two on either side of us, and a roughly rectangular area between them the size of a large tennis court that must have been used as some kind of assembly area. I headed toward the door of the nearest building, and Ha scurried in front, opening it before me. The walls were made of some kind of adobe, daubed a deep red but chipping so badly as to form a sort of pinto effect with the natural ocher beneath it. As Ha opened the door, I could see that the inside was rather well lit through large, open window spaces with no glass on both sides of the building. The thatched roof was high enough for a number of irregular shelves to have been erected, and quite a bit of equipment was stored on them. There were only two Vietnamese soldiers inside, squatting on the floor at the far end of the building. When they turned and saw me enter, they quickly stood up and greeted me simultaneously: *"Chau, Dai Uy."*

I waved a signal for them to relax and go about their business with my hand as I answered them, smiling, *"Chau, Ong."*

They stayed on their feet, however, watching my moves carefully. The room had a cement floor and was lined on both sides with what were obviously sleeping positions, either low, narrow wooden tables or straw mats stretched out in the dust, with small clumps of personal belongings, jars, clothing scattered here and there. I was struck by two things. First, this was certainly not up to any military standards of order or cleanliness that I was familiar with, although I was willing to grant a certain amount of irregularity to this unit because of its irregular, local-force nature. And secondly, these people were really poor! I mean, it was depressing enough to see young men sleeping on a corner of cement floor, but it became an even more pitiful situation when you realized that this was all they had! Or perhaps these were just the military-duty stations of young men who actually lived elsewhere in town with their families. I didn't know, and I didn't want to go through the hassle of trying to get the idea through to Ha in broken English, so I just continued to walk down the middle of the building, looking around carefully. Actually it could have been a combination: The guys who *had* a home elsewhere probably lived there most of the time, but the men without any other base, and with little or no personal property, lived right here, on the dusty cement floor. I started to feel sorry for the little guys, but then I remembered the farmers' huts I had been inside, which didn't offer much more in the way of creature comforts, and I realized that the soldiers were probably perfectly content sleeping on the floor. After all, it wasn't that much different from a barracks anywhere in the U.S. Army, excepting the limited comforts of a bed and the spotless condition insisted on by sergeants. And if they were a bit sloppy, so what! There were still thirty or forty grown men sleeping in here every night. As I walked, two frightened white chickens darted out from beneath one of the small table-beds on my right, and I noted white droppings on the floor behind them. What a story this would make back in the World: "I went into a Vietnamese Army barracks building where the sergeants were *so* chickenshit that—" But no, the people who hadn't been here would never believe it.

I heard someone enter a door on my right. It was a short, wiry sergeant who must have been in his fifties, to judge from his gray hair and wrinkled face. He saluted me, and a lot of gold showed in his wide smile.

"Chau, Dai Uy."

"Chau, Trung Si."

A burst of smiling Vietnamese to Ha, who relayed it. "Suh, he want know why you heah?"

"Tell him I just came by to see what the men were doing on a day off. Ask him where everybody is."

Ha spoke to the sergeant, got a response, then turned back to me. "Suh, he say some work for Dai Uy Trung, some fix road, some fix boats."

"Oh, okay, just wondered. Thank you, Trung Si." I waved my hand at him, and he saluted me. I returned his salute, then moved toward the door. I was obviously intruding; maybe this hadn't been such a good idea after all. I stepped back out into the glaring sun, then paused briefly as Ha scurried out after me. "Okay, Ha, I think I'm just gonna walk around town a little bit now, take a look around. You stay here and do whatever you were doing when I got here."

"Yes, suh."

I turned and looked at him, smiling at his eager innocence. "Relax, Ha, ain't nobody gonna hurt you." He looked confused at this, not sure what I had said. I raised my hand to him as I turned away. "I see you tonight, Ponderosa, eight-thirty, we go province chief house, get briefing for operation tomorrow, ya?"

"Yes, suh, eight-thutty, me come you house."

"Okay, Ha, see you then."

I moved back out the gate and turned right, moving farther away from the center of town, still following my curiosity. It was becoming increasingly apparent to me that this town was little more than a gathering of poor Vietnamese, and the richest man in town was probably the province chief, Colonel Tran. I had been inside his house and had been less than impressed with how he lived—or at least that part of his house that was open for briefings. I continued down the main road for several hundred meters, then turned left down a rather wide road, flanked on both sides by walled-in private houses.

As I looked around, I noted a tall redbrick steeple off to my right. That must be a Catholic church, clearly built by the French. I wondered if it was still in use, if perhaps there was a French priest there, and I decided to stop in and see. I walked another hundred meters or so, then made my way down a smaller street that led to a large, open square in front of the church. No one was in view as I made my way across this brick square. It must have been lovely once, and I wondered what it had been used for. Had there been open-air ceremonies held here, weddings, baptisms, funerals? Or had this been just the gathering place where, in the absence of rain, celebrations took place, congratulations were extended, or tears were shared? It didn't matter, really, for now the whole area had an abandoned look. Yellowed grass grew up between the dark, splotched bricks, the thin sprigs brushing my shins as I walked toward the church. The corners on the steeple were blackened; the tile roof was neglected. As I came closer, I could see jagged corners unrepaired where time or hostile missiles had enforced their will. I saw a large chain across the front door and stopped when I realized that I wouldn't be able to get in.

It was a long way back, and it started to rain soon after I headed home. When I finally walked into the Ponderosa, I exhaled a deep sigh of psychic relief. The radio was braying some loud rock music from Saigon, but I ignored it, warming to the comfort of a secure, dry refuge, with no one to bother me for at least three more hours. I took off my shirt and hat and walked into the bedroom. Jerry and Norm were stretched out in their racks, and I sat down on mine and quickly unlaced my boots. They both woke up when I entered, and Jerry stretched luxuriantly, then turned to me, smiling. "Hey, Dai Uy, have a nice walk?"

"Hunh."

"Hey, whatsa matta? Sounds like rain on the roof."

"Yeah, it's rainin' like a muthafuck." I stood up, my boots off, and slipped my wet pants off, then started to crawl under my blanket and poncho liner.

"Discover anything interesting?"

"Fuck, no! That's the last curiosity walk I'm gonna take!"

"Well, I think I'll go down to the compound. Hey, Norm, wanta come?" Norm was scrambling out of his bunk as I dissolved into mine. "We'll get you up for supper, 'kay, Dai Uy?"

"Hunh." I was falling asleep as I heard them walk out the front door.

Norm awakened me around five-thirty, and I felt much refreshed as I pulled on dry fatigues. Somehow, the waves of depression that had begun to crash through my head as I had started to walk home had been calmed. I just refused to think about those "heavy" questions for now, knowing that they'd return in due course. Jerry, Dick, and Jesse were at the club. After Norm and I filled our bellies with mystery meat, scalloped potatoes, and fruit cocktail, we read paperbacks until after eight, when we heard Ha arrive at our door, still nervous, even in the dark. We zipped over to the province chief's house.

The next day's operation would be near the Coconut Grove, and I decided Norm and I would accept a late lunch offer from Bob Coffee, who was on the advisory team in Hoa Dong, the district in Kien Hoa province where the grove was located.

We finished our walk in the sun around noon, as predicted, and

Norm and I climbed into the backseat of Bob's jeep as the troops from the 44th were climbing in their trucks for the ride back to Kien Hoa city.

"It's almost noon. You guys wanta go see Madame Nhu's house, and then we'll come back to Hoa Dong 'n' eat?"

"Sounds good, Bob." We were now approaching the main Kien Hoa–My Tho road from the south, and we could see Hoa Dong three or four clicks away off to our left. Alex, Bob's enlisted driver, turned left on the main road, and we zipped down the road past the Hoa Dong turnoff. Alex turned right at the next road, leaving Hoa Dong behind us, and we drove toward the large white Nhu houses several clicks away. We slowed as we approached the first house, where a coil of barbed wire was stretched across the narrow dirt road. A young Vietnamese soldier came scurrying out of a clump of trees, carrying an M-2 carbine and hatless. He pulled the end of the coil back, clearing the road, and stood stiffly at attention, presenting arms awkwardly. His face was stretched into a strained grimace, and he looked incredibly sloppy, shirt dirty and unbuttoned, dirty, stained pants, bare feet. I had clapped my helmet back on, and Bob returned the salute as we drove by. "Jesus, Bob, you really got the ragtag guys guardin' the gates, dontcha?"

"Aw, shit, man, those guys do nothin' but lay around in the sun all day, supposedly guardin' these houses. We've got a platoon of the popular forces permanently assigned over here. They can't leave, don't go on any of the operations, none of that shit."

"How'd that happen?"

"Ah, it's political. The Ngo family still owns these houses. You know Madame Nhu was married to one of President Diem's brothers, the guy who ran the national police. Their family name is Ngo, their first name—they do that different from us. He got killed when Diem did, back in 'sixty-three, I think. Ol' Madame Nhu, the Dragon Lady, was in Rome then, and I don't think she's ever been back. But they still own the houses, and she pulled enough strings to get this platoon assigned to guard them permanently. They stay in this little triangular fort the French built, up here on the right."

Ahead of us some fifty meters, on the right, was a small fortress with earth walls maybe six feet high. Alex parked the jeep next to it, and we climbed out. A lieutenant came scrambling over one wall of the fort, pulling his shirt on as he did so and saluting Bob. Bob returned the salute, then began talking to him, obviously the platoon leader, in Vietnamese. I walked around the back of the jeep, examining the fort. Six or seven white chickens wandered freely over the walls and around the bunker, pecking idly at the ground. I turned back to Bob, who had finished his conversation and was walking toward me. "Hey, Tom, the platoon leader told me he's got a squad in one of these houses; but the others are empty, and he doesn't think we ought to go in them, we'd have to break in. C'mon, let's go look." I followed as he and the platoon leader started across the front lawn of the nearest large house. The grass was long and unkempt, reaching up to the middle of my shins. The grass that grew out of cracks in the wide steps that led to the huge front door, tightly shut, told of disuse. We moved around the left side, then up another set of steps and in a smaller door. The ceilings were very high, and the house was amazingly cool and pleasant. There was no furniture at all, but the rooms were large and open, with tall floor-to-ceiling windows that opened onto small balconies. The floors were alternately hardwood parquet, dry and aching from years of neglect, and smooth, brightly colored tile. We came to a main central hallway, which led to a wide staircase. Halfway up these broad stairs was a landing, which led on either side to another flight of stairs that mounted to the floor above. I was very impressed as I ascended; it was clear that whoever built this place had been wealthy and important. I presumed that these houses had been built long ago by Frenchmen, and I could see the unmistakable skeleton here of bygone glory. I rounded the corner and followed the staircase that led to the right. When I reached the top, three Vietnamese soldiers, two in a semblance of uniform and the other in his underwear, had gathered at their platoon leader's call. He explained something to Bob, who then turned to Norm and me.

"This is half the squad that mans the position in this house; they've got a thirty-caliber machine gun mounted in one of the corner windows back there." I looked in the direction he pointed and, sure enough, saw a machine gun mounted in an open window, with two more Vietnamese soldiers squatting next to it. Bob walked down a hallway, and I followed him. He stopped in an open doorway and gazed in as I approached him. "Whatsa matter, we catch 'em eatin' lunch?"

"Yeah, and they're not supposed to leave the gun, ever. Look at this shit."

I leaned in the doorway and followed his extended finger with my eyes. "Holy shit!" The room was huge and must once have been a ballroom. On the far wall, some twenty meters away from us, was an enormous decoration. It was a large rectangle of some kind of dark red semiprecious stone, inlaid into the wall. In the center were two large Oriental characters, each taller than I, made of mother-of-pearl and inlaid into the red background. "Jesus, Bob, how old is this house?"

"I don't know, but the district chief told me these houses were here when he was a little kid in the twenties, and the French people lived here."

"Well, whoever built this house must have put those characters in there, right?"

"Seems like it, but if they're Vietnamese, then that must have been a long time ago, because some French priest converted the written Vietnamese language from Oriental characters into Western—what do we call 'em, Roman characters?—so that they began to use the same alphabet we do back in 1890 or so, right after the French government declared that Indochina was part of France. So this house must have been built before then if those characters are Vietnamese."

"Ask the platoon leader if he knows what it means."

Bob said something to the platoon leader, who answered him, and Bob relayed it to me. "Means 'long life.' "

"No shit! I'll bet it really says, 'Frenchy go home!' "

We both were grinning hard now, and Bob made a halfhearted swipe at my ear from two steps above and behind me, which I easily dodged, breaking into a galumphing gallop down the remaining stairs and then jogging out into the middle of the wide hallway. I stopped in the middle of the house, spread my arms wide, threw my head back, and closed my eyes. Then I slowly started to revolve in a circle, moaning out loud, "All-you-ancient-ghosts-and-spirits-still-inhabiting-this-house, I'm-waiting-f-o-o-o-o-r y-o-o-o-o-o-o-o-o-u! All-ee-all-ee-in-come-free!"

Norm and Alex were sitting on the stairs, and the Vietnamese platoon leader was standing behind them, grinning but slightly bewildered. Bob stopped laughing and said something to him, and the two exchanged several sentences.

"Hey, he says there's some kind of important religious temple out back, with an old priest and his wife who are supposed to be magic."

"Magic, huh? What can they do?"

"He says they can fly, and they can make themselves invisible."

Before I could respond, a piece of plaster the size of a grapefruit fell from the ceiling and smashed onto the tile floor across the room. We all ran.

Norm's voice chased me outside: "Hey, that's your fault, Captain Carhart. You were callin' the French ghosts, and they came to pay you a visit!"

"Hell, I was gonna laugh about the magic this priest and priestess can do, but now I'm not so sure. What are they, Buddhist?"

"Sorta, they're a sort of splinter sect of Buddhists. Wanta go see 'em?"

"Fuckin' A, let's do it!"

Bob turned and spoke in the doorway to the platoon leader, who soon appeared and walked by us down the steps, beckoning us with his hand as he passed. Shit, this looked like a *real* adventure! I didn't expect to see people fly or disappear, but I'd play their game, just to get a glimpse of what was going on. We all were silent now as we walked around the house, then down a path through the trees that soon led into a thickly overgrown section of what could only be called jungle. We all had our weapons, and even though we were being guided by a supposed ally, I was happy to feel the warm comfort of the strap tugging at my shoulder.

After a few minutes we came to a small clearing in front of what looked like a house, but with carefully woven latticework walls. A step up from what the farmers lived in, that was for sure. The platoon leader had disappeared inside, and he quickly returned, followed by two very old Vietnamese, white-haired and wearing floor-length white silk cassocks. The man had a long, wispy white beard growing from his chin, and they both wore white brocade sandals. They bowed deeply to us, and we four Americans bowed reverently back. They smiled as Bob exchanged a few words with them. Then they invited us inside with their gestures.

Incense had been burned here, and there were four elaborately decorated tables, one against each wall, each bearing ornate metal boxes surrounded by small figurines of Oriental people assuming different positions: some standing; some sitting; some bearing heavy loads on their shoulders. Each box had a small door in the center of the side facing us, and each was surmounted by a white seated Buddha. The effect was indescribable; there was no question but that we were now in the inscrutable Orient, strangers in a strange land. The old Vietnamese couple bowed again, smiling, and led us through another door.

Now we were in a darkened room with little light. A large unlit candle, affixed to the hub of a wooden wagon wheel, occupied the center of the room. The wheel lay flat on a small pile of rocks that was in the middle of a pool of water. The woman spoke to Bob, and he relayed the message to us: "This pool is fed by a stream from one side of the room, and it goes out the other side, and this woman told me there are two fish in the pond that are she and her husband."

I leaned over the pond, and sure enough, I could see the large red fish almost motionless in the pool of water. "She says those fish are her and her old man, huh?"

"That's what she says, but don't ask her anything, Tom, please. After that bit with the plaster falling down, I'll believe in any kinda juju they tell me in this place."

We all smiled and bowed slightly to the couple, and they led us out another door. We were right near the door we had entered, and we all bowed again. I noticed that although the woman had a wrinkled face, she had a slender body that seemed awfully limber for such an old woman. Then I noticed that her white silk dress was almost sheer and that she wore nothing beneath it; I could easily see her large breasts, not sagging any more than those of a twenty-year-old girl, her brown nipples clearly visible through her dress. I was stunned, but then she bowed again, we bowed, and she and her husband disappeared back inside what must have been a temple. I looked at Bob, my mouth open. He was smiling but wasted no time, motioning to the platoon leader that we wanted to go back to our jeep at the big house. I was dazed as we walked back through the patch of jungle. That woman had the face and hair of an old woman, and I hadn't questioned her age until I saw her body through her dress. Her body looked like that of a teenager! She was even very large-breasted, by Vietnamese standards, but her breasts didn't sag at all. How was that possible? And why had she said that she and her husband were those two fish? What did it all mean?

We piled into the jeep and started down the road, back toward Hoa Dong. "Hey, how 'bout those fish? What was the story on that?"

"Shit, don't ask me, that was all mystery to me. Hey, and did you check out that woman's body? Christ, her tits made her look like some fucking teenager!"

"Yeah, I caught that. Shit, I don't know. It's just one of those mysteries of the Orient, I guess. Whadda you think?"

"Shit, man, I don't know, I'm glad we got out of there before she turned me into a fucking toad!"

"Shit, Tom, no problem there—you already *are* a fucking toad!"

I knocked his hat off and mussed his hair as he leaned forward in mock defense, yelping softly through his laughter. We were quickly back at the road, then made our way down the track that led to the main gate of Hoa Dong, a kilometer ahead of us. The alert guard saluted us very neatly as we sailed through, and then we pulled into the district chief's compound and stopped the jeep in front of the main house. We moved inside, into the large kitchen, where a long wooden table was already set with plates, utensils, Styrofoam cups and a large pitcher of iced tea. A Vietnamese woman magically appeared through a door, bearing a large bowl of steaming rice, followed by a younger girl, carrying a bowl of what looked like mixed vegetables and chicken. Bob went right to his place at the far end of the table, then indicated open places to Norm and me. "Sit down, sit down, let's eat! Looks like we got chicken stew today. I think you'll find we eat pretty well out here." We dug in and ate a hearty meal. When we had finished, the older woman reappeared, this time carrying a plate of papaya and pineapple slices. "Wow, you guys do eat well!"

"Yeah, let's take our coffee and dessert out back on the veranda."

We settled into deck chairs under an awning and began chewing fruit and slurping coffee. The sun beat down on the baked, dry paddy fields beyond the low wall fifty meters away. The ribbon of road lay still in the distance, the poplar trees that lined it shimmering in the absence of any breath of a breeze. It was very hot, and I was grateful for the shade. We chewed the fat for an hour or two, then I stood up and stretched. "Well, I guess we'd better get back to town." Norm and I strapped our cartridge belts on, then picked up our weapons and helmets where we had left them by the sink, and moved out into the dry, dusty area in front of the house. We shook hands, thanked Bob and Alex for their hospitality, then climbed into our own jeep and buzzed out of Hoa Dong and back toward Kien Hoa city. I sat back in my seat, sated and content. Somehow, the war didn't seem all that bad.

Dai Uy Trung

SOON ENOUGH, the full-blown rainy season arrived. One operation folded into another, and while there were occasional contacts on the flanks, the VC always melted away—were *allowed* to melt away—and there were always enormously inflated body counts given to us that we had to report to Ringmaster, the American headquarters in Kien Hoa. Yet I never saw a single VC body.

Weeks slipped by, and I became increasingly weary of the charade going on around me. *The Stars and Stripes* reported on the Democratic National Convention in Chicago and how Mayor Richard Daley's police had smashed the masses of antiwar demonstrators. But the demonstrators were college kids, and they weren't armed; they were just out in the streets, screaming and making nuisances of themselves. What had happened at home that our police were smashing the heads of our kids? Was it true that they all were cowards and had only self-preservation in mind? Granted, the war seemed to be a fiasco here in Kien Hoa, but my memories from the 101st were vivid. We had been fighting there and kicking ass; wasn't that what it was all about? Weren't we fighting to guarantee that the Vietnamese people would be allowed to choose their own form of government, to protect them from the Communist hordes, who tolerated no dissent or minority position but always took power through brute force, never through the ballot box? Hadn't there already been one election, which was seen as a fair, open, expression of popular will? Or were we, the soldiers, being lied to and made fools of as well? It all seemed so fucked-up. . . .

After reading about the Chicago riots, Dick and I went on an operation with the 44th, accompanied by the 52d. We were down in Hoa Binh, moving across open rice paddies, and right away we made contact. Trung made sure he was hiding safely whenever gun-fire rang out, but I had to hand it to him: He didn't withdraw but kept his troops moving forward, all three companies deployed on line. At one point a long burst of RPD fire from a hidden position swept through the trees over our head, and Trung threw a shitfit, scrambling into a ditch, then laughing at the close call.

Then a long flurry of RPD fire broke out, five hundred to a thousand meters off to our right front. "Who the fuck is that? The Fifty-second is over there, right?"

"They're supposed to be, sir, sounds like they've got their tit in a wringer." Muffled explosions, from grenades or mortars, were now mixed in with gunfire, and then we could hear the answering fire of M-2 carbines and .30 caliber machine guns with which the Ruff Puffs were armed. They were outgunned, no question, but at least they were firing back. The two lead companies in our battalion were about three or four hundred meters to our front, and Trung was talking to them on his radio.

Then I got a call from the 52d. "Tiger, this is Silver Knight, over." Silver Knight was a young Lieutenant Matheny, new in prov-ince and in-country, whom I had met only once at the club.

"Tiger. Go."

"This is Silver Knight. We have fixed a Victor Charley unit; they are staying and fighting. But if you can come up on our left, then we should be able to trap them against the river. Over."

I pulled my map out of my pocket and flipped it open on my knee. A sudden gust of chilly wind filled with heavy rain made me turn my back. I quickly scanned the map, seeing that a watercourse two or three kilometers long was shown on the map between us, and there was also thick underbrush several hundred meters wide indi-cated. "Roger that, Knight, it looks like we've got quite a barrier between us. If we can't find a path through that, we'll have to hump three or four clicks before we can support you. Lemme check with the locals, be back in zero-five, out." I turned around and saw Ha twenty meters away. Dick stood with him, but Trung and his boys had disappeared. I started striding toward Ha. "Hey, Ha, where is Trung?" He gave me a perplexed look, then pointed off to his right. As I approached him, I saw a small hut I hadn't noticed before. "C'mon, Ha." I strode toward the hut, Ha and Dick in tow, yelling as I walked. "Hey, Dai Uy Trung! Dai Uy Trung!"

I rounded the corner and almost ran into one of Trung's lieuten-ants, coming out the door. I stopped, sensing an opportunity. I grabbed him by the sleeve and pulled him over against a tree, as Ha and Dick caught up with me. I opened the map and pointed at the watercourse between us and the 52d. "Ha, ask Trung Uy if there is some way we can get through this stuff. Is road or trail or path not shown on map? Tell him we must get there beaucoup fast."

Ha ran it off in a hurry, and the Trung Uy nodded, pointing with his finger at the map. "Yes, suh, he say dere is small road en breech ova wata, dis place." The Trung Uy was now pointing vehemently toward the tree line three hundred meters away, then tapping himself on the chest. "Suh, he say he live dis place, he show way."

"Okay, great, wait a minute." I took the horn from Dick. "Silver Knight, this is Tiger, over."

"This is Silver Knight, over." The gunfire was raging now.

"Tiger, have found a guide and a way to get through that barrier. We should be moving directly. Are you taking incoming mortar fire? Over?"

"This is Silver Knight, negative on that, but we're pretty pinned down. Would appreciate your coming up on our left flank; then we got him. Over."

"Roger, on the way, out."

I went into the hut and found Trung sprawled in a hammock strung between the two vertical roof supports, his satraps squatting docilely around him. I stopped and waited until Ha came hurrying up behind me. "Ha, tell Dai Uy Trung we must go this place, now. Beaucoup VC, and the Fifty-second says if we come fast, we trap VC." I was gesticulating at my map, then laid it out on the floor. I took care to indicate precisely the point we would pass through the brush and over the watercourse.

Trung looked down half-interestedly as Ha rattled off what I had said. Then he waved his forefinger from side to side, saying something to Ha. When he was through, he lay back in his hammock and closed his eyes while Ha translated to me. "Suh, Dai Uy Trung say no way to go dis place, is many trees, no road. He say we wait dis place, mebbe VC try to exape dis way. Den we shoot."

That mealymouthed, candy-assed coward! He just doesn't want to get wet! An edge of fury crept into my voice as I spoke to Ha. Trung's eyes opened, and he slipped up in the hammock until he was almost sitting up. "Ha, you tell Dai Uy Trung that there *is* a way through the trees, and I've got somebody to show us how to go. And tell him that the Fifty-second is fighting hard and needs our help, and I know we can get there. So if we don't go right now, then tonight, when this is all over, I'll tell Colonel White, and he'll tell Colonel Tran that the reason we didn't go to help the Fifty-second was that Dai Uy Trung refused to go. And we'll see how he likes *them* apples!" Trung listened silently to Ha's quavering voice.

When Ha was through, Trung stood up, then snapped something to his radio boy, who came scrambling over. He delivered a curt message into the handset, then strode outside and started off to the right, his minigoons scrambling to keep up with him. I was still pissed-off, but at least I had gotten some action out of Trung. Ha was jogging off to my left and a little behind me, and then I heard Dick on my right: "Looks like you finally got 'im off 'is ass, sir." I turned and looked into his wide grin and had to smile myself. The gunfire had really slacked off now.

"Well, let's just hope we get there before it's all over. Sounds as if the party's breakin' up anyway."

On my left front I could see one of the companies moving across rice paddy dikes. As we got to within a hundred meters of the edge of the jungle, the first company had about half disappeared in single file down what had to be a narrow path, and the men of the second company were just arriving at the jungle's edge, milling around with their friends from the first company. I blew out a long, slow breath of anger at this. If a mortar round or a hand grenade or even a burst of AK fire ripped through that crowd, they deserved it. Fuck! They knew the rules; they were just oblivious to them. What the hell to do?

Suddenly cries went up from the group within the wood line, and they started tumbling back into the clearing as if they had seen a ghost, screaming and babbling to each other. The gunfire had grown hotter now, but it was still more than five hundred meters away. I turned and asked Ha what had happened. He said he didn't know but ran to catch up with Trung and find out. He was still talking to him when we reached the edge of the jungle, and the point man came scrambling out of the jungle, wiping the sweat from his forehead and neck in a most ostentatious way. "Ha, what's the matter, did he get shot at?"

Ha turned, now only ten meters away. "No, suh, road has bomb trick."

Dick was right behind me. "I think he means a booby trap, sir."

Ha looked perplexed, trying to think of how to express the idea. "Ha, you mean booby trap, bomb buried under road?"

"No, suh, bomb on stick, string on tree, when solja walk, hit string, bomb esplode, boom! No mo solja."

"You mean a booby trap." What the fuck should we do now? The gunfire was still churning. I reached for the radio horn.

"Silver Knight, Tiger, over."

"Tiger, this is Silver Knight, over."

"Tiger, we have arrived at that barrier I spoke of earlier, but it seems to be booby-trapped. I'm going up to check it out but we'll probably be delayed. Over."

"This is Silver Knight. Roger that, but we could sure use your firepower, we still can't move. Over."

"Tiger, roger that, doin' the best we can, hope to be there soon, out."

Well, fuck, let's take a look at this booby trap. "Ha, tell the point man I want to see the booby trap." There was quite a bit of stumbling and jumping around, and finally the point man went back to the path at a point where it led into the heavy brush, beckoning to me to follow him. We crept down the narrow, winding path for perhaps fifty meters. Finally, at the edge of a sharp turn the point man froze and pointed around the corner. I edged my body out to a position where I could see around the sharp turn, and there, sure enough, was a wire across the path at ankle level. The point man burst past me and ran back in the direction we had come. Then I was alone in the jungle. What to do now? The MACV rules we had learned at Di An strictly forbade disarming booby traps. Too many people had died that way since the traps themselves were often booby-trapped; you think you have disarmed it, and you set off something bigger nearby that blows your shit away. The rules were that you blew all booby traps in place. But how the fuck could I blow this one in place? You couldn't even see the fucker until you were five meters away, and that was just plain too close. If I turned back, and we went around the watercourse, we wouldn't get there for another hour, and then it would probably be over anyway. But now I had really put my ass in the wind. I had crept down this path alone with the point man, and if I came back sheepishly with nothing but the agreement that yes, the trail is booby-trapped, let's go around, I would have lost enormous face in front of every Vietnamese private, and they all would laugh themselves silly over that American Dai Uy who talks so big but doesn't have any balls. Well, I at least had to take a closer look.

I slipped to my knees, then to my belly. Slowly, slowly I crept down the path, studying every vine, every leaf, every clod of dirt.

Jesus, what the fuck am I doing? I don't know the first thing about booby traps or how to disarm them. All I can see is that wire in front of me.

When I got to a point where I could have reached out and grabbed it, I froze again, then looked down it to the right. It seemed to be tied around a small sapling just off the trail on the right. Then I looked to the left. My heart was genuinely in my throat, and my breathing came in short, shallow gasps. I could see the wire disappear into a bush, and I crept closer, running my eyes along it, now less than six inches away from it. The cold sweat of terror ran over my brow and down the back of my neck. Please, God, don't let me fuck up; I don't want to die. Lemme see, now, remember, don't touch anything. They've got pressure detonators, and release detonators, and push-pull detonators. Christ, they've got you coming and going; this time I'm really gonna eat it. I moved my head slowly, gingerly along the wire to the left.

Then, suddenly, I saw it! Behind the bush the wire was attached to a U.S. M-48 hand grenade! I breathed a small sigh of relief. At least it wasn't a five-hundred-pound bomb or an artillery shell—if that was *all* there was. I carefully moved my eyes along the wire. It was hooked over a rubber band that was around the grenade. The pin had been pulled, and the rubber band held the spoon on. I see, someone catches the wire with his foot walking down the trail, pulls on it, which pulls the rubber band off, and that allows the spoon to fly off, and four seconds later it explodes. Okay, that looks simple enough. Now, is *that* booby-trapped, too, so that if I grab it and hold the spoon on with my hand while I take the wire off, something else will blow? I slowly moved my eyes the length of the wire, off the trail on the right, taking care to touch nothing. I looked really close at the way the wire was wrapped around the sapling, noting that it was simply wound around itself, then abruptly ended. No other hand grenade, no other traps apparent. I slowly moved my eyes back down the length of the wire and saw no other connections.

Now, what was holding the grenade in place? I drew my face to within six inches of the grenade, then saw that it was wired to what looked like a stake driven into the ground. Hunh! That looks pretty straightforward! I can just pull that fucker out of the ground, and then we can walk down the path. Hunh! Wait a minute, now, not so fast, think this one out 'cause we're playin' for all the marbles. What else could happen? I stopped and stared at it, listening to my trip-hammer heart and my harsh breathing. Well, I couldn't think of anything. I listened for a moment. The gunfire had slackened, but there was an AK or RPD burst, then another one. Silence. Then a long RPD burst. Fuck, time's awastin'.

I carefully, cautiously extended my hand above the grenade, then slowly lowered it. I gripped that cold hunk of steel for all I was worth, tightly squeezing the spoon to the body of the grenade. Then I started twisting my hand, loosening the short stake in the ground. All at once it gave and came up free in my hand. At the same moment I suddenly realized that it might be seated on a pressure-release detonator on top of a buried five-hundred-pound bomb. My heart stopped. I was sure I was dead because of my stupidity! I waited with bated breath, a second, then two, then three, then four. Nothing happened! My hand and arm were shaking, but I had actually disarmed the booby trap. It was nothing sophisticated, just a hand grenade and a trip wire. I unhooked the wire from the rubber band, threw it to the ground, then started back down the trail. I still wasn't completely safe. I could still fall down, or my sweaty hand could slip, and the whole fucking thing could just spontaneously go off and blow me away. I had never before or since walked so carefully, all my attention devoted to the lethal load clasped in my sweaty palm. Then I was at the edge of the jungle, walking back into the clearing.

I heard Dick's voice. "Whyncha try ta undo the fuse, sir?"

"Good idea."

I stopped and very gently tried to turn the spoon. Then the seal broke, and I slowly unwound it, separating it and the fuse from the killer body of the grenade. After a few revolutions the heavy metal body filled with C-4 explosive clunked heavily at my feet, and I threw the spoon and fuse twenty feet in front of me. It fell to the wet ground, and all the Vietnamese soldiers around shrieked and scrambled away. Four seconds later it exploded like a cherry bomb. I bent over and picked up the explosive body, its stinger now pulled, then turned and looked for Ha. He stood twenty meters away, shaking like a leaf. "Ha!"

"Yes, suh."

He came running over, and I held the defused grenade out for him. The acrid smell of cordite still hung in the air from the blown fuse. "Here, give this to one of Dai Uy Trung's men; tell him to get rid of it. Then tell Trung the booby trap is gone; we can move down the trail."

"Yes, suh." Ha looked around him, suddenly lost, but already the first company was streaming back down the trail. I felt a relief that it is difficult to describe, as if my life had magically been restored to me. My throat felt dry and parched. I grabbed my canteen and took a long pull of water, then another. I walked around a little, trying to look as if I were studiously observing the movement but actually grateful, saying little prayers of thanks. When Dick called me softly, I turned, noting that it was now our turn to enter the jungle, following Trung's group.

After crossing a narrow footbridge over a stream, I turned and held out my hand to Dick, who filled it with the handset. "Silver Knight, Tiger, over." No answer. Moving through the jungle now, I could see the clear sky of open spaces no more than fifty meters to the front.

The radio suddenly came to life. "Tiger, Tiger, this is Silver Knight Oscar, over." His sergeant. Something must be up. "Silver Knight Oscar, this is Tiger, go."

"Tiger, this is Silver Knight Oscar, Silver Knight is hit. We are all alone, could use some help. Over."

"Tiger, roger, how bad is he? Over."

"Silver Knight Oscar, he's hit in the leg, I think it's broke. Like I said, our allies done split. Appreciate it if you could come get us. Over."

"Tiger, roger, we're just comin' out of the woods. What's your location? Over."

"Silver Knight Oscar, I can see your troops, am poppin' smoke at this time. Over."

I depressed the key instantly. "Don't do that; you'll mark your location for the bad guys." Too late. I could see yellow smoke billowing up out of a clump of trees a few hundred meters away. "Silver Knight Oscar, I see yellow smoke. We're on the way, out."

I handed the handset back to Dick, talking to him as I did so. "Call Ringmaster and tell them we need a dustoff for an American, would ya, Dick? Hey, Ha, where's Dai Uy Trung?"

Ha appeared on my left. "He ova dere, suh." Ha pointed to a clump of reeds by the edge of the paddy, and I strode toward it, Ha running to keep up with me. Then I saw Trung sitting at the edge of a dike, drinking from his canteen. Motherfucker's probably takin' a nip of booze, I thought, pissed-off and frustrated.

As I approached him, I turned to Ha. "Ha tell him an American is hit with the Fifty-second. I need a platoon to go with me and Trung Si Lightner to help them."

Ha turned and spewed something to Trung, who instantly answered him. Ha turned back to me, that old frightened look spread across his face. "Suh, he say all soljas in Foty-fo busy dis place. No can send to Fifty-two."

"No, Ha, just tell him I need some men to go with me, in case we hit VC." The 44th was lined up on their bellies at the crest of a high dike, occasionally shooting back, but for the most part just hiding from the VC fire. The area we would have to cross was open, but most of the distance could be covered if we crouched over behind the other dike.

Ha was talking to Trung, who gave a curt reply, not even looking up. Ha turned to me again, trembling now. "He say no can do, sorry, suh."

That asshole! I turned on my heel and strode away. I had gone two or three steps when I turned back to Ha. "C'mon, Ha, you're comin' with us. Tell Trung we go Fifty-second, by the smoke." I turned and walked away, furious.

Dick fell in beside me, still talking on the radio. We had covered no more than twenty meters when he talked to me. "Dustoff is on the way, sir. Should be here in about twenty minutes."

"Okay, Dick, thanks. I think we'll be okay if we stay behind this dike. I see two dikes we'll have to cross, but we'll all run over them together when we get there, shouldn't be any problem."

The rain had stopped now; but the sky was still overcast, and in spite of the slight chill in the air, I was starting to sweat freely. That prick Trung wouldn't even send a squad to protect his fucking adviser! White was gonna hear about this! I devoted all my attention to covering the ground as quickly as I could, hoping that no VC squad would beat us to the yellow smoke. We crossed the two dikes uneventfully, and although there were occasional rounds zipping over our heads as we moved, I was sure they were just stray shots. We entered a clump of trees, and I immediately saw a pale-faced sergeant standing nervously behind a tree with an M-16 in his hands. He turned to us as we approached, and then I saw a body stretched out at his feet, moaning. The sergeant sounded relieved. "Jesus, it's good ta see ya, sir! Dintcha bring no Ruff Puffs?"

"Just my interpreter. Fucking asshole battalion commander wouldn't send any men with us!"

"Well, I know what ya mean, sir. Fuckin' Fifty-second started takin' casualties, and then they just hatted up and split! Lieutenant Matheny here was tryin' to stop 'em when he got hit."

"Well, the dustoff is on the way."

I bent over Matheny, whose eyes were closed. "How you feelin', Matheny?"

His eyes opened. Tears were welling up and trickling down his face. "Not so good, sir, I think I broke my leg."

"Well, the dustoff is on the way, but we're gonna have to carry you a ways, get you out of the woods and out of the line of fire." I stood up and looked around. There was another high dike a hundred meters or so to the rear, away from the enemy fire. "Okay, we're gonna have to carry him some. Let's try to get over that dike there. Sergeant, you and I'll carry his shoulders. Dick, you try to carry the leg. And try to be gentle." We stooped and put his arms over my shoulder and that of the sergeant, then slowly lifted him. A sharp cry told us we had made a wrong move. Then Dick was able to lift both legs, and we started to move. After about twenty meters we got to a small trail that led to the dike, and the going was easier. Matheny was biting his lip and occasionally emitting grunts of pain. The poor guy was in agony. We walked as quickly as we could, trying not to hurt Matheny any more than necessary.

After a few minutes we made the crest of the dike, then gently laid Matheny down on the other side. His sergeant had torn Matheny's pants open where the bullet had gone in and tied a bandage over the wound. The bandage was soaked with blood, and more blood ran through it and onto the ground. I took the bandage off my own LBE, then bent over him. I had to cut the first bandage off with my knife, then tried to wrap the new one around the wound. Shattered bits of bone were all around the large exit hole on the front of his thigh, and I could feel a smaller hole on the bottom of his thigh, freely bleeding. What the fuck do I do? First, I stop the bleeding. Matheny's eyes were closed, and he was moaning softly. I detached the shoulder strap from his M-16, then slipped it under his leg. I pulled it as tightly as I could, but the bleeding continued. Christ, he must have lost a lot of blood since he got hit. I took his sheath knife out of the holster on his hip and slipped it through the sling, twisting it to form a tourniquet high on his thigh. I turned the tourniquet tight, then tighter. The bleeding stopped, just as if I had turned off a faucet. I heard a banging noise in the background. Then Dick bent over me.

"Dustoff is comin' in, sir. I just talked to him. Gonna pop smoke 'n' bring 'im in."

"Okay, Dick, tell 'im we need a stretcher and some albumin. This guy's lost a lot of blood."

I looked back down at Matheny. His eyes were still closed, and he was breathing more softly now, not even moaning. I hoped he wouldn't lose the leg. Then the noise was louder, the blades of the helicopter swirling purple smoke all around me. I held my hat on with one hand and the knife-tourniquet with the other and, squinting my eyes, turned to watch the slick settle in thirty meters away. When it touched down, two men jumped out and came running toward us, one holding a folded-up stretcher. One flopped down next to Matheny and almost instantly slipped a needle into his arm. It was attached to a long plastic tube, at the far end of which was a clear bottle of albumin. The other medic had opened the stretcher, and the albumin bottle holder handed it to me, indicating that I should hold it aloft as they put him on the stretcher. Silver Knight Oscar took it from me, I held on to the knife handle as they picked him up, and the four of us trundled over to the slick, ducking as we ran under the hammering blades. While they loaded the stretcher, I leaned over to the medic and yelled in his ear, *"Put the tourniquet on zero-five ago. Lost a lot of blood."*

He nodded, then turned and yelled in my ear, *"It's okay, we'll have him in the hospital in about one-five. He'll be all right."*

I stepped back. The medic vaulted into the slick after the stretcher, and the helicopter jumped into the air, beating its way powerfully up and off to the left, toward Can Tho, some seventy kilometers away. I stood there with my feet rooted to the ground as the slick slowly slipped from sight, its roar now only a faint banging in the distance.

A quiet voice snapped me back to reality. "Okay if I go in with your people sir?"

"Huh? Oh, yeah, sure, Sergeant. Hey, what's your name anyhow?"

"Sergeant Martin, sir."

"Okay, Sergeant Martin, just hang with us, we'll get you in somehow. Let's try to get back over to the Forty-fourth right now."

"Okay, sir. Looks like ol' Lieutenant Matheny got him a clean ticket home."

"Yeah, he won't be comin' back to the Fifty-second. He's goin' back to the World."

We fell into silence, trudging along. There was no more gunfire now, and I could see and hear the loud troops from the 44th along a dike that was at right angles to us a few hundred meters away. Cold raindrops hammered the bill of my baseball cap, soaking my shoulders, trickling unheeded down my neck and over my shoulders. Then Dick was at my side. "Sir, I reported that the dustoff was completed. They advised that the operation's bein' terminated. Dai Uy Trung's got the word. We'll be extracted from a road back where the Fifty-second come from."

"Okay. Why don't you tell 'em Sergeant Martin here is with us now?"

"Already done that, sir. They also said Colonel White wants ta see ya when we git in."

"Yeah, well that's great 'cause I wanta see him, too."

We continued to trudge on, then rounded the end of the dike and melted into the mass of milling bodies. I saw Trung twenty meters away, then went over to the base of the dike, slumping down into a deep squat and rubbing my face slowly with both hands. I smelled the strong odor of blood and realized that both my hands were still crusted from working on Matheny's leg. Well, hell, if Colonel White wants to see me, I'll go in wearing blood; no sense gettin' pretty for him.

Ha came up and told me Trung had killed two VC while we were with Matheny and he wanted to show us the bodies. I stood up and stretched and started to wearily walk after Ha's bobbing figure. Then I saw Trung, standing triumphantly over two prostrate figures clad in black pajamas. He was laughing with the milling diminutive figures who always surrounded him. He saw me and raised a hand exultantly. "Dai Uy, Dai Uy, look you, VC! VC! Me shoot!" I walked up to the VC, both of whom lay on their chests. I stuck my toe under the arm of one, then flipped him over on his back. He was dead, all right, with a bullet hole through the front of his neck. Trung was now holding two weapons in his hands, an AK-47 and an SKS bolt-action rifle, and shaking them victoriously in front of him.

He ran off another mouthful to Ha, who turned to me with that same hesitant look. "Suh, he say he . . ." He was struck for the word, and I tried to help him.

"What, killed the VC and captured these weapons?"

"Yes, suh, he say he surry you go becuz afta you go, VC attack. He keel dem wif he own raffle."

I looked over at the triumphantly grinning Trung. He wore a

small revolver in a flap holster at his side. The only time I had ever seen him fire a rifle had been at sparrows. I thought there was not the slightest possibility that Trung had actually killed these two. But someone clearly had, and he was taking the credit. Well, what could you do?

"Okay, Ha, tell Dai Uy Trung very good, well done, I call in report to American headquarters." I turned to Dick and called the body count in to Ringmaster.

We moved out in Trung's wake, walking for no more than an hour, until we came to the string of trucks on a dirt road. Norm was waiting for us in the jeep. The rain had stopped, but the sky was clouded over. Much of the blood that had covered my hands had been washed off in a watery red rinse, and the rest had dried and was now crumbling off. But my pants and shirt were still splotched with dark brown stains of dried blood, and there still was an awful lot of blood on my forearms. We rode through town in silence. When we arrived at the compound, I turned to Norm. "Norm, you can take Dick home. I've gotta see Colonel White. I'll call you on the radio when I need a ride."

"Okay, sir."

Dick climbed into the front seat, and Norm backed around.

I turned and walked up the stairs into the building, down the halls, and around the corners until I stood in front of Jim Claiborne's desk. "Hi, Jim, understand Colonel White wants to see me."

"Yeah, he's goin' through paperwork now. Go ahead in."

I walked over to the colonel's office door and knocked twice.

"Come in!"

Well, here we go. What can he do, send me to the Nam? Send me to the line? I walked in and stood in front of his desk. "You wanted to see me, sir?"

"What's the matter, Capain Carhart? Don't you salute or report to your commanding officer anymore?" Frost and fire came out his mouth as he fired that machine-gun burst of words at me.

Oh, boy! Hang on tight, here we go! I slipped my heels together, straightened my body to an approximation of rigidity, and slowly raised my bloody hand to my brow, looking straight ahead at the wall above White's head. I drawled my report out as slowly as I dared. "Sir, Captain Carhart reports to Colonel White as ordered."

He snapped a quick salute at me. "At ease. Sit down." I sat stiffly in the gray folding metal chair at the side of his desk. "I've got some very bad reports about your actions today, Captain Carhart."

I was stunned. "From who, sir?"

"From Dai Uy Trung." I looked down at my feet. Of course! That little asshole! "He says you did a whole bunch of things that are either against the rules or very insulting to our Vietnamese allies and make us look bad. For instance, he says here that you disarmed a booby trap by yourself, against his advice. He said that he told you it could be blown in place, but you wanted to act like a hero, so you disarmed it yourself. Is that true?" I sighed deeply. That skinny little prick!

"No, sir, it's not true. I mean, it's true that I disarmed a booby trap; but it was in order to get through a thick growth of jungle, and there was no other way. We were trying to get over to support the Fifty-second. They had a contact, and I was trying to get there as fast as we could. We had to go through a strip of jungle, and all of a sudden the troops came screaming back down the path, saying there was a booby trap. And Trung, without even looking at it, said we'd go around it."

"So why didn't you do that?"

"Here, sir, I'll show you." I pulled my map out of my thigh pocket and opened it on White's desk, rainwater and bits of crap scattering over it, bringing a frown and a grimace to his face. "Here, sir, the contact was here, with the Fifty-second, and Lieutenant Matheny asked us to come and help him out, so maybe we could trap the VC force against the river. We were over here, on the other side of this green strip and stream. Well, as you can see, it runs about two and a half clicks farther to the south, and another five or six to the north, behind us, back the way we had come. Now the map doesn't show it, but there's a trail right about here that cuts through the jungle and a bridge over the stream. We had just started down the trail when the point man came to the booby trap, and they all came runnin' out of the woods, screamin' like wild Indians. I went down the trail, and I found that it was just a wire tied across the trail, attached to an M-forty-eight hand grenade. All I did was pull the grenade out of the ground, take the fuse out, and let that blow. Then we all moved down the trail and hooked up with the Fifty-second."

"Well, I don't know what they taught you at Di An, Captain, but it's a direct violation of MACV rules to disarm a booby trap. You're supposed to blow them in place. Didn't you know that?"

"Yes, sir, but it just wasn't possible here. You couldn't even see the grenade until you were less than five meters away. So I couldn't have shot it, and I didn't have fifty feet of string to tie to it and yank when I was a safe distance away. And time was important, sir. We had to use that trail, and I had to make a decision right away. I did, and it worked."

"That's no excuse, Captain. You should have blown it in place or gone around it. You used poor judgment, and you broke the rules. You're lucky you didn't get killed, but you were wrong in what you did, dead wrong!"

I sighed and looked down. What could I say? If I had taken the easy way around, then we might not have gotten there for hours! And Matheny might still be lying there, might have bled to death, might have been overrun and killed or captured by the VC. Sergeant Martin, too.

"Dai Uy Trung also says that you yelled at him before this, embarrassed him in front of his men, called him a coward and humiliated him. Then he says that later you showed yourself to be the coward, and he personally killed two VC after you and your sergeant ran away because you were afraid. What about that?"

Jesus Christ! I sighed deeply. "Sir, I think we've got some real problems. First of all, when Trung says I yelled at him and called him a coward, that was after Lieutenant Matheny had called and asked for help, and then I took one of Trung's lieutenants aside and told him through my interpreter where we wanted to go and asked him if there was a trail. He said there was and offered to guide us. Then I went inside this little hut where Trung was layin' in a hammock, drinkin' out of that canteen he carries booze in, and I told him about the contact. He said there was no trail, and we had to stay right where we were, in case the VC came running toward us. I told him that I knew there was a trail, and I showed him where on the map; but he still refused to move. So then I told him that if we didn't even try, I was going to report that to you, and you'd surely tell Colonel Tran, and that did it. He popped up and ordered the moveout. And then, after we got through the jungle, I got a call from Sergeant Martin, with Lieutenant Matheny, sayin' that Matheny was hit and that the Fifty-second had abandoned them. The firefight had virtually ended by then, so I asked Trung for a squad of men to go with me and my own NCO over to Matheny's position, which was only three or four hundred meters away across rice paddies; but he refused, so finally I left with just Sergeant Lightner and my interpreter. We got there, and Lieutenant Matheny had gotten shot through the thigh, and I think the bone was broken. He bled like a stuck pig, as you can see"—I held up my hands demonstratively—"but I put a tourniquet on, and then the dustoff got there and took him away. We went back to Trung, taking Sergeant Martin with us, and then Trung had two bodies and two weapons, which he showed to me, grinning like an idiot, saying that I had run away, and he had killed the two VC himself—which, by the way, I don't believe for a heartbeat, but there were the bodies, so I called the body count in."

I finished talking, and we sat in silence for a few seconds, Colonel White drumming his fingertips on his desk, staring out the window. Finally he sat up in his chair and looked at me. "Well, you may be interested to know that Lieutenant Matheny is all right, and he did get his thighbone broken, so he'll be going home."

"That's good to hear, sir."

"Yes, well, that still doesn't clear you for that booby trap incident. I think you were grossly mistaken in your judgment on that, and you did break the rules. And the rules exist for a reason."

"But, sir," I protested, "I was the main man on the ground, and sometimes the rules *have* to be broken! And I was the only one who could tell close up what was possible and what wasn't."

"That may be, Captain, but I told you, you certainly could have gone around."

"But, sir, what if we had? Do you think Lieutenant Matheny would be dead now, or would he just be a VC prisoner? Him 'n' Sergeant Martin, after they got abandoned by the Fifty-second?" I had him there.

He hesitated for a few seconds. "Why couldn't you have broken a new trail through the jungle for ten meters or so and gone *around* the booby trap position?"

He had me there. It was something that had never even occurred to me. Now it was my turn to hesitate. "Sir, I—it was—the jungle was just too thick, sir. We couldn't have done it." My ass, I thought. I just hadn't even considered that obvious move.

"Well, I can't imagine jungle so thick you can't wade through it with a whole battalion of men for ten or even twenty meters; that wouldn't have slowed you up much. Still, there's no sense crying over spilled milk. Dai Uy Trung is mad as hell. He may be an incompetent, but there's nothing that can be done about that right now, he's the commander. He has already said, over the radio, that he won't allow you to go to the field with him again, but Colonel Tran thinks we can calm him down."

He drummed his fingertips on the desk for fifteen or twenty seconds, looking down. Then he stopped and looked up at me. "I want
you to take an in-country R and R. I wanta get you out of province
for a week or so. By the time you get back maybe things will have
calmed down. Go see the first sergeant; tell him I told you I want
you to leave on the first flight to Saigon tomorrow morning. From
there, I think you'll go to Vung Tau, but call back in about a week
and check in with Captain Claiborne, got it?"

"Yes, sir."

"Okay, I still think you were wrong about that booby trap, and
I'm not just kidding around. From now on play by the rules. But all
in all, I think you did pretty well today. I may even put you in for a
medal for that dustoff action."

"A medal, sir?"

"That's right."

"But, sir, I didn't *do* anything."

"Well, you let me be the judge of that. Now get out of here and
forget the war for a week." He was smiling now.

"Yes, sir." I soared out of his office.

Proust

WHEN I ARRIVED at Tan Son Nhut airport in Saigon next morning, I lined up at the "in-country R&R" counter. I was soon scheduled to leave on a flight to Vung Tau later that afternoon. Vung Tau, known to the French as "Cap St. Jacques," was a coastal town that had apparently been a resort town forever. It wasn't as good as going to Hong Kong or Bangkok or Sydney for a week, but a four-day stretch there was better than nothing!

There was a wide, sandy beach with water-skiing, fishing, and skin-diving facilities; there was horseback riding; there were plenty of American movies being shown—hell, they even had skeet shooting, crazy as that sounds. Looking at their brochures, I was convinced that anyone using the skeet ranges needed to have his head examined. But most important, there were plenty of bars, all booming with the latest sounds from back in the World, and all overflowing with clouds of gorgeous Vietnamese hookers, whose heavenly sensual services were available for a truly modest fee. The town was carefully insulated from the war on a peninsula: No weapons allowed, no violence, no worries—it sounded great! But as I waited for the flight, whatever temptation I felt gradually faded as I thought of Jacqueline and Kinou.

After lunch, I told the NCO behind the counter that something had come up at my unit and asked him to hold my name for a couple of days, assuring him that I'd get back to him. He wrote my name on a slip of paper, put it in a special folder under the counter, and smiled as he wished me well and assured me that I'd have a slot open if I came back within a month. But other than that, I was off their books and on my own. I smiled back as I thanked him, then headed for the main PX. Sometimes it was a real asset to be a captain in the army.

I bought some civilian clothes in the PX, and a case of duty-free liquor. I purchased several bottles of the finest French wines, liqueurs, and, of course, champagnes: What the hell, live now, for tomorrow we may God-knows-what. And since I would be living it up with a Frenchwoman, the champagne was a perfect finishing touch.

Jacqueline was surprised and delighted when I arrived around six, and simply had Thi Teu stretch the dinner she was already preparing. Kinou was all joy and laughter, and soon I was rolling on the floor with him, playing away. Then I showered, changed into civilian clothes, and we had an elegant meal, highlighted by the wine I had brought.

The champagne was still chilling in her tiny refrigerator when Jacqueline and I put Kinou to bed. Thi Teu had disappeared, leaving us alone sipping Grand Marnier as I tried to explain my presence. I had told her right away that I'd be staying for a week, which both she and Kinou found wonderful news. Now I was fumbling, not sure of what I felt or what I should say. I told her I felt my love for her growing, but there were problems, the difference in our ages not being the least of them. . . .

She silenced me with her soft fingers on my lips. *"Je sais, Tom, je sais."* She told me she understood everything. Then she told me of a European tradition, built on centuries of war raging across the countryside. It was very common there for an older woman to adopt a young soldier, to become his *marraine de guerre* or "godmother of war." She would write him letters, send him cookies, knit mittens for him in the winter, do her best to take care of his psychic needs, giving him the hope of a safe base, a refuge from the storm. And sometimes, if they were together, she would offer him the flowers of physical love. It was a wonderful tradition, one she felt she was fulfilling with me. As much and as long as I needed her, wanted to love and be loved, she would be my angel. But the moment I left, she knew it was over, and that was the way it was. Ours was one of those nonpermanent relationships in life that would be as full and as deep as we wanted it to be, nothing more, nothing less.

I was amazed by her candor, her sensitivity, her love, her full, radiant, deep beauty. I pulled her close and kissed her, softly at first, then with mounting passion. She gently raised her arms and stopped me, looking deep into my eyes. "Remember," she said to me in French, "that whatever happens to us this moment, this week, can never be taken away, and will burn brightly in my heart forever. Nothing that came before matters, nor anything that might come later. For now, and in this moment forever, I will love you as fully as man can be loved by woman."

I was stunned and felt myself dissolving. I too, I told her, would love her as much this week as woman could be loved by man. In a burst of passion, we made love right there on the couch. Afterward, I brought an icy bottle of Moët et Chandon champagne in from the kitchen while Jacqueline turned over the record. She nestled under my arm as we touched glasses and soared up to heaven together with the opening clarinet solo of Gershwin's "Rhapsody in Blue." Truly, I was *chez moi.*

Jacqueline began telling me the story of the madeleines as related by Marcel Proust. Madeleines are a simple sort of sweet muffin, and Proust wrote about how the taste of one as an adult instantly awakened memories of his early childhood. As I listened, I recalled the sweet tang of freshly picked raspberries and sun-splashed memories of preschool joy at Grandma's farm in Eagle Mills. Proust, Jacqueline told me, used madeleines to show how we wrap time and reality around ourselves and all of life as a sort of malleable cloak that is far more controllable and changeable than we consciously realize.

As she talked, I became fascinated, and then thirsted beyond all reason to read his work. I begged Jacqueline to dig his books out, and after a brief search in her bedroom, she handed me two paperback volumes entitled *À la recherche du temps perdu.* These were only two volumes, she told me, out of a total of seven or eight. But these, *Du côté de chez Swann,* would give me a full sense of his ideas.

That was a Monday night, and before we went to sleep Jacqueline promised to take Friday off, that we might have a long weekend together.

Tuesday morning, hugs and kisses, then I was left alone. I poured myself a huge mug of coffee, ensconced myself comfortably in a corner of the couch, and opened Volume I: *"Longtemps, je me suis couché de bonne heure . . ."*

It was a deep and complicated book, but it fascinated me. My French was not as good as I had thought, and I soon began jotting down a list of page numbers, marking the margins where I would ask Jacqueline for clarification. Each evening, after Kinou was asleep, we spent hours going over Proust and his thoughts, and I was astounded by the shallow, unquestioning nature of the life I had lived. I challenged so little, I accepted so much; truly, my dreams had been too firmly limited by what others had told me. . . .

By Thursday night, I had finished Volume I and had read about twenty pages of Volume II. And I had skipped over so many confusing sections of the first volume that I was embarrassed. But Jacqueline only smiled and told me that many before me had found Proust to be stormy water. I swore to myself to finish it before returning to Kien Hoa, as an intellectual exercise, if nothing else, for someone whose education had focused too much on numbers and not enough on life. For the first time, I began to regret my limited exposure to literature, to the thoughts and dreams recorded by others who had passed this way before me.

But this long weekend belonged to the three of us. On Friday morning, Jacqueline released Thi Teu until Monday, and I took a cab to Tan Son Nhut, where I replenished our liquor supplies. I went heavy on the champagne.

I was back before noon, and Jacqueline had prepared a picnic lunch in a basket. I wrapped a bottle of white Bordeaux wine in a tablecloth, and the three of us strolled down the avenue. The sun was warm on my face as we ambled along, Jacqueline under one arm, Kinou skipping and dancing before us, the personification of laughing, bubbling innocence and joy.

We came to a small park, and after walking around ugly coils of barbed wire, I spread the cloth on the grass and we lay down. French bread, pâté, Brie cheese, grapes, a glass of wine—what more could there be to life? Other children were in school, adults were working, and we were alone except for the indolent South Vietnamese troops who seemed to be just hanging around the street corners. But in my civilian clothes, I pretended not to notice them, and they seemed not to notice us.

When we had finished eating, I kicked a soccer ball around with Kinou for an hour or so, while Jacqueline sat quietly knitting. Then the sky clouded over, and raindrops sent us scurrying back to the apartment. That evening, several other teachers from her school stopped in for a drink, and while I was delighted to be so completely immersed in a French-speaking world, I was happy when they left. Jacqueline and I went to bed early and drowned in lovemaking.

We spent most of Saturday indoors at the Cercle Sportif while the rain came down. Well rested, I was delighted and stimulated by hours of conversation with and about the French. Kinou was happily playing with friends from school, and when it got dark and people began to leave, I was sorry. We ate supper in a restaurant with two French couples who were friends of Jacqueline's and a slew of children. Then we went home and put a sleepy Kinou to bed. After a glass of brandy, Jacqueline led me into her garden of delights.

On Sunday morning, we went to mass in the huge cathedral only a few blocks away. We went to the late service celebrated by a French priest whose Latin lines, from my own Roman Catholic altar-boy childhood, were as familiar to me as my own name. As I sat there in civilian clothes, listening to his sermon in French with ostensibly my own French family beside me, I began to feel confusion over my immediate future. Another afternoon socializing with delightful French people, capped by another passionate night with the woman who was now truly my French lover, was beginning to have its effect: Did I really want to go back to being an American soldier at war?

But on Monday morning, I knew my week was up, and reality returned. As soon as Jacqueline and Kinou had left for school, I put my clammy fatigues back on and walked around the block to the Majestic Hotel, where I was able to use the military phone to call Captain Claiborne in Kien Hoa. He told me the moment for my return was not yet right, but probably would be within a few days. He asked that I check in with him each morning.

I went back to Jacqueline's, changed back into civilian clothes, and started anew on Proust, Volume II: *"Ainsi revenait-elle dans la voiture de Swann . . ."*

I was antsy in the evening, and my questions about Proust were hurried and perhaps superficial. Jacqueline sensed my growing tension despite my denials, and soothed my cares away. That night, we reached new heights of ecstasy.

Tuesday morning, Claiborne told me probably Thursday. The cancer in my belly began to swell, and I focused intently on Proust. That evening, Jacqueline told me that she would take Wednesday afternoon off for another picnic while Kinou stayed in school.

Wednesday morning, Claiborne told me that, indeed, Thursday was the day when I would be expected back in Kien Hoa. I gritted my teeth, skipped the big, complicated chunks, and plowed through the rest of Proust. I heard Jacqueline come in the door as I raced through the last page. I saw her shadow, silently waiting, as I read the last line aloud: *". . . et les maisons, les routes, les avenues, sont fu-gitives, hélas! comme les années."* I clapped the book shut as I stood up, and we embraced. I was trembling ever so faintly.

She packed our picnic lunch as I told her I had to go back the next morning. I was trying to explain how much I had gotten out of Proust as she came out of the kitchen and put her arms around me, then silenced me with a finger on my lips. She held me for a moment, then returned to the kitchen. She came back with the picnic basket on one arm, holding a cold bottle of champagne aloft in her other hand, a loving, enigmatic smile sweeping me behind her as she swirled quickly out the door and down the stairs.

We were alone in our park; even the South Vietnamese Army guards on the street corners were unnoticed. As we ate and drank, she told me she knew this was the last time she would see me, and that was good. Her fingers on my lips quickly silenced my protests, and I let her talk. I would be going back to the States in just a few months, she said, and I had a bright future before me that would surely include a loving wife and wonderful children. What we had together could never last, wasn't meant to last. But she was happy and grateful that I had shared a piece of my life with her, however limited. It was better not to drag it out, she said, to let this week we had spent together serve as the capstone to our love that she would always treasure. She asked me not to tell Kinou when he came home that I would never see him again, he was too young to understand.

She drained her glass and asked me to pour her a refill. I did, then she leaned forward, held my cheeks in her dove-soft hands, and gave me the sweetest, gentlest kiss of my life. She pulled her head back slightly and whispered that she was glad I had read Proust, that perhaps now I would understand her when she said she would love me as much as woman can love man this moment forever.

I choked up. Then I tried to blurt out my feelings, but her fingers on my lips quickly silenced me. Don't talk, she said, just think about what I have said, and you'll know that I'm right. No regrets, no melodrama, just a bright, happy moment that would live in our hearts forever.

She smiled her enigmatic smile, and I smiled with her. I managed to tell her how magnificent this time had been, and our smiles were beyond control. We finished our champagne in silence. I was happier then than I had ever been, and Jacqueline had given me memories for a lifetime. *Quel beau geste,* I thought, *quel beau geste.*

We finished the champagne and walked home arm in arm.

Kinou was there, and I felt nervous playing with him, but covered my confusion with laughter. After supper, that tired little boy's fight to stay awake soon failed, and we tucked him gently under the covers. Then Jacqueline took me to her bed for the last time.

I was awakened by the morning sun through the window as Jacqueline slipped out of bed. I turned over and dozed, but Kinou's laughter seemed to be calling me through a fog from the kitchen. When she came back in, I rolled onto my back and opened my eyes, and she bent over and kissed my lips quickly. Then she stood back up, smiling as brightly as I had ever seen her. *"Au revoir, mon amour,"* she whispered, blew me a kiss, whirled out the door and was gone.

She said *"Au revoir,"* which means "until we meet again," sometime, somewhere, rather than the dreaded *"Adieu,"* which means "Good-bye forever."

I slept for another hour, then got up, shaved and showered, and dressed in that familiar olive-drab suit. I left a note on her dresser that said: "I love you as much as man can love woman this moment forever." I took a cab to Tan Son Nhut, and was soon flying back to Kien Hoa.

Debriefing

DICK WAS WAITING in our jeep at the airport. As we rode into town, I asked him how things had gone in my absence.

"Well, shit, sir, we've only been on two operations since you left. They got in a big cluster fuck yesterday afternoon, stayed out all night, we got a bunch of our troops killed, didn't get any of them. Lieutenant Carmack 'n' Norm were out there, spent the night in a rice paddy. They're gettin' a big pep talk at the compound right now."

"Holy shit, what happened?"

"Ah, it seems they stumbled into a main force battalion on their way to the Coconut Grove for R and R. Somebody fucked up, and they didn't know where our operation was goin' on, and we just walked into it. Ol' Colonel Tran wanted to trap 'em until this morning, when he thought we could get some tac air in to do a number on 'em, but they just slipped away durin' the night."

"Jesus Christ! What's Jerry say?"

"Ah, he's all pissed-off at Trung. Wait'll you talk to him; he's really bullshit."

"Okay, let's go right to the compound."

There was a crowd of jeeps in the parking area, so Dick left ours on the street. There was a sort of sunken area on the back side of the house, covered with an opaque glass roof. Chairs had been set up there, and it looked as if all the advisers in province were sitting there, raptly listening to Captain Claiborne read statistics on ammunition consumed, artillery fire, other administrative bullshit. Dick and I slipped down the stairs and tiptoed up to Jerry and Norm, who sat in the next to last row. I silently slipped into an empty seat

251

next to Jerry, then stuck out my hand to both. They whispered greetings.

I turned my attention back to the stage area as Dick sat down next to me. Jim Claiborne had just called Captain Roberts, the province S-3, to the stage. Roberts looked a little too Prussian for my liking, back ramrod-straight, fresh, tight fatigues with sleeves rolled just so, short white-wall haircut, one of those stateside ascots, artillery red, making him look that extra touch spiffier. My resident bias against artillerymen as REMFs masquerading as grunts was intensified before he even opened his mouth. And when he did, the deep voice that boomed out belied his almost frail body. He was a good speaker, though, and gave what I had to admit was an excellent pep talk, going over the statistics with emphasis where necessary: "And while it's true that we suffered seven dead and thirty-two wounded and recovered only four VC bodies, I can assure you, with all the firepower we put into their position, they dragged away a lot more dead bodies than we did."

He finished his talk with a flourish, a fist upraised for emphasis. He held the pose for a few seconds, then turned and stepped back from the edge of the stage. Again silence. Then everyone began to stand up and drift off. There were occasional shouts of greeting, a burst of laughter here and there, muffled curses—the usual army postbriefing noise.

I stood up and stretched, then turned to Jerry. "So how was it?"

"Unbelievably fucked-up. C'mon, let's go home, I'll tell you all about it." It was a quarter to five as we walked out through the slackening rain and got into the jeep. Jerry drove, so he could sit in front and talk to me, and Dick and Norm jumped into the back seats. I started to talk as we pulled back out onto the street. "So tell me about this operation."

"Aw, Christ, it was typical Trung shit. We were on one of those safe 'search-and-avoid' sweeps, with the Fifty-second up in front of us, going by a big clump of woods. A couple of our boys from the right-hand front company were goin' through it, not expectin' anything, when they walked into a fucking hornets' nest, RPD fire up the ass, and two of 'em got killed right off, a whole bunch shot up. We still didn't know what was goin' on; this was around four o'clock, when we were almost in sight of the trucks. Anyway, they came runnin' outa there lickety-split, and ol' Tran happened to be upstairs in a slick he got from Can Tho for the day, so he landed near us and told Trung to get his troops lined up on our side of the woods, behind a dike that ran about fifty to a hundred meters away from the woods, depending on where you were. So we get all lined up, and we're throwin' all kindsa fire into the woods and gettin' a lot back.

"Meanwhile, Tran was on the horn to the Fifty-second, and he got them all lined up on the other side of the woods, and then he got some more ash-and-trash troops, you know, bridge guards, town defense platoons from Hoa Dong and Hoa Binh, the PRUs, I don't know what else, and then, by about five-thirty he was sure we had them surrounded. Christ, there was a lot of fire comin' outa those woods, and Tran was runnin' around, almost frothin' at the mouth, and his G-two had told him that he thought we had a VC main force battalion trapped. Then he called in artillery, and they fired eight rounds of one-oh-five in there, but then that was all they had, so he sent his helicopter back to Can Tho, pleading for an emergency re-supply of one-oh-five ammo, even though it was gettin' dark. We had the fuckers surrounded, although I can't believe it was a battal-ion, unless they were standin' on top of each other, probably more like a heavy or reinforced company. Oh, yeah, they had at least two fifty caliber machine guns in there, and they were keepin' a lot of heads down.

"Anyway, just at six o'clock, as it was gettin' dark, the slick was coming back to pick Tran up, to take him back to town. Before they got back, they called on the radio and said that they couldn't get the ammo in until the next morning, but it was loaded on trucks, ready to go. So Tran took Trung aside and told him that he was in com-mand through the night, that he was supposed to hold the bad guys in, and then Tran left. No sooner did he leave than all the fire stopped, and about half an hour later it was just like old times: The troops were standin' up, walkin' around, laughin', and talkin'. I tried to get Trung to tell them to shut up, but Trung was doin' the same thing; he said the VC have to sleep, too. So there was this is-land in the dike, you know, one of those raised areas about twenty or thirty meters square where the farmers store their grain and keep their water buffalo, that kinda shit, you know?"

We were driving past the Jade Pool now. "Anyway, the troops started gathering in little groups there; nobody wanted to stay be-hind the dikes or in the paddy waters, God forbid. So they're gath-erin' in little groups, and Trung is up there with 'em, walkin' around, laughin' and talkin' with them, and then they started lightin' *fires,* fer chrissake, and cookin' their supper! I really got scared at this, and I sent Ha to tell Trung not to pull this shit, but Ha came back and told me not to worry, Trung said he knew what he was doin'. Now Norm and I were on the dike about twenty meters away, and as soon as Ha came back with that message, we moved another twenty meters away and got down—they weren't gonna get my ass!" We stopped in front of the house and started to walk in. "So we're just layin' there, and things are gettin' louder, laughin' their asses off, musta gone on for half an hour. Then, all of a sudden, two RPDs open up from the woods and just blew the fuck out of 'em. They got two more killed and a whole shit pot wounded."

As we walked in the house, a smiling Jesse came out of the bedroom and greeted us. I noted a slightly pudgy Vietnamese woman, looked maybe thirty years old, busy mixing something in a skillet on the stove. "Hi, sir. This here's Co Lun, our cook. Supper'll be ready soon."

She turned to me and smiled, a round face flashing a lot of gold and ivory. *"Chau, Dai Uy."*

"Chau, Co." I casually wondered if Dick and/or Jesse were fucking her. Jerry had gone into the bedroom with Norm to dump his weapon and field gear, and I followed them. "So what happened?"

"Oh, so Trung comes stormin' by me with all his little buddies, and most of the idiots on the island were followin' him, so Norm and Ha and I did, too. He went about another hundred meters away from the woods, and he came to a farmhouse, which he just barged into. When I got there, he was inside the big dirt bomb shelter all the gook farmers have built into their houses, and he wouldn't come out. I sent Ha in, and he came out sayin' that the VC had launched an attack, and he was havin' one company come back to this house to use as a ready reserve in case the VC tried to get out. Then Norm and I and Ha went back to the original dike, and there was nobody there, so we went down the dike about two hundred meters, with no one there, until we finally came to the left-wing company. These guys were bein' pretty good, stayin' behind the dike, but there was a lot of laughin' and ass grabbin' goin' on, even though we could hear a lot of gunfire from the other side of the woods, where the Fifty-second was. Anyway, we settle down, and at least it's not rainin', and we start to eat cold Cs.

"Then, after a while, we're lookin' back at that island where we had been 'cause we hear all kinds of noise comin' from there. After about twenty minutes of hearin' hoots and laughter and calls from down there, we see a fire, and then another, and pretty soon, there's five or six fires goin' down there. I got the company commander we were with to put a call on the radio to whoever was down there and tell them to put the fucking fires out. And he calls them up, finds out it's a platoon from the right-wing company, and he's talkin' to some guy there when, all of a sudden, those same two RPDs open up again, and there's a lot of screamin' and then silence. By this time, the fires are out, but, I was just fuckin' disgusted! Norm and I stayed there all night, took turns sleepin', and when I was on watch, around two A.M., I hear more laughin' and grab assin' from the island, and I look down there, and there's three more fires, bigger'n shit. But I just ignored 'em, and finally, at first light, around six, everybody gets up, and Trung comes back to the dike with his company, but there's not a peep from the woods. We just sat around for a couple hours, and then, around eight-thirty, the one-oh-fives open up, and they fired about twenty or thirty rounds into the woods. We stayed out while the Fifty-second came through the woods on line and got on our side, but there wasn't shit in the woods. They said that they had gotten four bodies on the other side, but I never saw 'em. Anyway, they brought us back into town, got here in time to have lunch at the compound, where I heard there was a lot more shit goin' on, especially where the PRUs were hooked into the Fifty-second. Apparently the VC tried to bust out there during the night but bounced off and went back to the woods. Obviously the second time they tried, they went through a big hole, maybe the hole in our line, I just don't know."

"Jesus!"

"Well, shit, you get what you pay for. Then we got called in the afternoon and told there was gonna be a big debriefing at fourteen hundred hours, so Norm and I went down there, and you walked in at the end."

"Hunh. So basically, it was just the Forty-fourth and the Fifty-second out there, right?"

"No, shit, no, I told you, Tran got every swingin' dick in a uniform he could find out there. There must have been ten or twelve American advisers out there. Colonel White had a mobile operations center over with the Fifty-second; he really thought they were gonna trap a battalion of VC, but I guess they showed us a thing or two."

Jesse came in from the kitchen. "Supper's ready, sir."

"Okay, Jess, thanks. C'mon, Jerry, Norm, let's eat. Sounds like you guys had quite an experience out there."

"Fuck me, sir!"

We all laughed as we sat down, and then, as we were finishing our second helpings, Jess jumped up, mumbling through his full mouth that he had forgotten something, and went back into the bedroom, returning with a handful of letters for me. "This came in the mail for you while you was gone, sir."

My heart leaped up—mail! For me! I carefully leafed through the letters. They were all from my family, a letter from my parents in Tokyo, one from my little sister, Brita, who lived with them there, one from my sister Sally in Boston.

I cracked a Budweiser and withdrew to my bunk, AFN playing softly in the background. I read Brita's letter first—earnest, concerned teenager, high school cheerleader, trying to bring some cheer to her big brother who was off in the war—and I could tell from the tone of her questions and comments that she thought I was being shot at all the time, had to hide in a hole at night. Well, there had been a time, but no longer! Still, I had to chuckle at her youthful concern, and the love that flowed out of her letter warmed me inside. I put it aside and picked up Sally's letter. She was ten years older than Brita, and her status as a young adult came through in her message. She was worried about my safety and tried to show her concern but in a way that wouldn't come across to me as a challenge to my own feeling of manhood—a sort of withdrawn, approving, caring emotion. It was mostly a message of support and—glimmering through some of her carefully chosen lines, when she spoke of how she explained my present existence to friends and neighbors— pride. I put her letter with Brita's, to be reread later many times, but now for Mama!

She tried to treat me as a grown man, a warrior off on a challenging adventure of his own choosing, but it didn't come through as cleanly as had either Sally's or even Brita's attempts to cloud and disguise deep emotions. Mother was so worried that after a few sentences, she descended directly to the fears that visited her constantly for me, with entreaties to wear my military rubbers when I went to school in the rain. It was a long letter, mostly newsy, but interlaced with emotional support, fear of the unknown, and promise of prayers that she hoped would ward off all evil and keep me safe until I was returned to the secure guardianship of her watchful eye and warm embrace.

I sighed deeply as I finished, wondering if the boxes of Bering cigars that she kept sending and that theoretically followed behind as I kept changing jobs would ever catch me. Christ, there must be at least four boxes that had been sent out like pigeons in my wake and still flowed behind me, moving at the panic-free velocity of army administrative leisure. Unless, of course, the enlisted mail clerks had discovered what the uninsured boxes contained, in which case they were even at that moment being smoked. Or, of course, unless one of the pony express riders had ridden into an ambush, in which case the local VC commander was taking his ease, helped along by those coronas royales. Well, hell, *c'est la guerre!*

I wallowed in homesickness, but finally, trying to rid myself of the burden of all this turmoil, I stood up and went to the door. The rain had stopped, so I pulled on my cap and stepped out into the full dark, heading for the club.

When I arrived, I found MAT 85 at the table in the corner with Red. The laughter they shared soon snatched me up, and I dismissed all my silly thoughts. The only life to be concerned about was here and now in the Nam, right here on the ground in Kien Hoa. This was to be a night of cutloose, free exhilaration, reinforced by the knowledge that tomorrow might bring the rubber bag. I drank and laughed a lot that night, closing the club after two and somehow making it back in safety and crawling into bed.

The next day Colonel White called me in to his office for a pep talk and a warning. He emphasized that I was in a position to advise, not to command. Trung was the commander, he reminded me, and his word was law. It was most important that I not interfere with his command function or even make it look as if I might. I was there if he needed me, but until I was called on, I was to maintain a low profile and keep my mouth shut. I said nothing.

After that life slipped back into the traditional tedium. "Search-and-avoid" missions dissolved into each other without distinction as the rainy season brought deeper rice paddies and wetter walks. And the rain came down.

Phoenix

ON ONE PARTICULARLY UNEVENTFUL OPERATION we had stopped in a cluster of farm huts, and Trung had disappeared with his satraps. I had taken refuge in one house with Dick and Ha.

Suddenly there was an uproar in the clearing on the other side of the nearest house, soldiers laughing and shouting exultantly, yelling something about VC. I turned to Ha, my eyebrows asking him what was up. He shrugged as he answered, "Don' know, suh, dey say sumting 'bout catch VC."

We all stood up and walked around the house, arriving as Trung himself did. There, twenty meters away from us, five or six of his soldiers were pushing a young girl, wearing black pajama pants, a white blouse, and a conical straw hat. I stayed put, not wanting to get involved, and turned to Ha. "Ha, go see what happened."

He walked over to the group, where one soldier was now talking with Trung. More howls of delight, this time with pushing and shoving. Trung disappeared into the house again as Ha came back to me. "Suh, dis gul VC, se hide in hole, dere, sojas find, bring dis place. Dai Uy Trung say ask her questions, make her drink wata until se talk."

"What?"

"Suh, you know, dey make her take wata in face until se talk."

"Oh." I turned to Dick. "I guess that means they're gonna torture her until she talks. Better call in the fact that we took a prisoner."

"Okay, sir."

We had been told in advisory school to discourage torture; but as Colonel White had reminded me, I was not in command, and he had told me to ignore theft, rape, arson; I guessed that torture was included among the crimes I was not to notice.

Dick and Ha and I squatted under the tree and watched as they tied the girl prisoner's elbows behind her back. Her hat had fallen to the ground. They forced her onto her back in the mud and pulled her head back until it was flat on the ground. Then two men stretched a strip of cloth over her face, holding her head back on the ground by maintaining pressure on both ends. Two other men knelt on her upper arms, pinning her tightly on her back. Two more men carried a heavy urn of water over to her, held it over her face, and tipped it until a steady stream of water spilled onto the cloth that covered her face. She immediately began to thrash, kicking wildly and trying to wrench her head out from beneath the cloth. But the men held her tightly in position, and the water kept pouring down on her face from the enormous urn. I quickly realized that while she might be able to hold her breath for twenty or thirty seconds, eventually she'd have to breathe through the cloth, and she'd have to breathe in the water. Obviously, from her wild lunging, it must be horrible.

They poured for what seemed like two or three minutes, just to make sure that she got a good dose. Finally they stopped pouring, and the cloth was taken off her face. She coughed and choked as she continued trying to tear herself free, to no avail. A first lieutenant leaned over her face and shouted several questions down at her. She just kept choking and writhing from side to side, refusing to meet his eyes. He stepped back and, with a wave of his hand, indicated that the torture should resume. They threw her head back down on the ground, covering her face with the same rag.

The pouring and thrashing resumed. How sensitive these barbarians can be, I thought. I stood up and turned my back, starting to walk away. I felt nauseated when I heard the lieutenant yelling behind me, intermingled with her choking and her soft responses. I turned around and saw that she was sitting up now, talking as she choked, her dark face turned to crimson around her flat nose. So they got her to talk. What the fuck does she know, some little secretary or messenger?

I turned away again and paced around, joined now by Dick. He spoke softly to me. "I'd like to git one a them little fuckers that's so brave torturin' girls in a dark alley, sir. Show 'em a thing 'er two 'bout bein' a man." I nodded but felt so sick that I couldn't say anything.

We turned and trudged the several hundred meters to the row of trucks, where Norm was waiting in the jeep. "How'd it go today, sir?"

"Shitty. No contact, but they captured a teenaged girl they said was VC, so they tortured her until she talked."

That seemed to stun Norm, and he was silent for a few seconds. "Did Dai Uy Trung know about this, sir?"

"He ordered it. Anything happen in town today?"

"Oh, yes, sir. Colonel White called Lieutenant Carmack in this morning and told him the same things he told you, not to do anything on operations but walk along, not try to volunteer any help. Then he said we wouldn't be going out on an operation again for at least a week or ten days. Seems the Forty-fourth is gonna get M-sixteens day after tomorrow, and it'll take at least a week for them to go to the range and learn how to take them apart and clean them."

"Hunh. Well, that suits me just fine."

When we pulled into the Ponderosa, Jesse and Jerry were eating in the kitchen: fried hot dogs, bags of Fritos stolen from God knows where, and cans of fruit cocktail. It wasn't bad, and we told the story of the little girl getting tortured again. Jesse, who had two teenaged daughters, was revolted.

As we were eating lunch, Red knocked on the door and asked me to step outside for a minute. He told me he was trying to organize a group of Americans to go out with him and a group of his Hoi Chans to hit a VC "safe house" where, according to his intelligence reports, two VC big shots from out of province were staying with five or six bodyguards. He said that if I would agree to go along with him and some Hoi Chans, he knew of about six other Americans who would come.

"How would Colonel White feel about this?"

"I think he knows what I'm doing but I'm not going to rub his nose in it."

"When do you wanta go?"

"Tomorrow night, before those guys move again."

"Well, the timing is good—we don't have another operation for the next week or so."

He grinned. "I know."

"Actually, I'm gettin' pretty tired of this Mickey Mouse 'search-and-avoid' crap with the Ruff Puffs, and we saw some pretty rotten stuff today. Okay, I'm in. What time?"

"Twenty-two hundred hours tomorrow night. I'll show you

where we're goin' on the map, then we go do it. Can we use your jeep?"

"Whoa, hold on, Red. We'll bring our jeep, but what about a rehearsal?"

"What's that?"

I smiled. "Boy, you really are new at this. We've got to run through it first, Red; maybe in your backyard after the map check. Wait a minute." I turned and yelled in the front door: "Hey, Dick!" He came out, and as we filled him in, he was eager to play. "And Red, when you recruit these other Americans, tell them to paint their faces and the backs of their hands with green and black camouflage sticks, bring their M-16s with one bandolier of ten magazines, and one canteen of water. Twenty-two hundred tomorrow."

"Okay, Tiger. Do you want to be the commander for me?"

I shook my head. "No, Red, Phoenix is your show. You've gotta stay in command, but I'll be there to help you out. Don't worry, you'll do fine."

The next twenty-four hours flew by. I had told the others in MAT 85 the broad outlines, that we would be going out with Red and some others on an operation, but no one else was to know about it. We all went to the club after supper as usual, but Dick and I drank Cokes, and around nine, we slipped back to the ranch. We painted our hands and faces with green and black camouflage sticks, then drove over to Red's with our weapons, bandoliers, and web gear.

When we walked into Red's house, we saw a number of camouflaged faces we had just seen naked in the club, and we smiled conspiratorily, shaking hands and slapping backs without much comment. Red showed us on the map where we were going, then started to fold up the map, but I stopped him.

"Hey, Red, what about a rally point?"

"What's that?"

"Jesus! Well, in case something unexpected happens and everything blows to shit, we wanta set up rally points where we can reassemble later. Here, let's make this trail intersection we pass through a click before the target our only rally point, other than that, meet back at the jeeps."

In addition to me, Dick, and Red, the other Americans were a captain, two lieutenants, and three sergeants. The captain and one of the lieutenants wore Ranger tabs on their shoulders, so I knew they'd be all right. I was a little antsy about some of the others, but we were only moving on trails to a specific target house, and even the Americans who were a little green should have no problem; they had enough balls to volunteer to go outside the walls at night, so I was sure we'd be all right. I was further reassured by the five Hoi Chans we had, who used to go on night strikes all the time.

Even though this was Red's show, I helped him as we went out back and formed up in position for movement. One of the Hoi Chans was the point man, a position he was used to, then Dick, then another Hoi Chan who was a former platoon leader, then me, then Red, then an American sergeant carrying the radio, then the others. I put the Ranger captain next to last, so he would run our maneuver element if we hit anything on the trail. Then I coached Red as he walked us through slipping up to the target house, moving into an L shape some thirty meters from it, and blowing it away. I was pretty satisfied as we loaded ourselves into the jeeps.

We arrived at Hoa Bo before midnight, left our boots in the jeeps, and moved out in bare feet, just as Vietnamese farmers did: Boots were too noisy and far too heavy in the steady mud. After a couple of hours, we reached the target house, but crossed sticks on the trail had signaled to our alert Hoi Chan point man that the house was empty, as it proved to be. It was a tedious and frustrating walk back to the jeeps.

The next run was scheduled two days later, this time in Hoa Dong, up north of the Madame Nhu houses. For this trip, Red insisted on adding one new American lieutenant and two more Hoi Chans, for a seventeen-man team. I argued against it, but he was the boss, and he really wanted the extra firepower, so I relented. But I didn't like moving with so many men—in the dark it would be hard to keep track of who was on our side if we got fired up. When we reached the target house, we found that it had collapsed, partially burned down; not a soul around. What rotten intel this had turned out to be! The long walk back to the jeeps again was very frustrating.

The next evening Red told us that his intelligence reports all said that the two big shots had split up and were now traveling around province separately, with two or three bodyguards each, doing political recruiting and holding award ceremonies for some of the local VC. A number of us suggested breaking down into six- or seven-man teams, and he agreed that was probably the smart thing to do. He had gotten several reports that day on one of our targets down in Hoa Binh, and would probably want to try to hit him within the next few days. I volunteered to go with Dick, and Red said he wanted to tag along. I hesitated.

"Okay, Red, that's fine, but if we're going to do this in a small group—just us and maybe three Hoi Chans—I want to be in charge. Nothing against you personally, but I think Dick and I have done more of this than you, and I want to call all the shots. You'll be just another rifleman, okay?"

He smiled and nodded. "Okay, this is your baby; I'm just an extra rifle. Why don't you two come over to my place tomorrow afternoon around four? I'll have more intelligence by then."

"All right, we'll see you then, but on this run, I want three Hoi Chans, including the point man we used, and the platoon leader, and one other."

The next day, just for variety, Dick and I had lunch at the mess hall in the main compound, then drove back to the ranch. When we walked inside, Jerry and Jesse and Norm were playing Monopoly. "Hey, where didja get that?"

"First sergeant gave it to us. Wanta play?"

By a quarter to four Dick, Jesse, and I were on the verge of bankruptcy, all our property mortgaged. Jerry was hanging on, doing okay, but Norm had hotels on Boardwalk and Park Place. I glanced at my watch and called a halt to the game. "Wait a minute, duty calls! I declare this game suspended. Dick and I are going on an operation tomorrow night for Red and the Phoenix program, but nobody can find out about this, understand?"

"What're you gonna do?"

"Never mind, we're goin' out in the boonies with some Hoi Chans, just like before, and we've gotta be over at Red's house at four. I'm tellin' you this only in case we don't come back; at least the rest of the team'll know we didn't desert. I'll tell you more about that tomorrow night. For now nobody says anything about that, got it?"

Solemn nods around the table.

Norm spoke up. "We gonna finish the game tonight when you get back, sir?"

"Shit, you asshole, you're ruthless, aren't you?"

"No, sir, I just like to win, that's all."

"Nah, shit, I concede, Norm, we all concede. Maybe we'll play another game tomorrow."

"We've gotta give the game back tomorrow, sir."

"What?"

"That's right, sir, it's the only one in province, and we get it for only a couple of days at a time."

"Well, we'll see about that, but right now Dick and I have got more important games to play. C'mon, Dick."

It started to rain again as Dick and I made our way over to Red's house. We walked into his office, where he sat at his desk, looking at a large map. "Hey, guys, you're just in time. C'mon over here and look at this." We gathered around him at his desk. "Okay, we're down here in Hoa Binh. If you follow this main track out of Hoa Binh for about four or five clicks, you come to this main canal. Now you go along the canal—there'll be a path on top of the dike—about four clicks, you come to a little cluster of hooches, right here, see that?"

"Yeah."

"Okay, now a couple hundred meters off to the southwest here, on this little trail, there's an intersection with another trail—it's not shown, but it's right about here. There's a farmhouse at that intersection, and nobody lives there; it's a safe house for VC cadre. We've had three reports, since yesterday morning, that one of our targets is stayin' there. Two separate groups of VC leaders visited him last night. And there are either two or three other guys there with him, probably bodyguards. How's that sound?"

"How reliable is this intelligence?"

"Oh, it's usually pretty reliable. But this time we've got three independent reports on this."

"Okay, sounds good. What about the Hoi Chans? Can you get AKs for 'em?"

"Yeah, I got three, but two of 'em would rather carry M-sixteens if you can pull that off."

"Shouldn't be any problem. I'll bring 'em over tomorrow night, twenty-two hundred. Short rehearsal, then we go."

When we got back inside our house, the other three team members ran back to the table like so many kids. The Monopoly board was all set up and ready to go.

"All right, Norm, this time *I* get the fucking dog!"

"All right, sir, but I get the race car." We were quickly involved in the game, and when Co Lun arrived to make supper, we all were totally engrossed. We ate over the board without even looking up. By eight o'clock Jerry and the shoe had blown us all out of the water. There was minor fussing over this game, and before we went to the club, we agreed to play a rubber match the following day. I acceded to Norm's demand for the dog in advance. Once we got to the club, Norm and Jesse and Dick elected to see last night's movie over again, but Jerry and I sat on the back porch and drank beer. When Red arrived around ten, he joined us, and we strove valiantly to harmonize for an hour or so. Nothing was mentioned about the operation the following night, and when the movie broke up after eleven, we all piled in the jeep and went home.

The next morning I was up with the sun around six. After the usual morning ablutions Jerry and Jess went down to the compound to look for some reading material, and Dick and I walked over to the fish market on the other side of the main town square. It was a bustling, noisy affair, and we stood on the side, just observing. After a few minutes of this, we walked across the main street and sat down at a table on the sidewalk in front of a small café and drank bitter French coffee. We talked about the war in general terms, about the rumors that a peace was coming under a neutralist government, about the proposed combat jump that the 2d Brigade of the 101st was supposed to make, about rumors that the jump would be made onto the main airport in Hanoi, and that after they had taken that, the whole division would be flown in and would storm town. Even as we traded gossip like this, we knew it was bullshit, but it passed the time. We finished our second cup of coffee, paid up, and strolled back to the Ponderosa in a now-rare burst of sunlight.

The jeep told us Jerry and Jesse were back, and when we walked into the kitchen, they were arguing with Norm about who got the dog. The board was all set up as we took off our hats and sat down in our places, and I quickly settled the argument. "All right, Jerry, I did say last night that Norm could have the dog for the first game, but *that's it.* Somebody else gets it this afternoon, okay?"

"That's all right, sir, I only need it for one game to set myself up right."

"Okay, *roll!*"

We were quickly off and running, and with this last day of possession of the game, there was little thought of anything else. But after a while, Jerry and I managed to carry on a semiwork conversation while it was somebody else's turn.

"Hey, while Jess and I were scoutin' for books and magazines, I ran into ol' Captain Claiborne; he wanted to talk to me."

"Yeah? What'd he have to say?"

"Well, take your turn; then I'll tell you."

"Okay, wait. Seven. One, two, three, four ... Atlantic Avenue! I'll buy it."

"You haven't got enough money, sir."

"Bullshit, how much is it, two hundred?"

"Two-forty."

"All right, I'll mortgage, let's see, I'll mortgage the B and O Railroad and, uh, and the Waterworks. Now gimme Atlantic and twelve dollars. So what'd he say, Jerry?"

"He said the Forty-fourth is gonna be issued the M-sixteens tomorrow, and they've got a special ARVN armaments squad that's gonna teach 'em how to strip it down, clean it, and fire it. And they'll be startin' out to the range in Hoa Dong day after tomorrow, one company at a time. He said we should go out to the range and show our faces occasionally, but that we won't be goin' out on another operation for at least another week." Norm's dog had just landed on my mortgaged B&O railroad.

"You asshole!"

"Sorry, sir."

Jesse rolled the dice, and I turned back to Jerry. "Hey, Jer, okay it I borrow your M-sixteen tonight?"

"For what?"

I shrugged my shoulders. "I just need another M-sixteen tonight, that's all, and a bandolier of ammo."

It was Jerry's turn to shrug his shoulders. "Sure, I'm not gonna be usin' it tonight. Here, gimme the dice." He rolled snake eyes. "Fuck! Two! Community Chest!" He picked up an orange card from the stack in one corner of the board and read it to himself silently, then threw it disgustedly down. "Take a ride on the Reading. Who owns that, you, Jess?"

"Yeah, but it's mortgaged, so yer safe, sir."

"Whew! Hey, Dai Uy, I assume that if my weapon gets used tonight, whoever uses it'll clean it before I get it back."

Dick had just rolled a ten and landed on Boardwalk. "Fuck! That's you, right, Norm?"

"That's affirm, no houses, no hotel, that'll be fifty dollars, please."

"Aw, fuck!"

"Shit, Jerry, we use it tonight, I'll have it shinin' like a diamond in a goat's ass for ya tomorrow mornin', wait 'n' see." I rolled a seven, landing on Community Chest next to Jerry. "Well, let's see what we got here: 'Go to jail, go directly to jail, do not pass Go, do not collect two hundred dollars.' Shit, I'm just gonna stay there for three turns, there's gettin to be too many minefields around the board, and I need some money!"

Dick wouldn't let that pass. "Shit, sir, only way you're gonna make any money is ta balls it out and get by 'Go' a couple times."

Norm rolled a six, landing him on Park Place. "Park Place, I'll buy it. Now that means I've got both Boardwalk and Park Place, so here's another four hundred dollars; I'll take a house on each one, please."

"Hey, where the fuck you gettin' all that money from?"

"I been savin' it, sir, I let you guys fight over Baltic and Ventnor, and just lay back and wait for the big ones."

"Well, fuck, now I *am* gonna stay in jail for a while!"

By lunchtime Jesse and I both had gone bankrupt. Jerry was in deep trouble, with all his property mortgaged, but Dick had hotels on several properties. Norm was Daddy Warbucks, his holdings arrayed before him like so many carefully arranged crown jewels. The board was ringed with green houses and red hotels, most of which belonged to him. I stood up and stretched. "Well, you guys can knife each other in the gutter if you want to, but I'm goin' down to the compound to check the mail."

Jerry was quick to chime in. "Let's go. C'mon, Norm, game is called on accounta rain, three-way tie at the close, new game starts after lunch."

Norm squawked as he stood up. "Sir, that's no fair. I won, or I woulda."

"All right, you won, but you ain't gettin' that fuckin' dog this afternoon."

Norm shrugged, repressing his cat-that-swallowed-the-canary smile. "Okay by me, sir, I don't care what piece I use."

"You prick, you're gonna get to use a piece a shit after lunch. I'm gonna make you lean on it, too, so it gets under your fingernails!" We were laughing and jostling like children as we streamed out to the jeep through the sheets of warm rain, piling in and tooling down to the compound. We spent hours there, shooting the shit with the other bored advisers who were also sitting on their hands. The rain finally let up around two-thirty, and we drove home.

The game cranked up again, and we whiled away some otherwise deadly hours by watching the dice send us merrily down the pike toward the Great American Dream Machine. I got the dog and, just as anticipated, was starting to shoot into the lead when, at five-thirty, a jeep crumbled over the gravel and stopped out front.

Jess stood up and looked, then quickly returned to his place. "First sergeant, sir."

"Aw, fuck, I'll bet he wants the fuckin' game!"

He was knocking on the door, and Norm let him in. He took off his hat and turned his attention directly to me.

"Evenin', sir."

"Hi, Top, what can I do you for?"

"Well, sir, this is the only Monopoly game in province, and there's some guys that signed up for it that were supposed to get it this morning."

"Well, shit, I understand, but we're right in the middle of a game. Can't we get a one-day delay on that, give it to you tomorrow?"

"Well, hell, sir, I'd like to do that for ya, but if I did it for you, then I'd have to do that for everybody, and the people who're next—tell ya the truth, sir, Colonel White wants it. He's gonna teach Colonel Han how to play tonight, and he just sent me down here to get it. Otherwise, I'd let you keep it for as long as you want it."

"Take the fucker, Top."

I went in the bedroom and stalked over to the window, seething. As I looked out, I watched Top hustle out, game under one arm, and leap into his jeep. Then he cranked it up and was gone. I walked back into the kitchen, where the rest of the team still sat dejectedly in their places. "We got enough steaks left for supper?"

Jess jumped up and opened the refrigerator. "Shit, sir, we got fifteen or twenty left. We better start eatin' 'em 'fore they go bad."

"Okay, let's have a steak dinner tonight." I went back into the bedroom and flopped on my rack, pulling an old *Sports Illustrated* out of the duffel bag where I had stashed it. But I had barely started rereading it when the aroma of steaks cooking reached my nostrils. Soon we were eating, and the food did a lot to revive our spirits. After I had finished, I went over to Red's house, where I asked him for the latest intelligence. He had had one new report around noon that the VC political guy was still in the safe house. Word was out he would remain there for another forty-eight hours. Our strike was still on. I went back to the Ponderosa bedroom and lay down, having asked that Dick and I be awakened at nine-thirty. I slept like a log.

At nine-thirty I woke before Norm even touched my arm, quickly recovering my awareness of where and who I was. I pulled on my Tiger fatigues, then triple-checked my weapon, my bandolier, my knife, the two grenades I would carry in the waist pockets of my shirt. I pulled my boonies hat down over my eyes, ready to go.

Dick spoke his first words to me as I bounced up and down, making sure everything was strapped down tightly enough to be silently secure. "Dontcha wanta wear camouflage stick, sir?"

"Oh, yeah, almost forgot."

Dick and I painted each other's faces black and green with the thick waxy camouflage, then did our own hands, sleeves rolled down and buttoned tight. Like two ghosts, we stepped into the kitchen, where the three others sat idly playing poker for matchsticks. "Hey, Norm, I forgot to ask you, can we use your weapon and bandolier?"

"Sure, sir." He stood up and walked into the bedroom to get it.

"Same promise as for Jerry—we'll have it clean for you tomorrow." He shrugged.

At twenty-two hundred hours Dick and I went to Red's, where we had a map check. Two of the Hoi Chans knew this safe house and suggested a longer approach route to avoid sentries. We agreed to that, then walked through the attack in Red's backyard.

Red and the Hoi Chans climbed into his jeep, and Dick and I climbed into ours. There was a light mist, but we took the top down, so we could unass it in a hurry if need be. Dick didn't turn the headlights on, and the full moon strained through the heavy cloud cover cast more light than I was happy with. We soon left town and slowly wound down the trail to Hoa Binh. Red had called there earlier to warn the American team that some of his boys would be coming in a jeep so that we wouldn't be fired up. We stopped the jeep just inside the silent, unwalled town, and Dick and I took our boots off and threw them on the floor in front. The wet mud was cold on our bare feet as we started to creep down the trail. I was impressed by the stealth of the Hoi Chans; they were head and shoulders superior to the Ruff Puffs, but now they were on our side, and I felt good. And if we had managed to convert them, surely others would follow. One day, I thought, the good guys all would be on our side, and the VC would just disappear.

After an hour or so we turned south on another main trail. I was high and light inside, my adrenaline pumping furiously. I was conscious of that old feeling of controlled fear, dancing with death, that

I kept harnessed. It was a good feeling, all my senses alert to everything.

After another hour the point man stopped briefly, then stepped delicately off the trail to the right, threading his way through low underbrush toward a tree line a few hundred meters distant. We all followed silently, stepping through a narrow stream of cold water, then up into the stiff, short weeds that reminded me how sensitive my bare soles were. Inside the tree line the point man had stopped with the platoon leader. When I drew close to them, they signaled that the house was off to the left. I nodded and waved them on, and our stealth increased as we crept through the trees. After another few hundred meters we came to the edge of an open field. The platoon leader pointed to the dark form of a house some hundred meters away. I slipped the safety switch on my weapon to automatic as we moved onto open terrain and crept toward the house.

Halfway across the field I became aware of the noise of background radio hissing and a voice in Vietnamese from the house, obviously a radio transmission being received there. Low light outlined two window openings in the side of the house we were approaching. Then there was silence again, and the loud voice of someone talking, obviously sending out over the radio, could be heard. Then silence, the hissing radio noise, and another broadcast coming in. We were getting close now. We climbed onto a low dike, still thirty meters from the house. Just like our rehearsal, the men in front of me went off to the right. I followed them for ten meters or so, then stopped and got down, turning to look behind me. Red and the Hoi Chan who followed me had moved forward thirty meters, on the left side of the house, and I saw Dick moving past me, no more than ten meters away. Another garbled communication was coming in over the radio in the house. Then a metallic click told me it was being shut off. I turned quickly back to the house, in time to see the faint light in the windows go out and shadows move as a door facing us was opened. Then several figures moved out into our sight. We could hear their conversation as they came out, and I knew I could wait no longer.

I poured eight or ten rounds into them on automatic, the immediate supporting fire from weapons on both sides of me blowing death through the straw walls of the house. Two figures slumped to the ground outside the door, and I put the rest of my first magazine through the house at knee level, swinging my weapon from side to side to assure that no part of the grass-walled building was ignored.

I quickly jammed another magazine into place and put another ten rounds out below knee level, to get anyone on the floor, and put a few random bursts through at head level, then through the roof, just to make sure.

When my second magazine was expended, I seated another, chambered a round, and stood up. Within a few seconds firing had ceased, and I dashed forward, Dick on one side of me, the former VC platoon leader on the other. Then I was inside the door, the platoon leader pressing by me on my right. I pulled my flashlight out of my right thigh pocket and scanned the interior with the red beam. Two inert bodies lay on the floor. I saw the house bomb-shelter bunker, tossed my other grenade in it and rolled away. As soon as it blew, the VC platoon leader was peering inside it. He moved back toward me, shaking his head negatively as he came.

We turned to the two bodies on the floor inside. One of them was an older-looking man with what looked like thin gray hair. Red came up behind me as I grabbed his black pajama shirt and turned him over on his back. Pinned to his shirt was a brass star with a small hammer and sickle and some Vietnamese words below it, all bordered with red, no bigger than a silver dollar. I quickly undid it and stuck it in one of my breast pockets. Dick had stooped over the other body, then was suddenly beside me, his harsh whisper startling me. "Two outside look like just guards, sir, this un, too. Whatcha got here?"

"I dunno. I think this is our boy. Look at what he had on his shirt." I pulled the pin out of my pocket and showed it to Dick.

"Wow! Must be the guy!"

I pulled a small leather satchel out from under his body and leafed quickly through the papers that were falling out of it. There must have been more than a hundred pages, most of them typed, some forms, others just written on blank paper. "How many weapons we get, Dick?"

"Three AKs, sir. This old dude didn't have one."

"Yeah, okay, we gotta get outa here. What'd we miss?" I waved the flashlight quickly around the one-room house again. Then I saw the radio, a U.S. Army PRC 10 model, several jagged holes torn in it by our rounds. I pulled it away from the wall it was leaning against and looked at the frequency it was tuned to. "Looks like eighty-five point zero zero. Dick, remember that in case I get greased on the way back."

"Roger, sir, eighty-five point zero zero."

I looped the strap to the leather satchel of documents over my shoulder, then stood up. "Okay, let's go."

Red was still reading, so Dick went over to him. "Goddammit, stop reading! You can do that later. We gotta get the fuck outta here!"

Red obediently stuffed papers in one rucksack and picked it up. He may have been a captain, but Dick outranked him on this mission.

We moved back outside, and the VC platoon leader was instantly in front of me. Then we were moving back toward the tree line, the point man out in front where he should be. I was feeling full and cocky now but trying to bring myself down off this emotional high, just in case we ran into some shit. But it was hard to do, I felt so elated. Goddamn, but we caught 'em with their pants down! God*damn*! Four of those fuckers, three bodyguards and our target with a satchelful of documents. And Red had a whole rucksack full of stuff! What could they be? Pay records for the local VC? But then I didn't even know if they got *paid*! Well, in any case, it sure looked like we had nailed one of the two guys Red was after.

Now we had to get away from there in a hurry. There might have been a couple more bodyguards hiding near the trail intersection that we had crept around, and I didn't want to run into them. The point man understood that with no words spoken, and he was almost running through the woods and the weeds, then back up on the trail on the crest of the dike. We hurried through the farmlands. Then we were back at our jeep, exhausted but elated. I tied my boots on, then went over to Red and the Hoi Chans and clapped them on the shoulder, looking into each of their faces as earnestly as I could in the dark. "Good job!" I whispered to each one. "Good job! Good job!" They may not have spoken English, but they got the message.

I was so high I was ready to burst as I slipped into the front seat. Dick turned us around, and we headed back to town. Our ride was silent despite our elation; this was no time to drive into some shit. Lights out, we regained Kien Hoa city uneventfully and soon were driving into Red's compound.

I dropped the brass star pin and the satchel of documents on Red's desk, then Dick and I went upstairs and used soap, hot water, and washcloths to scrub the camouflage off our faces and hands. When we came down, Red was still reading documents from his captured rucksack. We went out to his garage and cleaned our weapons. The Hoi Chans gave us Jerry's and Norm's in like-new

condition, and we stuck our heads back in the door to tell Red we
were leaving. He was still reading.

"Hey, Red, we'll see you around noon!"

He looked up, startled, then remembered and smiled. "Yeah,
okay. Boy, we really got some g-o-o-o-o-d shit here. We got our
man, all right, and he had some stuff on him. C'mon over after
lunch."

I opened my eyes to the steady drumming of heavy rain on our
tin roof. My watch said that it was a little after eleven. Dick was the
only other person still in bed. I walked into the kitchen, where Jesse
and Norm were at the table, reading letters. "Mornin', troops."

"Mornin, sir, how'd ya sleep?"

"Okay, I guess."

"How'd things go last night, sir?"

"Good. Hell, great! We got four VC, and one of 'em was an old
big shot, wearin' a Communist party star pinned on his black pajamas."

"Goddamn, sir, sounds like you done okay."

"Yeah, I'd say we did. Hey, Dick!" A muffled groan from the
other room answered me. I walked back in the bedroom, reached up
onto Dick's upper bunk, and slapped him in the butt as I called him
again. "Hey, Dick, c'mon, get your ass outa bed. We got to get
cleaned up." After breakfast Dick and I headed for Red's.

We moved slowly up the steps and in the front door, past the
Vietnamese sergeant at the front desk and back to Red's office. He
was sitting behind his desk, shuffling papers. "Howdy, Red."

"Shit, what are you guys doin' up so early? It isn't even noon
yet!"

Dick and I laughed with him as we moved into his office and
closed the door.

"So how'd we do?"

"Oh, we done *great*! This is the biggest coup we've had since I've
been in province! That fuckin' guy we got last night is really a big
shot, apparently down here on a special mission from Hanoi with a
bunch of others. He and his friend, who's still runnin' around loose,
were takin' a little R and R in what they thought was a pretty safe
province for them—handin' out some medals and stuff—but boy,
has that ever changed now!"

"Hey, that's great, Red. What were those papers?"

"Well, from what I've seen already, it's really some good stuff on the VC infrastructure in this province and in a couple of others where he was planning to go—names, villages, everything! I've got people workin' on that right now, and it'll be goin' up to Saigon pretty quick!"

"Shit, Red, that's great!"

"Well, I wanta thank you two. I can't tell you how much this's done for us. And now that we've nailed the first one, we've suddenly got lots of good intel reports on his friend. So six more guys who went out with us on those first two runs are gonna put on a full-court press to run him to the ground, startin' tonight."

"Who's goin'?"

"Captain Murphy, two of the lieutenants that he liked, and three good Hoi Chans."

Murphy was the Ranger captain who had covered our asses on the big raids.

"Murphy's good; he'll get him."

"Boy, I hope so. If they get him before he leaves province, every political VC in the delta will hear about what happened to those two guys, and they'll have a few second thoughts before they come to Kien Hoa."

Two nights later, Murphy's team did nail the other guy and two bodyguards over in Hoa Dong. After that, Red was so happy we practically had to stand on his feet to keep him from floating away.

But for unknown reasons, I felt myself coming down hard; I didn't seem to smile much anymore, even at rare rays of sunshine sneaking through the omnipresent gloomy clouds. Dick and I and the rest of the team went through the motions of watching our Ruff Puffs at trainfire, but everything seemed pretty grim.

Imprudence

WE SLIPPED BACK into tedium, and a week later, went out on our first operation with the 44th, newly armed with M-16s.

We kicked off at eight in the morning, and for the first two hours it was the expected yawner. Then a couple of unexpected bursts of AK fire off to our right told us that the 52d had stumbled onto something. The fire escalated, and a call for help came over the radio. I was surprised to see Trung comply with the request, sending the word out to his company commanders to get on line across some rice paddies and move forward toward an indicated tree line. Within about fifteen minutes the thin line began to waver forward. We could hear occasional M-16 fire answering the AK noise to our right, and the sound stirred me; maybe now our troops, newly armed with M-16s, would be willing to fight. They still seemed green as grass, but they had to learn about combat sometime.

Dick and I stayed with Trung, and after his men were some fifty meters out, he and his command group very gingerly followed on a dike that separated two paddies. We were no more than thirty or forty meters into the paddy area when a long burst of RPD fire rang out from the wood line to our front. Four or five men in the company to our left were hit and went down in the ankle-deep water. There was some answering M-16 fire from our left, but our right wavered, then collapsed. The panic was contagious, and soon the thin line dissolved, as most of the Ruff Puffs threw their new M-16s down in the water, then turned and ran pell-mell for the seeming safety of the dike they had just left.

I was stunned. It became a farce as Trung and his boys shoved by Dick and me and lit out for the high bushes behind us. The retreating Ruff Puffs were still in front of us, but coming toward us at

breakneck speed, openmouthed and screaming. The company on
our left front was firing but also beating a less than orderly retreat. I
just couldn't believe my eyes!

Dick's voice caught me by surprise over my shoulder. "What
now, sir?"

"Shit, I ain't stayin' out here alone! Feets, what are you doin'
standin' there?" We both turned and jogged after Trung's group.

When we got back in the bushes with Trung's men, a frightened
Ha approached me. "Suh, Dai Uy Trung ask fo atiry on dis place
fust. Den we attack."

"Okay, Ha, thank you." I moved over to the base of a nearby
tree and sank down to the ground, leaning against the trunk and ex-
haling deeply.

Dick was quickly beside me. "Hey, sir, they left a bunch of casualties out there, too. Poor bastards'll drown if they don't drag 'em
back."

"Yeah, you're right. Let's go see what's bein' done."

We stood back up and walked to the edge of the bushes, where
we could see the paddies stretched out before us. There were still
thirty or forty troops out in the paddies, most of them trying to pull
wounded back to the bushes. The RPD position, two hundred
meters away, was now silent. Off to our right we could hear occasional bursts of AK fire and answering M-16 fire. I was genuinely
depressed. What a sorry-assed mess.

We walked back to Trung's position, the area now filled with
wandering, frightened, weaponless Ruff Puffs, yelling at each other,
some of them physically shaking with fright. Sergeants and officers
were yelling and trying to herd them back into unit formations, and
Trung was busy talking on the radio. I went back to our tree with
Dick, and we slumped down on our butts. There wasn't much we
could do except wait for Trung to get his cry for help through to the
artillery pieces. I wasn't about to say anything to Trung, who was
now in a very delicate situation. I didn't think there was anything I
could say after the rout we had just witnessed that he wouldn't take
as a personal insult.

Several Ruff Puffs came out of the bushes from the direction of
the rice paddies, all carrying armloads of wet M-16s. Across the
paddies a slick was coming in low, still three or four hundred meters
out. The first man out when it landed was Colonel White, followed
by Colonel Tran. We all saluted, and Trung hurried over to Tran,
while a smiling Colonel White came to me.

"How's it goin' out here, Captain Carhart? We heard you got into a big fight trying to take a wood line."

I didn't know how to respond, but I figured the truth couldn't hurt. "Not too good, sir. We were movin' on line across some paddies when an RPD opened up, hit a few of our boys, and the rest of them wavered for a bit, then turned tail and ran."

"Huh. Just one RPD, you say?"

"Yes, sir."

"Dai Uy Trung told us over the radio that you were fired on by a reinforced company of VC. He said at least forty or fifty positions, and he just didn't have the manpower to complete the attack."

I shrugged. "Sorry, sir, one RPD. There might have been at the most two or three other AKs, but neither my sergeant nor I noticed them."

Colonel White looked at Dick. "That a fact, Sergeant?"

"Yes, sir, one RPD fired three or four bursts at the most."

"Hmm."

"You oughta be able to tell that from the casualties, sir. We only had three or four men hit, and I don't think anyone was killed."

"Yeah, Dai Uy Trung said he had five casualties. We're gonna take them out with us when we go; they're loadin' 'em now." We looked over at the slick, blade still turning, where wounded Vietnamese were being laboriously loaded through a side door.

"Well, Captain Carhart, all I can tell you is to try to support Dai Uy Trung. He hasn't got the best training in the world, nor do his troops; but they're tryin', and it's our job to help train them. So whatever you do, don't make Dai Uy Trung lose any face. We've already been through this, right?"

"Yes, sir."

"All right, you should have artillery support once we clear the area, and then you're going to try to take that wood line again. So stay with Trung and try to help him look good, okay?"

"Yes, sir."

We all saluted again, and Colonel White drifted back under the whirling blade and waited by the body of the slick for Colonel Tran, who was still huddled with Trung. Then Tran stood up, salutes all around, and he strode back under the blade and hopped into the slick, quickly followed by Colonel White. The beast reared back, shuddering, lifted off, and zoomed away from us some twenty or thirty meters above the rice paddies.

Dick and I walked back over to our tree and slumped down next to it. Gaggles of Ruff Puffs were milling around near the pile of weapons, pulling them out and examining them. A couple of sharp shouts from a Vietnamese sergeant seemed to quiet the tumult, and they formed two lines and began picking weapons up and walking away with them. Then came four sequential sharp explosions from the direction of the paddies—must be the artillery, I thought. Orders were passed, and the Ruff Puffs started to filter back through the weeds toward the rice paddies where they had earlier abandoned their weapons. Dick and I stood up together and moved toward Trung's command group. Soon enough they started to move, and we followed. At the edge of the rice paddies we stopped and waited. One company had been held in reserve off to our left, and the other two companies were very gingerly making their way across the paddies. We all stood immobile as they slowly swept forward, no enemy fire coming from the opposite wood line now. Maybe our artillery had been accurate, I thought, then instantly dismissed the thought from my mind. Knowing full well that artillery fire would follow, that one RPD had just picked up and split. We watched as the two companies reached the wood line, then disappeared into it. Trung was talking loudly on the radio; then he started back in the direction of the area where Colonel Tran and Colonel White had visited us. Obviously we weren't even going across those paddies. We waited there for half an hour or so, and then the two companies that had crossed the paddies rejoined us and we straggled back to the trucks.

When we returned to town, Dick and I both went down to the compound for the debriefing that was supposed to take place after each contact. When we arrived, Jim Claiborne told us that there would be no debriefing today. Apparently the 52d had been in an even messier situation than we had, and the word from Colonel Tran was that there would be no more operations for another week or two, while both battalions went back to the range with their M-16s. Again we Americans were supposed to show our faces occasionally but were to leave all the formal training to Vietnamese teams that were to come down from Saigon.

We were pretty depressed at the prospect of sitting on our hands again for several more weeks, but the first sergeant had some good news for us: Our unit had two slots for Hawaii in three more days. Dick was nearly dancing on the way back to the ranch. We already knew that he and Jerry would be going. They raced back to the compound to put MARS calls through to the World. When they returned, both were ten feet off the ground; in just a few days they would be united with their wives in Hawaii.

On the day they left for Saigon, to go through another day of processing before they left for Hawaii, we sent them off in good cheer. But after they were gone, time hung heavily on our hands. The training teams from Saigon hadn't arrived. I had nothing to read. There was nothing to do.

As the days passed, I recalled that Red had said earlier that he wanted someone to ambush the VC sampans that plied the river after curfew; maybe we'd take a prisoner or two and bring them back. I had hesitated about this before, but now, what the hell. The three Hoi Chans who had gone out that night with Dick and me and Red were good. And if I had a price on my head, they must have one as well.

I went over to Red's house in a clean fatigue shirt, lighting a cigar on the way. He was fumbling papers at his desk when I walked in. "Hey, Tiger, what's happenin'?"

I nodded to him. "I wanta take those three Hoi Chans out tonight, set up an ambush on the river."

"You mean up north of town?"

"Yeah."

"Great! But how come you're suddenly so eager?"

I shrugged. "I'm tired of sittin' on my ass. I wanta fight the war."

"Well, shit, that's great! I can get them for you, no sweat. What time you want 'em?"

"Send 'em over to my house around nine tonight."

"Okay, will do. Can you get 'em some M-sixteens again?"

"Yeah, I can do that, all three of 'em if they want."

"Well, I think they're gonna want only two. You gonna get me some prisoners?"

"Fuckin' A. Nine o'clock tonight, at my place." I started to walk out of his office, then turned. "And whatever you do, don't tell anybody where we're goin', I don't want a welcoming committee."

"No sweat."

"Okay, see you later, Red."

"Yeah, so long. Hope you have the kinda luck you had first time out."

I nodded, raising my hand to him as I walked out. I wasn't going to tell him that I was going out alone, I didn't want him or some other klutz going out with us to fuck things up. If Dick wasn't around, there wasn't anyone else I trusted, and I would just as soon go by myself. And whether they deserved it or not, I felt unspoken trust for the three Hoi Chans.

I wandered through town for the rest of the day and hardly even noticed the light rain that had started again. When I got back to the Ponderosa, it was almost six. I told Norm that I wanted Ha to be there a little before nine, then crashed into my bed, falling quickly asleep.

At a quarter to nine Norm tugged gently on my sleeve, and I was quickly awake. "Ha's here, sir."

"Okay, thanks, Norm." I got up, pulled my tiger fatigues out of my duffel bag, and put them on. Then I picked up my LBE, my sheath knife, two bandoliers of ammo, and my weapon, which I carried with me into the kitchen. Ha was sitting at the table, and he stood up as I walked in. "Sit down, Ha. I go out tonight with Hoi Chans. I want you to translate for me while I tell them what we're gonna do. Then you stay here just like last time until I come back."

I opened the door, waved the Hoi Chans in, and pulled my map out and laid it on the table as they sat down. "Okay, we go out this way, north of town. Then we go out here, up to this point. Then we wait along the river." I waited while Ha translated. "Okay, then we wait here. When a VC boat comes, we shoot, try to take boat, try to take prisoners. Then we take them this way, then back to town, *biet*?"

Again Ha translated. Han, the former VC platoon leader, pointed to a different point on the river, another couple of clicks from town. Ha translated his comments to me. "Suh, he say dis place betta fo prisnas. Dey stop VC boat, many time dis place, you catch easia."

I looked at the indicated point. Another couple of clicks, another half hour of humping. That put us about eight clicks outside town, about five from the main road where we would leave the jeep. Humph. "Okay, we'll go to that point. Any questions?" Since they had none, I went in the bedroom and got Dick's M-16 and a couple of bandoliers, talking to Norm as I went. "Norm, okay if we borrow your weapon again?"

"Sure, sir, it's right there by my bunk."

I scooped it up, along with two more bandoliers of ammo, then walked back into the kitchen and laid the weapons on the table. Two of the Hoi Chans picked them up and opened the bolts, checking the receivers. Then each seated a round. "Okay, Ha, you stay here until I come back."

I strapped our M-79 grenade launcher to the rucksack from on which our radio was mounted and stuffed ten rounds in my thigh pockets, in case I needed long-range explosive power, say, for a sampan loaded with flammables in the middle of the river. I looped two M-16 bandoliers across my chest, slipped into the radio frame, picked up my M-16, and walked out the door to the jeep. I started to take the top down. The Hoi Chans helped me, knowing better than I did how the tops disassembled. I slipped behind the wheel and cranked it up, the Hoi Chans leaping in with no need for instructions. I turned on the headlights, but as we approached the north gate to town, I turned them off and slowed down. I waved to the Vietnamese guards, who returned my wave, then flipped the radio on with my right hand and keyed the mike. "Ringmaster, this is Tiger, routine commo check. How do you read this station, over."

"Tiger, this is Ringmaster, read you Lima Charlie. How me? · Over."

"This is Tiger, read you same, thank you much, out." I put the microphone back down next to the radio. I didn't want to alert anyone to my going out on this run, but in case I got into some deep shit, I wanted some desperate last lifeline commo with the compound. Not that they would do anything for me in the dark, but still . . .

We drove two or three clicks with our lights out, then pulled under a low hardwood tree and stopped. I pulled the radio up on my back, chambered a fresh round, then took my boots off and placed them under the steering wheel. "Okay, let's go." We started to move silently, stealthily, swiftly. Adrenaline was churning through my system as we moved, and I felt good. We had five clicks or so to move, and after about an hour we turned left on a large, wide trail. Remembering the map, I knew that we were only a little more than a click away from where we were going. Suddenly I nearly tripped over a dark lump on my side of the trail. The rain had stopped; but the sky was clouded over, and night vision didn't carry very far. As I stepped over it, I saw that it was the body of a dark dog, lying on its side. Shit, dog meat was a delicacy here, I knew that much. But I wondered why no one had eaten it. Why was it just lying here in the trail? I figured it must have died, or been killed, after everyone had gone in for the night. But I rejected that even as I thought it, knowing that night was operational time for the VC; hell, they might even be holding political meetings in some of the hooches that we passed at a distance of less than fifty meters. I didn't want to get any closer to them, and the Hoi Chans were in agreement, steering wide for fear of setting up a howling of dogs. A dog on our left front actively began to yap at us; then came another's bark. Shit, I thought, let's get by this point. I was trying to hustle along, moving quickly now, to get away from those two barking dogs. Suddenly I saw it. Twenty meters away from me, in the middle of the trail, was another form, but as I grew closer, I could see that this one was lighter. It was another dog's body. Apparently dead. A whitish dog. Fear ran over my face like a rash, prickling the hairs on the back of my neck, freezing my arms and legs. I recalled that moment in Tokyo a couple of months earlier, when my sister Sally had warned me about a dream she had where I pass some dead dogs in the road at night while I'm with Vietnamese, and then I get captured. She had made me swear that I would avoid whatever that meant, and I had laughingly given her my word, thinking at the time that she had meant two dead dogfaces. And now here I was: two dead dogs in the trail I'm walking on at night with Vietnamese men.

Christ Almighty, I really could end up captured and dragged off to years of agony somewhere. Here I am, off in the middle of nowhere with three Communist soldier turncoats who are probably eager to sell my ass to their former commander—hell, maybe even their current commander, for all I know. What the hell is wrong with me? How stupid can I get?

I was immobile on the trail before the second dead dog. Other dogs were still barking, growing more insistent. The Hoi Chan who had been behind me stopped next to me, then urged me on with arms and whispered unintelligible Vietnamese. I wouldn't move, shaking my head no. Gotta think fast! I dropped to one knee in the trail, pulling the handset from the radio off my shoulder suspender where I had hooked it and began talking into it in a hushed whisper. I stopped talking and listened to the silence coming out of the earpiece, holding my hand up as if I were in some heated conversation. Han, who had been in front of me drifted back to my side and hunched down next to me, a quizzical look on his face. Then I stood up, hooking the handset back on my suspender, waving to the point man to join us. He didn't seem to understand, so I indicated to Han to get him, then pointed across a rice paddy to our right, showing that I wanted to go in that direction. Han ran down to the point man and brought him back. Then I pointed off to the right, showing through my impatience that we had to move fast. There was a moment of hesitation, during which the point man looked inquisitively at Han. But Han had bought it, and he urged the point man to do as I wished. We crossed fifty meters of rice paddy. I waved to the point man to continue going in the new direction, and he moved out.

I was breathing more easily now. Within about an hour and a half we came to the main road, and I knew that we must be four or five clicks north of our jeep. The point man stopped on the road and looked at me; but I urged him off in the direction of the jeep, and he moved out. Within less than an hour I saw the dark form of the jeep under the tree where we had left it, and I breathed a deep sigh of relief. I slid behind the wheel, not bothering to take the radio off or put my boots back on, and we started down the road toward town. When we got to within a couple of hundred meters of town, I sounded the horn twice, then turned on the headlights. We had awakened the gate guards, from their sleepy stares, but I waved joyfully to them as we drove in.

When I dropped everyone off at Red's, they all were giving me funny looks. I picked up the radio handset and pointed into it. "Beaucoup VC!" I exclaimed. "Beaucoup VC!" I waved my hand in the direction of the north gate, and they all smiled, seeming to understand that I had gotten a warning from the compound that there were a lot of VC moving into that area that night. They started to laugh and chatter among themselves in the Vietnamese way, then laid the two M-16s and bandoliers of ammo in the front seat. They raised their hands in farewell as I backed my jeep out the gate, and I waved my hand to them as I sped off. Fuck! Saved again! It was nearly three o'clock as I walked into the Ponderosa. I dropped the weapons on the kitchen table, laid the radio on the floor, pulled Ha out of bed, and sent him home. Then I stripped my Tiger fatigues off and left them on the floor, slipped into bed, and passed out.

The next morning, when I got up around eleven, I was still chilled by the experiences of the night before, and I decided I would have to go explain to Red. But what would I say? For the first time I had avoided combat. I dressed and walked out the front door, lighting a cigar as I moved. When I got to Red's house, I walked by the guard at the front door and into his office. He was pushing papers but sat back smiling when I entered. "Hey, Tiger, how's it going? We heard you almost ran into a main force VC battalion last night. Radio report told you they were movin' into the area."

"Shit, Red, I dunno, but I'll tell you one thing, I haven't been that scared in a long time."

"Okay by me. We'll have to mount up another raid soon. I understand that two more political dudes came in with that battalion, and I've already got a rough fix on where they're stayin'."

So there *was* a VC battalion that had moved in last night! Holy shit! We'da got creamed! "Where's that, up north of town?"

"Yeah, less than a click from where you were goin' with the Hoi Chans. I won't ask you what your intelligence sources are, but that kept us out of a messy situation."

I laughed out loud. "Shit, Red, kept me from gettin' dead is what it did!"

"Yeah, that's affirm! Tell me, did the boys on your team pick that up from some Vietnamese, or what?"

I held up my hands defensively. "All my sources are American, Red, and that's all I'm sayin'."

"Well, I don't think you got it from the compound 'cause when I went down there this mornin' to tell 'em about all the reports we were gettin' from our agents, they seemed surprised as shit! But maybe you were talkin' to Colonel White, that what it is?" I leaned back in my chair, smiling and puffing on my cigar, but not making a sound. "Shit, Tiger, if you're getting G-two reports from Colonel White, we've got to get together on our intelligence 'cause I sent your team out where you could have gotten burned last night, all because I never got the word on that VC battalion until this mornin', and that's a dangerous way to run a railroad."

"We'll see, Red, we'll see. Actually last night was just a lucky fluke. It wasn't Colonel White, and I don't know that it will ever happen again."

"Well, keep me in mind next time you hear something."

We shot the shit for another few minutes, and then I left and walked back to the Ponderosa. Goddamn, Sally! I had been ready to dismiss her comment about the dead dogs, but whether prescient or not, it had pretty clearly kept me alive the night before.

One morning a week later Dick got back from R&R. He and Jesse and Norm and I went down to the compound after lunch and had some coffee in the basement mess hall. Then Lieutenant Jim Brown, Jim Claiborne's S-1, who I hadn't exchanged two words with, plopped down beside me. "How's it goin', guys?" We all nodded a greeting. "Hey, I understand you guys were in some real shit there the other day out in Hoa Dong."

We all looked at him impassively. "What shit was that, Jim?"

"You know, that last operation, that shit with the VC main force battalion in the wood line."

My mouth broke into a relaxed grin, and I released a few involuntary chuckles. "Shit, you mean those three bursts from one RPD where our boys threw down their guns and ran?"

Jim was smiling with me, but his serious mien remained. "No, I mean the one where Colonel Tran led the assault on the RPD position personally and killed three VC with his pistol."

"What?"

"That's what it says in that recommendation for a Silver Star for Colonel Tran you signed."

"What?"

"Yeah, Colonel White had me look it over for administrative shit. You know, ol' Colonel Tran already got one Silver Star that Colonel White wrote up, and since this is his second award, Colonel White wanted to make sure nothing was wrong."

I was shaken. "Was this for that last action where the Forty-fourth threw down their M-sixteens and ran?"

Jim slowly nodded. "That's affirm. You were advising the Forty-fourth, they got pinned down, and Colonel Tran led the assault on one RPD position. He killed three VC, and the rest of them split. Least that's what the award recommendation says."

I was astounded! Everything we read about the war from home, even in *The Stars and Stripes,* which was supposed to be colored in our favor, was filled with stories of American lies and deceptions and bullshit that people in the World believed were the rule rather than the exception over here! Now I was getting dragged into this by way of forgery! "You say Colonel White's got this recommendation now?"

"Yep, gettin' ready to send it down to Can Tho." I pulled my cap on and turned to race up the stairs three at a time. I got to White's office door and burst in, my hat still on. I was angry, but it was best to start out by the rules. A surprised Colonel White looked up from his desk.

"Sir, Captain Carhart reports to Colonel White 'cause you said your door was always open and I got a beef!"

Colonel White returned my salute casually, then leaned back in his chair, curious at my sudden appearance. "Sit down, Captain Carhart. What seems to be the problem?"

"I'd rather stand, sir. I just heard that someone forged my name to a recommendation for a Silver Star for Colonel Tran for that fuck-up the other day in Hoa Dong. And I just want you to know that I didn't sign it." I was glaring at White now.

A moment of silence set in while Colonel White ran his hand over his balding scalp. "Captain Carhart, why are you getting so all worked up over a supposed medal?"

"Sir, everything I've seen from back in the World talks about how crooked this war is. I don't want to be a party to this fiasco if what I heard is true!"

"Look, Captain, you know this war is as much political as anything else—in fact maybe more so."

"Yes, sir, I understand that, but I won't be a party to a lie."

"Now settle down, Captain Carhart. I don't know what they taught you about war at West Point—I didn't have the privilege of going there myself—but you ought to know that getting along with your allies is an important part of fighting any war!"

"Sir, at West Point, they taught me not to lie, cheat, or steal, and that was for life, not just for four years. If my name goes in on a false sworn statement, I'll raise hell! I was there, and I saw that Colonel Tran didn't do anything other than get off the slick, talk to Trung, then get back into the slick with you and disappear."

"You know, you're not being very politic about this, Captain. If you just kept your eye on the ball and your career, you might end up getting a Silver Star yourself—if your commanding officer thinks you're doing a good job, as I do, by the way."

The easy way out. Play the game, and I'll get you a Silver Star. He half turned in his swivel chair, putting his hands behind his head and leaning back. "I agree with what you said about not lying, cheating, or stealing, by the way. But you've got to recognize, Captain, those are nice ideals in a world of absolutes. And out here in the *real* world, everything is relative! Those boyhood ideals are fine, but sooner or later you've got to grow up! And if you embroider a little bit on what somebody did, that's not the same as *lying,* for Christ's sake, that's just the only way to get somebody a medal, that's all."

"Then why wasn't I asked to write up the original recommendation, sir?"

He sat up and pulled his chair behind the desk, ignoring my

question. "You know, Captain Carhart, you haven't done a bad job since you've been in province, but my appraisal of you is starting to change real fast, so watch your step! Remember, I'm your commanding officer, and I write your efficiency report. Now I'm warning you, your attitude isn't doing you any good at all, and if you care anything at all about your future in the army, you're on very thin ice." I stood immobile, locked rigidly in a position of attention, sweat starting to trickle down my chest and sides. Colonel White took his time examining me. "Your pockets are unbuttoned, Captain, and that fatigue shirt doesn't seem to have been washed in a month! Is that any way to report to your commanding officer?"

I grated my teeth, then hissed an answer out. "No, sir."

"I can't hear you, Captain."

"No, sir!" He seemed slightly startled by my bellow. I wanted to dive across that desk and tear him apart.

"All right, Captain Carhart, you've informed your commanding officer about this supposed forgery. What else do you plan to do?"

I hesitated for a second, then: "I don't know what I'll do, sir, or what I can do. But if worse comes to worst, I'll fight it any way I can."

"All right, Captain Carhart," he said, looking down at papers on his desk, "leave my office and return to your quarters."

I stepped back and saluted him. "Afternoon, sir."

He touched his fingers to his forehead, still not looking up. "Afternoon."

Dick and Jesse and Norm were sitting in the jeep, and after I flopped into the front seat, we pulled out onto the road and headed for home. Norm was the first to break the silence. "How'd it go, sir?"

"Ah, not too good, he's madder'n hell at me. But I don't think he'll dare submit that forged recommendation now." We sat in silence for the rest of the trip, and as soon as we reached the Ponderosa, I went inside and plopped into my bunk. A short time later Norm came in. "It's a message on the radio from the compound for you, sir. You're supposed to report to Colonel White ASAP."

I looked up into Norm's eyes, not understanding for a moment. Then it all flooded back to me. That bastard! I suppose I'm gonna get my ass chewed again, but fuck it, what's he gonna do, send me to the Nam? "Okay, thanks." Well, I guess he's had long enough to stew.

Norm followed me out, and I glanced back at him. "I'll run you down there, sir."

The ride was silent. Then we were there, and I stumbled out of the jeep and up the stairs into the cool, high-ceilinged house. I exhaled strongly as I walked toward the man's office. Here we go. I knocked twice.

"Come in."

I stepped into the room, noting the first sergeant standing against the far wall. Must be here on some other administrative business, I figured. Well, let me have it. "Sir, Captain Carhart reports to Colonel White as ordered."

He returned my salute silently, then reached for a manila folder lying on a corner of his desk. "Captain Carhart, here is your two-oh-one personnel file, and the officer's efficiency report that I have just completed for you. There's a flight to My Tho in half an hour. You're to be on it with all your possessions. Tomorrow you will make your way to Can Tho, where you're being transferred. The first sergeant here will escort you back to your quarters to pick up your gear. Then he'll make sure you're on that flight. Army regulations require that I be available to answer any questions you have about your OER, so take a quick look at it and see if there's anything you want to ask me about."

I was stunned as I picked up the two-page OER. An officer was rated by two superior officers on the OER—his commanding officer and the commander's commanding officer. There were fourteen different categories, in each of which an officer received a rating with values from 1 to 10. The total possible score was 140. Most West Point graduates historically received perfect or near-perfect scores. If your score was lower than 135, then you were on a sort of probation, no longer a "golden boy" eligible for early promotion. If your score was lower than 120, then promotion would become a problem; you really had to excel in your next two assignments to stay up with your peer group. The total score I received from Lieutenant Colonel Mauve, the province American executive officer who barely knew my name, and Colonel White, Mauve's commanding officer and the province senior American adviser, was 78. I looked up at Colonel White. "Am I being relieved, sir?"

"Yes, I suppose you could say that. Any more questions?"

"No, sir."

"All right, you'd better get a move on to catch that plane. If you miss it, then I'll *really* be upset. Don't forget, tomorrow, you are to catch a ride from My Tho to Can Tho and report in to the Four Corps personnel office. Now move out!"

I took a step backward and saluted.

"Good afternoon, sir."

"Afternoon."

I walked out into the hallway in a daze. I turned to the first sergeant as we walked out the door. "Hey, Top, I've got my own jeep and driver here."

"Well, you can ride with him back to your place, but I've got to take you to the airport."

I moved down the stairs in a daze as the first sergeant got in his jeep. I flopped into the front seat of ours, next to Norm, and we moved out the gate.

"What happened, sir?"

"I'm afraid I got relieved by Colonel White. I'm off to Can Tho."

"Jesus Christ! What for, sir?"

"I dunno. I guess I gave him too much back talk."

"But, sir, they don't relieve officers for that."

"They do now."

"Shit, sir, I think you ought to go see the IG."

The IG, or inspector general, was a sort of ombudsman who was supposed to represent the individual soldier's interests when he got fucked by the army.

"Nah, I don't think so. Colonel White is my CO in a combat zone, and I'm pretty sure the army would back him up all the way on this. Hell, he could relieve me for looking at him cross-eyed if he wanted to."

When we got to the Ponderosa, I went in the bedroom and gathered up my few possessions. Before I realized it, I was packed and ready to go. I plopped my helmet on my head, hooked my LBE and two bandoliers over one shoulder, hooked the strap from my rifle over the other, and hefted my duffel bag back into the kitchen.

The first sergeant stepped forward and took it from me. "Lemme get that for ya, sir." He disappeared out the door, leaving me helpless with Dick and Jess and Norm. We walked back into the bedroom as I related my experience with Colonel White.

Jesse and Norm were shaken and didn't really know what to say, but Dick was outraged. "Shit, sir, I knew something like this was gonna happen. You didn't get relieved over that medal; this is all because of Phoenix!"

"What?"

"Hell, yes, sir. This province has *always* been safe for the VC, and the Ruff Puffs don't do shit, we all know that. Colonel White has had a sweet deal, no killin', no dyin', a 'pacified province' and a good OER for him! Shit, he's on everybody's 'good guy' list, and all he cares about is makin' general. He doesn't give a fuck about fightin' the war! In fact, he wishes it'd go away; it's only trouble for him. And then you come along, and in the last month, you've been out on three Phoenix operations...."

"Four," I corrected him. "I went out again while you were in Hawaii."

"Okay, four, and of course Colonel White knows that, too, and what's happened? Those two visitin' VC big shots got knocked off in the middle of the night, and a bunch of bodyguards, too, and now all the rules of the fuckin' game have been changed on White, and he's runnin' scared."

"C'mon, Dick, you know I wasn't that big a player."

"Bullshit, sir. You're the Tiger, everybody knows that. You go through this Ruff Puff advisory bullshit by day, but then you lead teams out at night and you kill people. And White just can't control you! You're makin' him look bad, because he doesn't do shit to even slow the Commies down, but you're out there blowin' 'em away, and you're completely out of control as far as he's concerned!"

"Dick, you're exaggerating things."

"No, I'm not, sir. White hates you, and he's afraid of you, and he'd do *anything* to get you out of his hair. And he was probably gettin' pressure from our allies to get rid of you, too. Don't forget how all our Ruff Puff operations have been compromised, and the VC sure don't want you around! So some piddly shit thing happens, and he kicks you out of province, and now he won't have to worry about his sweet deal and his nice letter from the province chief he advises. No, sir, you got relieved just because you were tryin' to fight the fuckin' war, that's all!"

Jess chimed in: "I think Dick's got somethin', sir. We been talkin' about it since you got called back to the compound, and we couldn't figger out any reason why Lieutenant Brown woulda told you about that forgery 'cept to get you so mad you'd lose your temper and go in and blow up at Colonel White."

Confusion washed over me. Why the fuck *did* Lieutenant Brown tell me about that forgery? He's White's boy, a super-REMF who sits outside his office and doesn't know me from the man in the moon. And he didn't *show* it to me, he just *told* me about it, and I went ballistic with no proof! Was I set up for this? Did they just tell me that knowing I'd leap into the fray so they could burn me?

I felt the weight of the world on my shoulders and collapsed on my bunk, burying my head in my hands. Dumb. Dumb. *Dumb!* And I sure went for it, didn't I?

I heard knocking on the door and the first sergeant's voice: "Let's go, sir, gotta catch that plane."

I stood up and shook hands with Norm ("You got fucked, sir, but I enjoyed serving under you"); then with Jess ("Amen, sir, sorry this is happenin' "), then with Dick ("You're the best commander I've ever had, sir; I'll never forget you"). I put my arms around Dick and we hugged each other hard. I stepped back and looked in his eyes. "Strike force!" I whispered harshly. Then I turned and was gone.

Refuge

I GOT TO MY THO and checked into the transient quarters, not really wanting to talk to anybody. I ate alone in the large mess hall, then started to walk around in the small compound, smoking a cigar. After half an hour of pacing I headed for the noisy club where my spirits were slightly recharged by the friendly American sound of Hank Snow drifting plaintively out of the speakers over the bar. I had really gotten to like country and western music over here, the only music there was that you could identify immediately as American—not English, not French, not German, not Russian, but American. I went to the far end of the long bar and sat on the last stool, starting my first beer five or six stools from the nearest American. I tried to think about North Carolina and my days at Fort Bragg, where this kind of music was lifeblood. I was feeling horribly depressed when a major sat down next to me. I turned, and he nodded to me. "Hi, Captain."

"Hi, Major." I glanced at his left hand and saw the West Point ring on his finger. I stuck out my hand to him. "Tom Carhart, class of 'sixty-six."

"Bill Smith, class of 'fifty-nine. What company were you in?"

"E-two. How 'bout you?"

"G-one."

A West Point graduate! Now maybe I'd get a sympathetic hearing! Now maybe somebody would boost my ego and make me feel like other than a criminal! "Whatcha doin' in My Tho, Tom?"

"Well, it's a long story, but I just got relieved of command in Kien Hoa this afternoon, and I'm headin' for Can Tho tomorrow."

"Oh. Okay. Well, nice meetin' ya." He stood up with his beer, smiling smugly, and moved away, striking up a conversation with men he knew farther down the bar. I put my beer down, tucked a dollar bill under the can, pulled my hat on and headed for the door, rage building in my head. What am I, a fucking leper? Goddamn ass-coverin' mealymouthed motherfuckers! Fuck 'em all! Goddamn REMFs! I somehow made my way back to my temporary bunk, where I ached myself to sleep.

The next morning I caught an early flight to Can Tho. I decided I would try to find Ron Marvin, a West Point classmate who was a staff officer for IV Corps, and see if he could get me a fair hearing. At the U.S. IV Corps headquarters in Can Tho, I walked into the main tactical operations center and asked where the G-3 air, or staff air operations officer, was. I was directed to another building, where I found Ron assembling a model airplane at his desk. He jumped up, a surprised smile on his face, and we shook hands and clapped shoulders heartily. I found myself smiling and ragging him in spite of my predicament. "Shit, Ron, I knew you were in the G-three air shop, but I didn't know that meant you made models!"

"Ah, don't give me that crap. This is for a going-away present for some air force general. What brings you down here?"

"Well, sit down, Ron, 'cause I'm in a world of hurt, and I need your advice." I quickly went over what had happened. Ron supported me fully, and he was a valuable ally.

What a difference a classmate could make! Earlier that morning, coming out of My Tho, I had been at the ragged edge of despair, and now, with nothing else having changed, I was almost soaring! And all because of a little encouragement and reinforcement from a peer! "I think Colonel Hazam'd like to hear your story."

"Who's he?"

"He's the chief of staff of Four Corps, and he's jumpin' through his ass over all the stories about lyin' and cheatin' that get into the press. He's just death on anybody who tries to pull a quick one."

"Sounds like my man! Is he a grad?"

"No, but he thinks a lot of West Pointers, and his son is a plebe right now. He also jumped with the one eighty-seventh in Korea, and he thinks a lot of the airborne. So if you get to see him as a West Pointer with the screaming eagle on your shoulder, you've got a lot goin' for you. I'll get to work on that this afternoon. I've got a special access to him."

I sat in Ron's room, nervously trying to read, but it was a wasted, wretched afternoon. He got back around five, and we went right to the mess hall.

Over supper Ron told me he had arranged an appointment with Colonel Hazam at ten o'clock the following morning. He said Hazam had a reputation as a straight arrow and a hard ass, but if I just played straight with him, I'd be all right.

My stomach was tied in a knot the next morning at ten as I walked into his office and saluted. He did look the part of the stern taskmaster as he gruffly returned my salute and told me to sit down. I gave him my 201 file with the officer's efficiency report, then sat tensely on the front three inches of my chair while he read it. Then he looked up at me. "What have you got to say for yourself, Captain?" I told him of the time I had spent as an adviser in Kien Hoa, including my operations with Phoenix, up to the eyewitness statement and the fury I had felt and expressed. He listened to me silently, then pitched my 201 to a corner of his desk. "In addition to being the chief of staff for Four Corps, I'm also the commander of the Forty-fourth Special Tactical Zone on the Cambodian border. How'd you like to be a tactical operations center duty officer for me?"

"I'd like that fine, sir."

"Okay, how much time you got left in-country? About a month?"

"Yes, sir, my DEROS is six December."

"All right, I'll send you out to Cao Lanh, and I'll tear this OER up, write you a new one on the basis of your performance for me. That sound reasonable?"

"Yes, sir, very reasonable."

"I hate to see a young man like you get your career messed up because of something political, so we'll start all over. You just consider yourself on probation, all right?"

"Yes, sir."

"Check with Major Williams outside. He'll get you manifested to Cao Lanh this afternoon."

I stood up and saluted, then walked out to see Major Williams. There would be a slick at two o'clock. I was to have all my shit out at the helipad by then. I walked back over to the main TOC, where I found Ron. "So how was he?"

"He reminded me of my father when I catch him in a good mood!"

"What'd I tell ya?"

"Yeah, he's sendin' me out to Cao Lanh to be a TOC duty officer for the Forty-fourth Special Tactical Zone. Said he's gonna tear up that dogshit OER I got in Kien Hoa and write me a new one on the basis of how I work for him."

"Hot damn, now you're in! See, I told you he'd do you right!" We went to lunch early and stayed late. Then Ron carried me and my duffel bag over to the helipad in a jeep.

Soon the slick was there, and I climbed on. An hour or so later, I got off in Cao Lanh. An enlisted man at the helipad pointed the TOC out to me. The American base there was inside a walled-in compound that was maybe two hundred meters square, and the TOC was inside a low stone building that stood in one corner. I went into the dark building, and after my eyes had adjusted to the dim light, I went over to the bank of radios that stood against one wall and introduced myself to the duty officer, a Captain Smith. He in turn directed me to another small building some hundred meters away, where I reported to my new boss, the S-3, a Major Brown.

Major Brown took me back to the TOC, where we went over the nature and basis of our unit. The 44th Special Tactical Zone was a strip some twenty miles wide that ran along the Cambodian border with South Vietnam, from the Parrot's Beak, northwest of Saigon, to the South China Sea. The 44th STZ was an American operation which attempted to limit the enormous influx of supplies and reinforcements flooding across the Cambodian border for the VC and NVA, supplies and reinforcements that had made the long trek down the Ho Chi Minh Trail through Laos and Cambodia from North Vietnam. We had the constant use of only Ruff Puff troops who happened to inhabit the small Vietnamese towns in the border region. However, we had massive use of U.S. air power and the scheduled use of elite Vietnamese forces, the marines, airborne, and ranger battalions that were kept in Saigon as a strategic reserve. Occasionally we had access to a brigade of the U.S. 9th Infantry Division, but only occasionally. There were about a hundred American servicemen at Cao Lanh, mostly administrative types, and we were inside a tight little fortress that looked as if it could be pretty easily defended.

I was assigned to the graveyard shift as TOC duty officer, midnight to 8:00 A.M., four days on, one day off. I slipped quickly into the routine and soon lost all track of the days and date. I was responsible for incoming radio messages, relaying them to forward units on call or to Can Tho when they were emergency calls for support, but mostly just ash-and-trash stuff: resupply requests, medical requests, R&R requests, you name it. I was really nothing more than a glorified telephone operator, passing messages on to Major Brown or his boss and the XO for the 44th, Lieutenant Colonel Blue. Colonel Hazam, the actual commander, never was able to spend more than a few days a month in Cao Lanh, and his deputy, Lieutenant Colonel Blue, ran most things for him. Not much went on. For unknown reasons, I found myself massively depressed.

After I got off at eight in the morning, I'd go to the mess hall and eat a big breakfast, then go to my small cubicle in the wooden barracks building, where I'd sleep until four or so. I'd get up, go out to the big open field outside the gate and join the daily tackle football game. Colonel Blue was always the quarterback on one team, and Major Fly, the supply officer, was the QB on the other. I usually played in the line somewhere or ran out for a pass with the eight other "deep receivers" on either team. It was something to kill the time. After the game we'd all flood into the mess hall, where we'd eat a hearty meal of mystery meat and reconstituted potatoes. After that I'd usually go to the club for a beer or two, but if I were going on duty that night, I'd leave by nine and go back to my room, where I'd write letters or read.

Otherwise, work at the TOC kept me busy. As the crossroads of so much information I was able to keep track of Communist resupply shipments over the Cambodian border into IV Corps. I learned that they were significantly reduced compared to what they had been before Tet '68. We weren't sure what that meant, but from the lack of Vietcong activity along the border or even throughout the delta, it looked as if they either were laying back to wait us out or were just plain whipped.

Westmoreland had claimed early that Tet '68 had been a major defeat for the Communists. At first the conflict between this official military line—always suspect in any true citizen army—and what you read in the U.S. press of the "great Communist victory" in Tet '68 was quite confusing. But with the passage of time it looked as if Westmoreland had been right. The Communists, especially the VC, seemed to have shot their wad. One never heard of operations mounted by main force Vietcong battalions anymore. Had we really killed them all off at Tet? They had gambled everything on one roll of the dice; but they had miscalculated, and they had lost big. No South Vietnamese forces had gone over to their side, they had held no populated areas except Hue for more than a few days, and when Hue was retaken after a month, it was discovered that the Communists had murdered more than two thousand civilians who lived in that city. While there may have been genuine political differences felt in South Vietnam before this happened, once it was made public, the general South Vietnamese population clearly hated and feared the Communists; they didn't want what had happened in Hue to happen to *them*!

I thought a lot about what Neon and others had told me back in Kien Hoa, as well as what I had learned in advisory school in Di An, about American intentions in Vietnam and how we intended to help establish a government that would evolve into a democracy. No doubt that was the program envisioned by our leaders; but those of us carrying rifles were not usually informed of high political maneuvering, and it wasn't all entirely clear to me. The generally accepted model, at least in the ranks, seemed to be Korea, and no doubt the people of South Korea were better off than those living under Communist rule in the North. South Korea, of course, certainly didn't seem to be a democratically governed country anything like what we knew in the States. But then *nothing* in this part of the world seemed like anything back in the States—another reason, perhaps, that we referred to home so matter-of-factly as the World.

Time suddenly started to rush by. Then, before I was really ready, I got my DEROS orders, and the magic date was December 2—a 4-day "drop" off the normal 365 days!

On December 2 I packed my meager possessions in my duffel bag, signed out, shook hands with the guys staying behind, and jumped on the slick for Tan Son Nhut Air Base in Saigon. I had not formally received an OER, but I knew Hazam's word was good. I was sure I had earned at least a passing grade from him, and an OER would catch up with me through administrative channels.

Once I arrived at Tan Son Nhut, I had some administrative lines to go through. There were only a few hours in which I might try to say a tearful good-bye to Jacqueline and Kinou, but I saw that big World Airways freedom bird gleaming on the tarmac, and it took my breath away. I decided it was best to leave things as we had. I would love her that moment forever. Then, before I realized what was happening, I piled on with other GIs and was shown to a seat.

I sat down, buckled in, and looked out the window. Strange, suddenly seeing Vietnam "out there." So much had happened; so many thoughts, memories, sensations flooded through my mind. The strong smell of burlap, of dirt, of shitters being burned out with diesel fuel. The stench of dead bodies in the hot sun. The ecstasy of a leisurely cold shower on top of Fire Base Birmingham, after weeks without having even taken off my boots.

One engine started, then another. Shot through the leg. Uncle Jimmy, Tiger Five, whispering to me in the dead of night, two inches from my face, as green tracers flashed over us down the hill. Cold rain trickling down my neck.

We started to roll forward, then turned hard to the left. Scrambling around near the top of that hill, then Speedy clutching at me: "My legs, sir, my legs!" They pull his dead body up into the dustoff from my arms, leaving me trembling, drained, and alone, soaked with his blood.

Somewhere far away, I could hear a stewardess droning over the PA system. Mobile Advisory Team 85 motoring into Go Cong, brimming over with eager anticipation. Naïve. Foolish.

We turned at the end of the runway, then stopped, and the pilot gunned the engines. Search and avoid. The mud. Dai Uy Trung. Neon. The Hoi Chans. Dick Lightner.

With a lurch we started to roll, accelerating quickly as the engines roared. Tan Son Nhut and Saigon beyond streamed by, blurring the window. Good-bye, eagle. Good-bye MACV. Good-bye Vietnamese people, good, bad, and indifferent. Good-bye, Jacqueline. Good-bye, Kinou.

We broke with the ground, and the wheels came up to a roar of approval from a hundred GI throats. We banked hard over Saigon, resplendent below as sunlight filtered through her French-planted hardwood tendrils and danced silently over her masonry features. Truly, the mysterious Orient. Good-bye, Vietnam. Good-bye.

Glossary

AFN: Armed Forces Network, a radio station run by the U.S. military in Vietnam, over which songs then popular back in the World were broadcast for the entertainment of U.S. troops

ARVN: Army of the Republic of Vietnam; the South Vietnamese Army

ASAP: As soon as possible

BOQ: Bachelor officers' quarters

BUY THE FARM: Die

CA: Combat assault—a helicopter-borne assault of U.S. troops into a contested area, usually resisted by Communist gunfire

CHIEU HOI: "Open arms" program, under which a Communist soldier would receive amnesty by surrendering to South Vietnamese or American forces

CLICK: A kilometer, roughly six tenths of a mile

COMMO: Communications

C RATION: A ready-to-eat, filling meal sealed in metal cans; not renowned for flavor

DEROS: Date of estimated return from overseas—the day one's tour in Vietnam ended and one returned to the World

DOGWOOD EIGHT: Radio code term used in the 101st for one wounded American soldier

DOGWOOD SIX: Radio code term used in the 101st for one dead American soldier

DUSTOFF: Medical evacuation by helicopter of casualties; the helicopter that effected such evacuations

FAC: Forward air controller, a light propeller-driven plane similar to a Piper Cub that circled above a U.S. Army unit in contact and provided a constant interface between the commander on the ground and tactical aircraft as they arrived on station

GOOK: An individual of Vietnamese ethnic origin; term sometimes expanded to include all individuals of Oriental ethnic origin

GREASE: Kill

H.E.: High explosive; used as a type description of bombs dropped by aircraft or shells fired by artillery

HOI CHAN: An individual Communist soldier who turned himself in to South Vietnamese or U.S. forces under Chieu Hoi program

HOOCH: Term used to describe rudely built or insubstantial huts or houses, either erected as temporary housing by soldiers on both sides or the dwellings of Vietnamese farmers

IP: Initial point, a geographic point from which a military operation would be launched

LBE: Load-bearing equipment, a system of web belts and suspender straps on which much of an individual soldier's gear was carried

LRRP: Long-range reconnaissance platoon or long-range reconnaissance patrol

LRRP RATIONS: Dehydrated rations carried by LRRPs; much lighter than C rations, therefore a much-longer-lasting supply could be carried by one soldier

LZ: Landing zone, an area cleared of trees and designated for helicopter landings

MACV: Military Assistance Command, Vietnam

MAT: Mobile advisory team, a group of American advisers normally consisting of five U.S. soldiers (one captain, one lieutenant, three sergeants) who advised South Vietnamese units

MEDEVAC: Medical evacuation of casualties to the rear, usually by helicopter.

NCO: Noncommissioned officer; a sergeant

NVA: North Vietnamese Army

O-DEUCE: Nickname for 2nd Battalion, 502nd Infantry, 101st Airborne Division

OSCAR: Radio slang for radio-telephone operator, an enlisted soldier who carried and sometimes used a unit's radio

PIASTER: Vietnamese unit of currency; official rate of exchange maintained was near one hundred piasters per U.S. dollar, although black market offered three or four times that rate

PIO: Public information officer

POINT MAN: The lead man in the Indian-file movement usually used on operations in the jungle by U.S. troops

PRUS: Individual mercenary soldiers who formed the provincial reconnaissance units in each province; reputations for effectiveness varied by province

PX: Post exchange, a small general store maintained by the U.S. Army for its members at its garrisons

R&R: Rest and recreation, a six-day period of leave offered to every U.S serviceman in Vietnam, which could be spent in Hawaii, Hong Kong, Singapore, Tokyo, Sydney, Bangkok, or Taipei

REDLEG: Slang term for artillery

REMF: Rear echelon mother fucker, term of endearment used by troops fighting the infantry war in the field for the 90 percent-plus of the U.S. military in Vietnam that supported them

RPD: Communist machine gun using same basic action as AK-47 but firing a 200-round drum with a longer barrel and a bipod; with an extremely high rate of fire, this weapon dumped out a lot of lead and death

RPG: Rocket-propelled grenade, an extremely effective Communist anti-vehicle or antipersonnel weapon, consisting of a rocket fired from a shoulder-supported weapon

RTO: Radio-telephone operator; see OSCAR above

RUFF PUFF: Slang term for regional forces and popular forces, South Vietnamese local military units roughly similar to the U.S. National Guard

SITREP: Situation report

SLACK MAN: The second man in an Indian-file movement; walking right behind the point man, he gave him immediate support, or "took up his slack"

SLICK: Nickname for HUEY general-purpose helicopters, by far the most commonly used type of helicopters in Vietnam

SPOOKY: Nickname for C-47 propeller-driven World War II cargo planes with six Vulcan Gatling guns, each of which fired 6,000 rounds per minute, mounted inside door. SPOOKY could linger on station, flying in a lazy circle, and pour devastating fire on a target designated by allied forces on the ground

TAC AIR: Tactical air support, usually a number of U.S. Air Force or Navy fighter bombers heavily laden with ordnance they would drop on enemy targets as requested by ground forces

TOP: Army-wide familiar nickname for a company first sergeant

VC: Vietcong, the Communist forces that purportedly consisted of men recruited from South Vietnamese society to fight against their government

WILLIE PETER: White phosphorus

WORLD, THE: The United States of America